Autobiographics

Reading
WOMEN
Writing

a series edited by
Shari Benstock and Celeste Schenck

Reading Women Writing is dedicated to furthering international feminist debate. The series publishes books on all aspects of feminist theory and textual practice. *Reading Women Writing* especially welcomes books that address cultures, histories, and experiences beyond first-world academic boundaries. A full list of titles in the series appears at the end of this book.

Autobiographics

A FEMINIST THEORY OF
WOMEN'S SELF-REPRESENTATION

Leigh Gilmore

Cornell University Press

ITHACA AND LONDON

First published 1994 by Cornell University Press
First printing, Cornell Paperbacks, 1994.
Second printing 1995.

Library of Congress Cataloging-in-Publication Data

Gilmore, Leigh, 1959–
    Autobiographics : a feminist theory of women's self-representation / Leigh Gilmore.
       p.   cm. — (Reading women writing)
    Includes bibliographical references and index.
    ISBN 0-8014-2778-9 (cloth : alk. paper). — ISBN 0-8014-8061-2
(pbk. : alk. paper)
    1. Feminist literary criticism.   2. Feminism and literature.   3. Autobiography—
Women authors—History and criticism.
I.   Title.   II.   Series.
PN98.W64G55   1994
809'.93592072—dc20   93-5982

The author gratefully acknowledges permission to use the following material: Excerpts from *Annie John* by Jamaica Kincaid. Copyright © 1985 by Jamaica Kincaid. Reprinted by permission of Farrar, Straus & Giroux, Inc., and Picador, a division of Pan Macmillan Ltd.
Excerpts from *The Autobiography of Alice B. Toklas* by Gertrude Stein. Copyright © 1933 and renewed 1961 by Alice B. Toklas. Reprinted by permission of Random House, Inc., and the Estate of Gertrude Stein.
Excerpts from *The Woman Warrior* by Maxine Hong Kingston. Copyright © 1975, 1976 by Maxine Hong Kingston. Reprinted by permission of Alfred A. Knopf, Inc., and Schaffner Associates.
Excerpts from *Zami: A New Spelling of My Name*. Copyright © 1982 by Audre Lorde, published by The Crossing Press, Freedom, CA 95019.
Excerpts from *Landscape for a Good Woman* by Carolyn Kay Steedman. Copyright © 1986 by Carolyn Steedman. Reprinted with permission of Rutgers University Press.
Excerpts from *Loving in the War Years* by Cherríe Moraga. Reprinted by permission of South End Press.
Excerpts from *The House on Mango Street*. Copyright © 1989 by Sandra Cisneros. Published in the United States by Vintage Books, a division of Random House, Inc., New York, and distributed in Canada by Random House of Canada Limited, Toronto. Originally published in somewhat different form by Arte Publico Press in 1984 and revised in 1989. Reprinted by permission of Susan Bergholz Literary Services, New York.

for my family

Contents

Preface

The aim of this book is to theorize the politics and possibilities of women's self-representation, to offer a feminist critique of autobiography, and to argue for a mode of reading that exposes self-representation as a contradictory code whose interruptive effects can be located in other genres. In effect, I wish to describe how the category of autobiography engages with other discourses of self-representation and to locate autobiographical authority in that engagement. Whether and when autobiography emerges as an authoritative discourse of reality and identity, and any particular text appears to tell the truth, have less to do with that text's presumed accuracy about what really happened than with its apprehended fit into culturally prevalent discourses of truth and identity. Thus, I read autobiography to discern how it engages with "truth" telling and "lying," those determinants of autobiographical authority, how it participates in linking identity to gender, and how it politicizes and aestheticizes that connection.

By placing "truth" and "lying" in quotation marks, I intend to indicate the extent to which they are constructs with histories. On the one hand, they form one of the most persistent binarisms for determining aesthetic and social value. On the other hand, many poststructuralists would take their thoroughly constructed status as something to be seen through, moved beyond, and rendered obsolete, the terms themselves participants in long-worn-out modes of thinking. I stand somewhere in between, for I believe it is crucial in a discussion of autobiography to examine, first, the discursive legacy of "truth" and "lying" in the ongoing project of self-representation, especially the attachment of "lying" to women's cultural productions; second, the kinds of human agency licensed or criminalized through these constructs; and third, the extent to which authority and power are structured through their historically shifting modes, for women and men, in relation to institutions. I offer this book, then, as an intervention in those constructions, if only for the time it takes to read and remember these words, and to break the link between "women" and "lying."

For the most part, feminist critics of autobiography have agreed there is a lived reality that differs for men and women and accounts for much of the difference between men's and women's autobiography. Just exactly how that difference might be represented is still an open question. Indeed, the desirability of difference as an organizing principle for feminist criticism is a newly open question. In her introduction to the first feminist anthology of autobiography criticism, Estelle Jelinek claimed that because women's lives are characterized by fragmentation, interruption, and discontinuity, so too are their autobiographies. Although this early insight introduced gender into a discussion from which it had previously been absent, it also risked reifying gender's most negative and least problematized formulations. Generalizations about the nature of women's lives are difficult to sustain when class, race, and sexual orientation are substantively and theoretically incorporated into analysis. And generalizations about how the organization of daily life "produces," or even "causes," autobiographical form depend on a kind of formalist gender logic that transcribes lived experience onto textual production and then presumes to read textual *effects* as experiential *cause*. When "experience" as a category of analysis is thematized rather than historicized and is used to cover the complex links securing "identity" to "gender" in the practice of "(self-) representation," it may play a role in the politics of interpretation altogether different from that its authors desire.

Nevertheless, until the feminist reinterpretation of autobiography, begun in the early 1980s with two important anthologies, Jelinek's *Women's Autobiography: Essays in Criticism* and Domna Stanton's *Female Autograph*, the study of autobiography was caught up in projects that further "genericized" a literary tradition. My critique of some feminist interpretations of autobiography, in fact, builds on the gains made by feminists. To distinguish my book from other feminist work on autobiography, let me say that my interest lies less in a theory of women's writing than in a feminist theory of autobiographical production. I emphasize feminist interpretation *in relation to* the discourses of self-representation as the site of my own critique in order to focus the following critical concerns.

First, the differences among women are so pervasive, specific, and significant to both political and aesthetic interpretations that any effort to consolidate "women" as a unified group risks homogenizing differences that feminists are now in a position to explore. Feminist interpretation that focuses on women's difference from men has been strategically advantageous in and out of the academy, but at the end of the twentieth century, we are witnessing the erosion of that position's benefits. The stresses within the political group "women" reveal the extent to which our feminist analyses have been limited by class and race bias and by an acceptance of gender and sexuality as essentially the same thing. The subject of feminism and the subject positions of women have been narrowed and unified in the name of political representation and social change. The result, however, has been registered as an increasing alienation of women from the name of feminism and the single identity of women as a social group or class. Many feminist interpretive strategies produce gender as a coherent category of analysis even as they fail to reproduce feminism as a political critique of much categorical thought. Although my own research on women's autobiography originated in an effort to discover underlying principles of continuity, that is, to produce women's autobiography as a knowable category, I became acutely aware of the extent to which autobiographers contest gender identity rather than simply enact it.

Second, I came to this project by reading autobiographies by women and discovering that although these were largely ignored in literary criticism, they nonetheless frequently occupied positions in other historical and critical discourses. How had autobiography studies resisted a range of self-representational texts by women when those same texts had demonstrated appeal to other audiences? In fact, in specific places and at specific times, debates over "what a woman is and should be" and "what a man is and should be" chart their course through autobiography, however a particular culture defines autobiography, and do so in relation to still other discourses in which the subject is engendered. Additionally, I found that the texts by men which constituted the emerging canon of autobiography are problematical as proof of the principles they have been pressed into service to demonstrate. Through what theories of representation and in relation to what values had Augustine's *Confessions* come to signify coherence, stability, and rationality? Through the delimiting of what contexts had *Walden* and *The Education of Henry Adams* become ungendered emblems of American self-disclosure? And further, how had the terrain of truth telling, which is structured through the complex relationship of disclosure and concealment as well as a less-than-uniform or demonstrable adherence to a contested rationality, come to be populated by male autobiographers whose texts did not easily conform to critical canons of propriety? These questions and others indicate the centrality of the function of criticism to my project.

Third, the emphasis in many feminist studies of women's autobiographies, diaries, and oral histories is on locating the similarity of
women's experiences. My own interest in women's autobiography
does not depend in any primary way on a shared "female experience"
to interpret the production of texts by women. There are those who
will find this approach politically limiting and others who will miss
the thematic continuity that makes the movement from cradle to autobiography to grave into a more or less shared story of female turning
points, crises, and conversions. I find, however, that in arguing for
the representation of identity, a crucial aspect of which is gender, I
cannot locate female identity and experience in a unitary, transhistorical female experience and female body and claim those as unproblematical and unifying grounds of meaning. For even if "woman" is a
gendered production of meaning occurring in autobiographies written by men and women and even when many women position themselves differently in relation to this figure than do men, a critical gap
still looms between anatomy and autobiographical destiny. To construe the translation of anatomy and even experience into textual
inevitability reduces the complex articulation of gender either to a
difference within the signifying subject or to a specific quality that
attaches to a variety of persons we call "women" in relation to other
totalizing ways of representing persons (e.g., class and race). Similarly, to assume that this translation takes place most automatically in
a particular form—autobiography—reduces the study of self-representation to a narrowly defined genre. Gender identity is frequently
contested by the writers I study here. For them, even when the non-
textual possibilities for changing normative heterosexuality, racism,
and classism—whether in relationships, communities, or profes-
sions—may not exist, the imaginative grounds for such praxis may be
constructed in an autobiography.

Thus, I would agree with Denise Riley's argument in *"Am I That
Name?"* (1989) that the differing temporalities of the category of
"women" reveal its synchronic and diachronic discontinuities more
than the continuity upon which some feminisms have depended.
While "women," as a category, is historically dynamic and even contradictory within contemporary formations, so too is it less than totalizing for individuals. That is, as Judith Butler writes, even if "one *is* a
woman, that is surely not *all* one is."[1] This argument, however, in no
way diminishes the material consequences of being interpellated as

---

[1] Judith Butler, *Gender Trouble: Feminism and the Subversion of Identity* (New York: Routledge, 1990), 3.

"woman" or a member of the category "women" by discursive and juridical systems. Arguing similarly against the grain, Butler asks whether the stability and coherence we attribute to the category of "women" for the purposes of grounding feminist politics and interpretation do not unwittingly participate in the regulation, reification, and maintenance of hierarchical gender relations. The effects of this thinking about "women" for a feminist theory of self-representation shape my analysis of the relations among gender, identity, and politics of representation as I negotiate within two histories: (one) the history of self-representation constructed by autobiography studies and (two) the contemporary discursive histories of specific autobiographical texts.

A focus on identity, gender, and the politics of representation entails viewing the criticism of autobiography as much more than commentary, primarily because it is that criticism's participation in mutually sustaining arguments about gender and genre which construe a self, a life worth telling about, and a history, in general, to be outside the authority of some. Further, those writers who have been programmatically placed outside the genre are always somehow "found" on the margins, the margins being construed as a "place" quite literally "without" history. Traditional criticism of autobiography has constructed a genre that authorizes some "identities" and not others and links "autobiography" to the post-Enlightenment politics of individualism or the post-Romantic aesthetics of self-expression or both. In contrast, much feminist criticism of autobiography has sought thematic, formal, and even broadly epistemological coherence among all women's autobiography, claiming that women represent the self by representing others because that is how women know and experience identity. This "self" that women represent has frequently been white, heterosexual, and educated; has sought identity in relationships rather than in autonomy; and has been conscripted as a player in the mother-daughter plot. Insofar as feminist criticism of autobiography has accepted a psychologizing paradigm, it reproduces the following ideological tenets of individualism: men are autonomous individuals with inflexible ego boundaries who write autobiographies that turn on moments of conflict and place the self at the center of the drama. Women, by contrast, have flexible ego boundaries, develop a view of the world characterized by relationships (with priority frequently given to the mother-daughter bond), and therefore represent the self in relation to "others." According to Mary Mason, this "other" or "others" may be represented as husband, children, even God, but in all cases the female self is depicted as profoundly influenced by the "other" and this primary relationship structures the autobiography. I argue, instead, that autobiography does not simply possess an experiential base from which it departs and which it seeks to depict.

The extent to which the "women" in "women's autobiography" have been stabilized, have been given a history, have had female identity conferred upon them and been seen as speaking and confirming this identity, obscures the broader ways in which gender is produced through the discourses of self-representation. I do not argue, therefore, from the premise that gender is a natural given; rather, bodies and identities are made knowable through a hierarchical and binary grid of "sex" which then makes gender intelligible (Butler, *Gender Trouble*, 151). Autobiography is positioned within discourses that construct truth, identity, and power, and these discourses produce a gendered subject. And while I am specifically interested in how women have negotiated these discourses, I do not assume that all women will negotiate them the same way. For all the instability and incoherence in the category of "women," as well as the category of autobiography, both generate a remarkable negative capability: both categories hold together disparate and contradictory interpretations of identity and history and collect an irreconcilable variety of experience and representation under a single name. The names of "women" and "autobiography," then, come to represent diversity as a natural and stable identity. Such is the logic of the name: here, it designates an ideological formation of identity and its representation through the terms "women" and "autobiography." Once those effects have been consolidated under a given name, the constructive dimension of that designation is obscured and seems simply to refer to something that was already there and waiting to be named.

The categories of "gender" and "women," like the category of "the individual," are problematized aspects in my study of self-representation. Both categories and the values that hold them in place have shifted considerably from Julian of Norwich's *Revelations of Divine Love* to Cherríe Moraga's *Loving in the War Years*, from Saint Teresa's *Life* to Minnie Bruce Pratt's "Identity: Skin Blood Heart." For most of the women I study, the practice of writing an autobiography allows a conceptual affiliation with certain attributes of "the individual," especially those related to self-definition. For many women, access to autobiography means access to the identity it constructs. Therefore, the distinction between self-representation as a political discourse and self-representation as an artistic practice is less important than their simultaneity of function in a particular culture and for specific audiences. Inasmuch as the "individual" is a discursive formation, autobiography is one of the major discourses through which it is produced and maintained. I would agree here with the structuralist (Lévi-Strauss) and poststructuralist (Derrida) insight that certain narratives offer structural or symbolic solutions to problems they cannot solve thematically. If the problem is the mystery of "identity," then a symbolic solution lies in the discursive production of autobiography's myth of identity. Similarly, "truth" can be seen as a conceptual problem that may be addressed, if not exactly solved, through an apparatus of truth production: the legal and spiritual confession or testimonial, the presentation of evidence, the specialized form of legal questioning. Autobiography seems to stabilize "truth" and a subject who may utter it. This is no less the case in autobiographies that invoke the therapeutic aspects of confession over the legalistic ones. Yet, both aspects offer a powerful promise to readers and writers alike: the remembering of a "truthful" subject.

I owe the first debt of gratitude to the women whose work is gathered in this text. Their writing has been my inspiration. Closer to home, I am grateful for the support I have had from family, friends, colleagues, and institutions throughout the writing of this book. Evan Watkins has participated in the full trajectory of its production, and I thank him for insightful comments throughout. Marcia Aldrich, whose own work proves autobiographical writing as a site of resistance, will recognize her signature throughout in the figure of the X. She has provided abiding friendship for which I am always grateful. Joseph Allen generously contributed his knowledge of everything from map reading to postmodern theory and, through his friendship and consistent challenge to all kinds of habits of thought, has deeply affected my thinking about identity and self-representation. Kathleen Ashley, Christopher Castiglia, Susan Sage Heinzelman, Kurt Heinzelman, Paul Jay, Françoise Lionnet, Nancy K. Miller, Shirley Neuman, and Sidonie Smith offered valuable comments on and encouragement for this book. Each stepped in at a significant point to restore momentum. Susan Heinzelman stepped in more than once and has offered encouragement through bright example. I have been well served by Bernhard Kendler and Joanne Hindman at Cornell University Press, and by Judith Bailey, who copyedited the manuscript. Celeste Schenck challenged me to develop my critical idiom and has my warm thanks. The anonymous first reader at Cornell has my deep gratitude for suggestions I everywhere tried to incorporate. I can only marvel at my students at the University of Southern Maine and Wellesley College who were astoundingly willing to take on the challenges of theory. Our theoretically informed political activism and politically informed exploration of theory taught me a great deal about feminist praxis and nonappropriative models of alliance, partnership, and coalition. I am still finding my way. My thanks especially to Mark Bishop, Gillian Harkins, Jim Jellison, Marlene Kenney, Joanna Piepgrass, Glen Powell, Jessica Reisman, and Tim Stover. Fellowship and research support was regularly offered by USM, which I gratefully acknowledge here.

Permission to draw on an earlier version of "A Signature of Lesbian Autobiography: 'Gertrice/Altrude,'" which appeared in *Prose Studies*, 14 (September 1991), is gratefully acknowledged here.

Finally, I dedicate this book to my family, a group of people who have considerably deepened my experience of life. I don't know how to thank any of them in conventional ways. I wonder, as is often said in dedications and acknowledgments, whether this book would exist without them. I know that the *I* who here writes *I* would not. So to my parents Natalie and Don Gilmore, my sister Sudee, my brothers Donny and David, my grandmother Cala Sue Henry Thompson, and especially to Tom Pounds, who honored what was at stake for me in this writing: here's something I made, buoyed by your inspiration and love; hope you like it. While my first thanks is to the writers I study, the ultimate thanks returns always to my family, my complicated knot of desire, love, and self-representation.

LEIGH GILMORE

Cambridge–Portland

Autobiographics

have been at the center of the production of autobiography. Auto-biography names the repeated invocation of an ideological formation that comes to seem natural—that is, in the simplest terms, that auto-biography is what men write, and what women write belongs to some "homelier" and minor traditions. While the full depth of the uncanniness (un-homelike-ness) of this home writing has yet to be explored, the projection of an all-too-familiar gender hierarchy onto texts through the terms "major" and "minor" has extended, in discus-sions of autobiography, to the persons who write. This gendered vision of the autobiographer affects the production and reception of women's self-representational texts. As the women I study here fre-quently point out, the dominant form of self-representational writing, historically variable and generically dynamic as it may be, seems to omit them not simply by oversight or accident. The very form of identity and authority it inscribes seems off limits. Autobiography, then, does not necessarily produce a fuller relation to the "real," to identity and authority, for women who write it. It may, as likely, prompt a profound renegotiation of the terms and forms of self-representation, one result of which is that women's autobiography cannot be recognized as "autobiography" when it is written against the dominant representations of identity and authority as masculine.

Such a brief circumlocution about the subject of women's auto-biography underscores the crisis in critical approaches to the dis-courses of women's self-representation. The crisis can be charac-terized as a kind of contractual dispute around gender and genre, in which the "terms" seek to define legitimacy within autobiography's discursive nexus of identity, representation, and politics. For all its synchronic and diachronic variety and density, gender (as female ID) persistently performs as incoherence, contradiction, and challenge within the discursive nexus named "autobiography." Interpretive frames that make autobiography knowable as a truth script for the representative man incorporate critical ideologies that take the subject and object of autobiography studies to be a man regarded by another man regarding *himself* (where *himself* is the shared referent of critic and autobiographer). Here, the subject position of woman autobiogra-pher so strains the discipline of autobiography studies that it has remained until recently a question beyond interpretation. One ques-tion many male artists and writers have been asking—"what is a woman that she could be represented?"—is transformed from a ques-tion about the object of representation when a woman becomes both the agent and the subject of self-representation. An inquiry into that project is profoundly marked by the ways in which critical, cultural, and aesthetic acts and their interpretations construe gender and representation as they are expressed in autobiography. For an exploration of the possibilities of women's self-representational writing is linked to the politics of self-representation. These acts and interpretations form a network for the production and understanding of self-representation within which both the materials of self-representation and the contexts for its understanding are reproduced.

When I began this project, the tools for finding and describing women's autobiography (its continuities, histories, and traditions) were inappropriate for what I call the discourses of self-representation. Not only could I not find women's autobiographies in critical studies, I could not consistently find them cataloged and shelved as autobiography in bookstores or libraries. Once I had found something that looked like an autobiography by a woman, an interpretation that already found me immersed in a problematical exercise in conjecture, how would I read it? What interpretive maps could chart the representation of a female or feminist subject? On one hand, when I began this book in the mid-1980s, the deconstructive map of misreading initially appealed through its ability to refigure "self"-representation and its resemblance to many women's a-centric texts. In its first incarnation in literary studies in the United States, deconstruction proved most effective, that is, most destabilizing, when it had a massive institutional and interpretive base within and against which to work. Clearly, this is not yet the case for Julian of Norwich's *Revelations of Divine Love*, with its marginal relation to literary tradition, although it is the case for Augustine's *Confessions*. On the other hand, the feminist archival tools of recovery prominent in the late 1970s and early 1980s weighted research toward the unpublished in a way that seemed to cede the field, in autobiography studies at least, to those published landmark texts (primary and critical) that already defined the terrain. For this project I needed different tools, different maps, and not ones that would locate women's self-representation either in relation to prominent features on a literary map of canonized works or in the authorized "sub"-genres to which they already belonged. In short, I discovered that a map for finding women's autobiography became a map for getting lost.[1]

---

[1] Many postmodern theorists have linked the mapping of space to the mapping of power, have used mapping both literally and figuratively, and have reached a variety of conclusions about the postmodern spatial order and its liberatory, confining, or panoptical possibilities. For example, Fredric Jameson uses the notion of "cognitive mapping" as an antidote for postmodern subjects who have lost perspective, or "critical distance," and are unable to locate themselves within multinational power relations. See "Cognitive Mapping," in *Marxism and the Interpretation of Culture*, ed. Cary Nelson and

In thinking about how this map could be read, Bakhtin's comments on the social audience are helpful both for what he notices and for what he makes it possible to notice:

> Each person's inner world and thought has its stabilized *social audience* that comprises the environment in which reasons, motives, values and so on are fashioned. . . . specific class and specific era are limits that the ideal of addressee cannot go beyond. In point of fact, *word is a two-sided act*. It is determined equally by *whose* word it is and *for whom* it is meant. As word, it is precisely *the product of the reciprocal relationship between speaker and listener, addresser and addressee*. Each and every word expresses the "one" in relation to the "other." I give myself verbal shape from another's point of view ultimately from the point of view of the community to which I belong.[2]

Although Bakhtin's description of the reciprocity of discourse has been widely influential, it seems to me his insights must be historicized and contextualized to be meaningfully applied to women's self-representation. For many women writers, the community into which one is born is not, ultimately, the community to which one belongs. Women who join convents, who cross classes and regions, who politi-

---

Lawrence Grossberg (Urbana: University of Illinois Press, 1988). Gilles Deleuze and Félix Guattari, in contrast to Jameson, explore mapping as a political construction of space, rather than its representation, and offer mapping as a way to redefine space as heterogenous, open, and variably negotiable for subjects. See *A Thousand Plateaus*, trans. Brian Massumi (Minneapolis: University of Minnesota Press, 1987). For related discussions, see Pierre Bourdieu, *Outline of a Theory of Practice*, trans. Richard Nice (Cambridge: Cambridge University Press, 1985); Bourdieu, *Distinction: A Social Critique of the Judgement of Taste*, trans. Richard Nice (London: Routledge, 1986); Michel Foucault, "Questions on Geography," in *Power/Knowledge*, ed. Colin Gordon (Brighton: Harvester, 1980); and Jacqueline Rose, *Sexuality in the Field of Vision* (London: Verso, 1986). From the viewpoint of social anthropology, Pierre Bourdieu's comments can be taken to illuminate the critic's situation: "It is significant that 'culture' is sometimes described as a *map*; it is the analogy which occurs to an outsider who has to find his [*sic*] way around in a foreign landscape and who compensates for his lack of practical mastery, the prerogative of the native, by the use of a model of all possible routes. The gulf between this potential, abstract space, devoid of landmarks or any privileged centre—like genealogies, in which the ego is as unreal as the starting-point in a Cartesian space—and the practical space of journeys actually made, or rather journeys actually being made, can be seen from the difficulty we have in recognizing familiar routes on a map or town-plan until we are able to bring together the axes of the field of potentialities and the 'system of axes linked unalterably to our bodies, and carried about with us wherever we go,' as Poincaré puts it, which structures practical space into right and left, up and down, in front and behind" (*Outline*, 2).

[2] V. N. Volosinov, *Marxism and the Philosophy of Language*, trans. Ladislav Matejka and I. R. Titunik (Cambridge: Harvard University Press, 1986), 86.

cize female identity, and who are lesbians locate themselves in complex relation to their communities or homes of origin and to the communities they join. Thus the nonreciprocity and the nonmirroring of many women as individuals by their social audiences makes Bakhtin's notion of "whose word it is and for whom it is meant" into a lifelong project rather than a simple description of communication. Moreover, the historical links among writers within a specific culture are obscured by the process of canonization and the history of criticism. We cannot tell from autobiography studies with *whom* many men were discursively engaged—neither whom they were addressing, ultimately, nor whom they were not.

The historical dimensions of self-representation have been severely limited by the values and methodology of many studies of autobiography. I begin, therefore, with the premise that women's self-representation describes territory that is largely unmapped, indeed unrecognizable, given traditional maps of genre and periodization. The historical communities in which women write, their choices to join different communities or to alter their given relation to a community in profound ways, and their relation to the male writers whose works have come to represent "autobiography" are little known within the bulk of autobiography studies. Thus instead of an introduction, which I cannot make, I offer a genealogy of the feminist interpretive strategy I call *autobiographics* and its relation to technologies of autobiography.

As Michel Foucault describes it, "genealogy is gray, meticulous, and patiently documentary."[3] Genealogy must find its subject in the act of seeking it, for history itself is part of the historicity of genealogical inquiry. Unlike historical inquiry, which already knows everything important about its subject and situation, "genealogy operates on a field of entangled and confused parchments, on documents that have been scratched over and recopied many times" (76). It is always a study of changed minds and catastrophe, of digressions that cannot predict or control their narrative ends. As Foucault conceptualizes it, history reduces while genealogy induces interest. As a model of desire, genealogy is all patience. Critical judgment is withheld and critical pleasure is gained through an engagement with diverse bodies of knowledge. Although Foucault's interest in holding off the moment of "truth," and his belief in the extension of his method, here understood as an analogy to sexual desire, is intelligible within the overall

---

[3] Michel Foucault, "Nietzsche, Genealogy, History," in *The Foucault Reader*, ed. Paul Rabinow (New York: Pantheon, 1984), 76.

dynamics of his work, genealogy proceeds through a diffusion of desire more interested in multiplying knowledges than in waiting for the right "one." I therefore affirm the limits of genealogy as my critical horizon for broadly methodological reasons: genealogy "must be sensitive to . . . recurrence, not in order to trace the gradual curve of their evolution, but to isolate the different scenes where [sentiments, love, conscience, instincts] engaged in different roles" (76). A genealogical introduction, then, is opposed to a search for origins even as it traces the temporary homes of meaning in a general attempt to understand where truth comes from.

If women's self-representational writing has no category with which it is identical, no single text that seems to mirror the larger familiar category of which it is another instance, that is because the organization of the history from which it seems to be excluded names it as "dis/organization."[4] To keep from getting lost in the usual ways—frequently by overrelying on traditional theories of interpretation and history which were developed to describe the literary characteristics of texts by mostly white, male, heterosexual-identified, non-working-class writers, and using this map to conclude that writers and theories other than the dominant ones must be "minor" or too difficult to assimilate—one must follow a route of estrangement from dominant codes of meaning and look again at the microhistory of cultural production and the critical histories of reception. But how does one map a field, map oneself in relation to a field, and learn to recognize an object on that map?

A brief excursus into map reading will illustrate what I am describing theoretically. Finding a subject, its history, and one's own relation to them depends on a belief in the cartographer's representation of reality, a map, which one holds in one's hands.[5] For example, I find myself on a map by sighting two prominent features on the landscape which correspond to two features on the map. I infer my position in relation to them and locate myself neither in the world nor on the map per se but rather in the convergence that authorizes the correspondence between a map and a world. I superimpose the two features I see on the landscape upon the map, find my desired destination in relation to them, and plot a course. Triangulation puts me on

[4] I am resisting here an approach toward women's autobiography that would analyze a series of paradigmatic texts, an approach taken by Mary Mason in her landmark essay on women's autobiography, "The Other Voice: Autobiographies of Women Writers," in *Autobiography: Essays Theoretical and Critical*, ed. James Olney (Princeton: Princeton University Press, 1980), 207–34.

[5] Conversations with Joseph Allen clarified the usefulness of this analogy.

the map, not in the world. I am, after all, already there but I lack bearings. I am lost.

Let autobiography studies stand for the map, the cartographer's representation of reality, here, the world of autobiographical texts. One finds oneself, then, in relation to features on this map; namely, autobiographies and studies of them. As a device for studying women's autobiography, the map seemed distinctly faulty. Did I even have the right one? Why couldn't I recognize the landscape? When I turned to women's autobiography, I found the spatiality conflicted and confusing (In what tradition does Saint Teresa belong? How to place Gertrude Stein in relation to other modernists?), and the prominent features offered less a way of arguing for the inclusion of certain marginalized writers within traditional genres than an argument for how they did not fit. Clearly, the map had been drawn to represent "reality" differently from how feminist critics of autobiography, dubious of "realism," would draw it. A map is, above all, an argument for realism; it is a truth-scape, made for an audience that, without it, is "nowhere." It offers a way to re-cognize what one is otherwise unable to know.

But the reality mapped by autobiography studies still poses problems for the person who is looking. The confusion generated by what autobiography *is* frequently manifests itself in *where* autobiographies are shelved. Sometimes autobiography is interfiled with biography, confirming William Spengemann's observation that autobiography is a subspecies of historical biography,[6] sometimes with history, confirming many of its practitioners' view that they are providing a "thick description" of their history and culture. Yet, women's autobiography suffers a deeper infelicity of organization. How might this affect readings of women's autobiography? What are the consequences of plotting a course with the wrong map? Small examples can be telling. While I was doing the initial research for this book, I learned a literal lesson about the difficulty of finding women's autobiography, a lesson that may illustrate what Adrienne Rich has called the "politics of location," which she describes in the context of self-representation: "I need to understand how a place on the map is also a place in history within which as a woman, a Jew, a lesbian, a feminist I am created and trying to create. Begin, though, not with a continent or a country or a house, but with the geography closest in—the body."[7] In a

[6] William Spengemann, *The Forms of Autobiography: Episodes in the History of a Literary Genre* (New Haven: Yale University Press, 1980).

[7] Adrienne Rich, "Notes toward a Politics of Location," in *Blood, Bread, and Poetry* (New York: Norton, 1986), 212.

search for Joyce Johnson's *Minor Characters* (1983), a book I knew was in stock, I turned to the bookseller for help after exhausting my usual strategies for tracking down autobiography. I learned that *Minor Characters* could be found in "Fiction"—fine so far: women autobiographers are frequently assumed to have "made it up"—under Kerouac, with whom Johnson had lived on and off for two years. Johnson nowhere describes *Minor Characters* as a biography, as readers of this introduction will no doubt already have surmised, but the classification signifies a fairly entrenched mode of "organizing" and, indeed, of valuing what women write about their lives.

Joyce Johnson begins *Minor Characters* by reading a photograph snapped at Columbia in 1945 of Jack Kerouac, Allen Ginsberg, William S. Burroughs, Hal Chase, and Neal Cassady. The photograph, a document from the prehistory of the Beats, is not from Johnson's own collection of memorabilia. "The snapshot is in a book now," she writes; "As I've grown older, the figures in the photo have grown younger."[8] The young men in the photo compete for the viewer's eye: Ginsberg by closing his own tightly, as if in defiance of the intrusion; Kerouac by welcoming the gaze, as he holds the viewer with his grinning intensity. By beginning her book with an interpretation of this photograph, Johnson simultaneously locates herself as both the writer of one book and the reader of another, for this particular photograph functions as a pivotal intertext. Johnson finds the snapshot in another book about this period of cultural history, in the appendix to a photo-laden documentary of the Beat generation in which women are mainly absent or underrepresented to the point of unrecognizability. In a gesture that refutes her position as a footnote to an era, Johnson re-places the photo at the beginning of her own book and rereads the place of women at the "end" of the other historical text. She was, after all, "there," as were the women of her generation, but nowhere represented.

The women, she finds, signify through their lack of visibility, through the stories not told of them, and through the critical representation of a literary and cultural movement filtered through the romanticizing haze of homosocial bonding. In order to establish another perspective that will enable her to "see" herself and other "minor" characters, Johnson reshapes the notion of insignificance within which women of her generation were known and, for a time, came to know themselves. Of some, such as Edie Parker, Johnson knows

[8] Joyce Johnson, *Minor Characters* (New York: Pocket Books, Simon and Schuster, 1983), 1.

little. When Parker splits from a short-lived romance with Kerouac, she "disappears." Johnson, however, makes this disappearance a feature of historical writing and examines its operation: "It was all over between [Edie Parker and Jack Kerouac], though, by January of 1945, and then Edie vanishes—at least from the literary histories—writing a pathetic letter to Allen Ginsberg, imploring him for a list of books 'like the ones you first read'" (3). Of others, such as Joan Vollmer Burroughs, whose death is the punch line to the question "*Ever hear the one about the man who played William Tell with his wife and missed?*" (5), Johnson writes against the "coldly stylized" narrative that memorializes Joan Burroughs as a joke. Johnson speculates from another perspective than the one authorized by the formal demands of the "bizarre anecdote." She probes, "But look at it another way," and offers that "maybe it was a knowing, prescient act of suicide on Joan's part, the ultimate play-out of total despair" (5–6).

Johnson seeks to situate women among women or at least within contexts that explain rather than sensationalize and dismiss them, partly for sympathy but mostly in order to interrogate the construction of women's lives as minor, insignificant, off the record. For it is within and against such practices that Johnson must locate herself and reorganize representation (literally, here, in the index of a book devoted to the history of the Beats) as she writes an autobiography: "I look in the index of the book with the snapshot of Jack and Allen and the others, and there I find: *Joyce Glassman*. And half a dozen page references, having to do with approximately one-twentieth of my life, 1957–1959, when I used to have that name" (6). Finding her way out of indexical representation and into self-representation depends for Johnson upon challenging an entrenched model of historical mapping, upon the rejection of a particular "place-name" that marked her identity in relation to one man and one aspect of his "world," and upon the persistent depiction of herself and other women as background features or ornamentation.

Johnson's interpretation of a photograph and a book index as places where women are *not* represented describes both objects from a perspective they do not immediately offer. Thus, she emphasizes the problem of spatiality with which I began: the general problem of finding women and the theoretical problem of remapping. For Johnson, the literal problem of exclusion is related to a perspective that excludes, a point of view that does not include women within the frame of reference, and thereby establishes the link between spatiality, or location, and epistemology, or, in this case, locating. The literal problems of spatiality are linked to the figurative problems of knowing and representing oneself in relation to a spatial grid of absence. Perhaps most interestingly, Johnson renders her previous dislocation as re-location in a way that comments upon the relation between spatiality and temporality, for Johnson now knows her place in that time differently; she re-presents her enforced absence as a historical construction, a narrative of a time in which she lived but of which she was not an official part. Temporality and spatiality are susceptible to re-vision in Johnson's self-representational project; indeed, to tell her story, she must revise both. And in so doing she demonstrates how both space and time are constructive dimensions of self-representation and not only the neutral organization of life to which an autobiographer may simply refer.

As Johnson's opening chapter also helps to make clear, a larger strategy for classifying women's autobiography than any particular bookseller's way of stocking the shelves is operating when the value and identity of *Minor Characters* is defined in relation to Kerouac. This strategy is indicated by the deletion of the marker of "self" as Johnson is transformed from woman autobiographer to a man's biographer. The refusal to acknowledge the link between the "self" of *auto*biography and the gender of the autobiographer participates in even broader strategies, for autobiographies perform powerful ideological work: they have been assimilated to political agendas, have fostered the doctrine of individualism, and have participated in the construction and codification of gendered personhood. Myths of American self-sufficiency, for example, of crafty capitalist know-how, and of gender, race, and class have been deployed throughout the history of American autobiography. Yet this has been a contested history, for the complex social authority autobiography comes to have at any particular moment in history or the value some autobiographies retain within literary and cultural traditions depends on a range of factors. In order to analyze that authority, interpretation must attend to the cultural and discursive histories of self-representation, rather than to some overarching explanation for the gendered differences between men's and women's autobiography.

To agree with the notion that gender is culturally constructed and that this construction is politically and ideologically interested in no way minimizes the effects of gender oppression on all women—neither on those who take gender as a "natural" property nor on those who interpret it as a cultural construction. For gender is both a *lived construction*, one that operates intimately and institutionally and is an integral aspect of all Western modes of hierarchy, and a *nonlived* (an impeding, even deforming) *ob-struction*. As an aspect, then, of

self-representation, gender attaches to a number of terms of value—
identity, authority, and truth, among them—and these attachments
are both resisted and inscribed in women's autobiography.

But how to find these on the map? The writers whose texts have
been used as the base of an argument for what autobiography is, form
a set of "exemplary" literary, political, and military men; they have
been seen (and this view persists) as singular figures capable of summing up an era in a name: Augustine, Rousseau, Franklin, Henry
Adams. Some feminist critics have taken these writers as a homogeneous group that forms, or has been formed into, a tradition against
which women write. As formulated initially by Estelle Jelinek, men's
autobiography follows patterns of coherence and unity and is characterized by a narrative that deploys the stable and autonomous *I* as its
hero. These values have been attributed to the canonical male autobiographers, however, through a patriarchally informed mode of interpretation. These canonical texts are themselves the site of far more
contradictory inscriptions of gender and genre than have previously
been thought *in autobiography studies*. The male autobiographies that
many feminist critics have claimed as models of unity and coherence,
such as Augustine's and Rousseau's, evidence the discursive and
ideological tensions of the models of personhood they invoke. My
own research has not borne out the claim that all men or all women
do any one thing in autobiography all the time.

In drawing a map for interpreting women's autobiography and other self-representational texts, I question the limits of gender as a
category of analysis in an effort to sharpen the critical and political
edge of feminist criticism, especially insofar as a focus on gender may
theoretically diminish the significance of sexuality, race, and class.
Gender is interpretable through a formalist logic by which the sex one
can *see* becomes the gender one must *be*. According to the formalist
logic of gender, the binary of sex (of which there are only two: male
and female) is the "natural" ground onto which gender as a cultural
construction is layered. Autobiography, then, according to this logic
of development, would translate the fact of sexual difference through
the experience of gender to its subsequent representation. In this
dynamic of production, autobiography is the last domino to fall: sex
becomes gender becomes experience becomes book. This domino effect in which sexual difference topples headlong into autobiography
describes the production of an *object* hammered into position by the
institutional inscriptions of gender, normative heterosexuality, class
positioning, racial marking, and a range of cultural coding that makes
us as legible as the other bar-coded items we consume. This object,

however, has been described as the self-standing autobiographical subject. I will focus on the relation between gender and autobiography as a way to interrupt the regular toppling of these dominoes. In particular, many of the writers I study here are lesbians. Their writing offers historical and cultural accounts of how gender and sexuality are not simultaneously known, experienced, lived, and represented. Indeed, their self-representational projects perform cultural work through autobiography focused on how sex does *not* become gender become heterosexual desire become female subjectivity. For many medieval mystics, as well as twentieth-century lesbian writers, conventional narratives of development, both cultural and literary, which conform to the logic of falling dominoes fail. They reveal the objectifying mechanism of subject formation.

The subject of autobiography, upon which so much scrutiny has recently focused, can be more accurately described as the object of production for the purposes of cultural critique. This object has been produced as *possessing* attributes whose meaning must be *acquired* for the requirements of legibility in the broadest sense, that is, for us to be read as subjects. Thus the ways in which an autobiographer variously acknowledges, resists, embraces, rejects objectification, the way s/he learns, that is, to interpret objectification as something less than simply subjectivity itself marks a place of agency. It is in this act of interpretation, of consciousness, that we can say a woman may exceed representation within dominant ideology. She exceeds it not because she possesses some privileged relation to nature or the supernatural. Rather, the discourses and practices that construct subjectivity through hierarchy must always be defended, their boundaries guarded, their rights maintained. Within these discourses exist unruly subjects who are unevenly objectified and who represent identity in relation to other values and subjectivities. In other words, if feminist theory describes women as "objects of exchange" in order to analyze social organization and to reveal the constitutively delimited sphere of possibility for women, my work builds from that critique to analyze how women use self-representation and its constitutive possibilities for agency and subjectivity to become no longer primarily subject to exchange but subjects who exchange the position of object for the subjectivity of self-representational agency.

The question of gender, then, cannot be explored mainly through the compulsory lumping together of all male-authored texts, on one side, and all female-authored texts on the other. Instead, I think, the question can usefully be enjoined at a more specific level, at the level of each text's engagement with the available discourses of truth and identity and the ways in which self-representation is constitutively shaped through proximity to those discourses' definition of authority. As useful as more monolithic claims about "men's" and "women's" autobiography have been to feminists during this crucial historical period in the institutionalization of feminism, generalizations about gender and genre in autobiography naturalize how men, women, and the activity of writing an autobiography are bound together within the changing philosophies of the self and history. As a hedge against this tendency, I will attempt to chart the terrain—the discourses of self-representation—differently by looking to noncanonical texts in order to understand how and in what ways women's self-representation occurs and in relation to what cultural institutions and forms it is written. To do so, I shift simultaneously within two critical discourses: feminist criticism and autobiography studies, and the differing temporalities of their subjects in relation to the differing possibilities of finding them. These discourses can be taken as different legends for a map that is still being drawn, and they should demonstrate that women's self-representational writing is bound up in still other discourses.

In the first chapter, I argue that there are not so much autobiographies as autobiographics, those changing elements of the contradictory discourses and practices of truth and identity which represent the subject of autobiography. Rather than attempt to reconsolidate the category of "autobiography" by causing it to "tell the truth" about women, I emphasize how the incoherence in the category can be used to further a feminist theory of autobiographical production. This emphasis gives conceptual precedence to positioning the subject, to recognizing the shifting sands of identity on which theories of autobiography build, and to describing "identity" and networks of identification. Through readings of Audre Lorde's *Zami* and Carolyn Steedman's *Landscape for a Good Woman*, I show how autobiographics avoids the terminal questions of genre and close delimitation and offers a way, instead, to ask: Where is the autobiographical? What constitutes its representation?

In the second chapter, the main concern is to explore how autobiography is located within a discursive field that engenders subjects and to intervene in the critical reproduction of that engendering. The problem of autobiography as a genre has been variously resisted on the following grounds. First, generic definitions of autobiography are an attempt to legitimate and canonize a marginal form of writing and, as such, almost always fail to win for autobiography the prestige of, say, the novel. Second, any interest in autobiography necessarily devolves from an interest in the author; thus autobiographical writing itself has no more or less intrinsically coherent or organizationally binding elements than the persons who write it. Third, auto-biographical writing can be expressed in a variety of genres and therefore has few meaningfully separable generic traits. In contrast to the category of "autobiography" indicated through this critique, I read a set of contemporary texts, focusing particularly on Sandra Cisneros's *House on Mango Street* and Jamaica Kincaid's *Annie John*, as examples of self-representation which call into question the constructed line between autobiography and fiction and explore them through autobiographics.

The critique of genre is further enjoined in Chapter 3 in which I describe confession as a discursive practice that both produces and polices "truth," "gender," and "identity." There I argue that auto-biography recuperates the technologies of self-representation present in the confession and deploys them to authorize and deauthorize certain "identities." Indeed, autobiography draws its social authority from its relation to culturally dominant discourses of truth telling and not, as has previously been asserted, from its privileged relation to "real life." I explore the extent to which the discourses of "truth" and "lying" underwrite aesthetic production and judgment through an analysis of how autobiography criticism participates in "policing truth" when it, in effect, criminalizes certain autobiographers.

In "Genders, Bodies, Identities," the fourth chapter, I elucidate the counter discourse of word/body deployed by medieval mystics in order to read Roland Barthes's description and enactment of a lover's discourse through two mystical texts. The medieval mystics' (self-) representation of the ecstatic body as the ground of and evidence for mystical rapture places considerable pressure on the Western foundations of autobiography in a particular way. Namely, it moves the body, so frequently absent from autobiography, to the thematic and epis-temological fore. This revision of the mind/body split results in a marked incoherence between the representation of "identities and truth" and the form that would contain them.

In Chapter 5 I explore how the gendered connection of word and body influences self-representation. Here, I read Genesis and *The Woman Warrior* as creation stories that deploy myths of human agency through representations of the female body. Both narratives represent the "creation" of gender as bodily violence. This analysis contextual-izes Cherríe Moraga's use of war metaphors and their relation to feminist self-representation.

In Chapter 6 I argue that Gertrude Stein rewrites the contradictory codes of gender, sexuality, and identity through the language of auto-biography. By doing so, Stein exposes and heightens the contradic-tory aspects of (self-) representation. Stein's career-long interest in autobiographical experimentation is characterized by a practice that reads autobiography against the grain of conventional interpretations not only in her disruption of autobiographical form, with its emphasis on chronological organization and narrative development, but also in her reinterpretation of the lesbian couple as the *I* of autobiography. I contextualize her experimentation within two histories: the emer-gence and submergence of a "butch-femme" semiotics and the devel-oping feminist criticism of autobiography.

I conclude by examining contemporary representations of feminist subjectivities and critical narratives of feminist "identities." Here I take up debates concerning feminist confession and the effect of femi-nist rhetoric on feminist self-representation. In this context I examine the construction of feminist subjects by Donna Haraway, Minnie Bruce Pratt, and Patricia Williams. Haraway's "cyborg," Pratt's "iden-tity," and Williams's "alchemist" indicate not only the possibilities for self-representation within feminist discourses of truth and identity but the politics of those representations as well.

1

Autobiographics

Self-Representation: Instabilities in Gender, Genre, and Identity

There is no gender identity behind the expressions of gender.
—Judith Butler, *Gender Trouble*

A genre, whether literary or not, is nothing other than the codification of discursive properties.
—Tzvetan Todorov, *Genres in Discourse*

You are of course never yourself.
—Gertrude Stein, *Everybody's Autobiography*

Autobiography provokes fantasies of the real. Its burden is not only
to represent gender, genre, and identity in any particular lived and
imagined configuration, but to posit a ground from which that configuration is thought to emerge. Gender, genre, and identity and, therefore, autobiography, are similarly "grounded" in metaphysics, in the
belief that representation is layered over substance. As my epigraphs
suggest, however, this seeming *real* is, in no small part, fantasy. In
several books devoted to (self-) representation, Gertrude Stein questioned how autobiography could be produced and what effects its
production would have on the identity of the autobiographer.[1] Stein
discovered how representing oneself to oneself and to others creates
enough discursive spacing to allow the autobiographer to see the
discontinuities in "identity" and to construe its representation as a

[1] The following works are central to an understanding of Gertrude Stein's experi-
ments in self-representation, autobiography, and biography: *The Making of Americans:
Being a History of a Family's Progress, 1906–1908* (1925; New York: Something Else Press,
1966); *The Autobiography of Alice B. Toklas* (1933; New York: Vintage, 1961); *Everybody's
Autobiography* (1937; London: Virago, 1985); and *Fernhurst, Q.E.D., and Other Early
Writing* (New York: Liveright, 1971).

problem in writing. Indeed, autobiography wraps up the interrupted and fragmentary discourses of identity (those stories we tell ourselves and are told, which hold us together as "persons") and presents them as persons themselves. Autobiography as a genre, however, has come to be identified less with these discourses and the act of piecing them together, than with master narratives of conflict resolution and development, whose hero—the overrepresented Western white male—identifies his perspective with a God's-eye view and, from that divine height, sums up his life. Scholars of autobiography have developed this master narrative into an interpretive grid and judged as worthy those autobiographers who represent themselves within its limits.

The limits of value in autobiography are demonstrated by the conflation of the value of the text with the value of the autobiographer. That is, the notion of what an autobiography is, which involves a judgment rendered within a network of identity-constructing discourses (such as the spiritual and legal confessions, certain religious and philosophical practices, psychoanalysis, and so on) is historically bound up with what we understand to be identity itself. Insofar as any notion of autobiography is necessarily enmeshed with the politically charged and historically varying notions of what a person is, we can focus on autobiography as a way to understand how (self-) representation and authority get linked up with projects that encode gender and genre. The encoding of gender and genre in the case of autobiography can be focused initially in this way: gender is produced through institutions and discourses that seek to divide and differently authorize persons as "men" and "women"; genre is produced by stabilizing and seeming to answer the questions: What is a "self" that it can be represented? What is autobiography that it can represent a self? We can see the ways in which autobiography is produced within discourses of identity that are powerfully informed by concerns about gender when we ask the definitional question that links gender with genre: What is women's autobiography?

The question turns for an answer in two directions: to its generic base—"What is autobiography?"—and to a question posed in increasingly sophisticated ways by feminists: "What are 'women'?"[2] Neither has a commonsensical answer and both have tumultuous recent critical histories. Autobiography, a discursive hybrid, has only

---

[2] See especially Judith Butler, *Gender Trouble*; and Denise Riley, *"Am I That Name?" Feminism and the Category of "Women" in History* (Minneapolis: University of Minnesota Press, 1988), for discussions of the conceptual, historical, and political instabilities in the categories "woman" and "women."

recently achieved the kind of critical respect and interest indicated by university press publications and panels at professional conferences, and it seems to have done so rather suddenly. In a recent book, one critic claims that suddenly everyone is interested in autobiography.[3] Yet, what it *is* is up for grabs. The struggle for the meaning of both gender and genre, a category autobiography still strains, is being waged, as it long has been, in the practice and criticism of autobiography. The following illustration of differing theoretical positions indicates one interpretive contest. At one end of the spectrum of interpretation, a poststructuralist position developed through deconstruction reads autobiography tropologically and construes the self as an effect of language, a textual construction, the figuration of what we call identity. At the other, a feminist position grounds autobiographical form and meaning in the experiences of the women who write autobiography and looks to women's lives for the framework to understand self-representational texts. But the analogy to a spectrum supports only one version of the debate, for feminist and poststructuralist critical positions refuse to delimit even this single controversy in autobiography studies. They form, rather, open sets with some shared, or partially shared, figures. What is significant here is how both feminism and poststructuralism become involved in producing the discourse of identity when both address the definitional questions related to autobiography.

Both gender and genre as they converge in autobiography are produced through a variety of discourses and practices that depict "the individual" in relation to "truth," "the real," and "identity." This relationship is no less constructed when it relies on "experience" for authority than when the individual is construed wholly as a reading effect, as a subject position, or as an object of discursive production. Following Michel Foucault (who described sex as a technology) and Teresa de Lauretis (who analyzed the technologies of gender) deeper into the technologies of autobiography (of self *and* self-representation), we may describe how certain discourses and practices produce what we have come to call autobiography and the autobiographical subject, as well as the values that subtend this category.[4]

Autobiography has been founded upon principles of identity: ontological, epistemological, and more generally, organizational. To

[3] Sidonie Smith, *A Poetics of Women's Autobiography: Marginality and the Fictions of Self-Representation* (Bloomington: Indiana University Press, 1987), 3.

[4] Michel Foucault, *The History of Sexuality*, vol. 1: *An Introduction*, trans. Robert Hurley (New York: Random House, 1978); Teresa de Lauretis, *Technologies of Gender: Essays on Theory, Film, and Fiction* (Bloomington: Indiana University Press, 1987).

question whether or not there is a self behind the autobiographical representation of self, a gender behind the representation of gender, a genre behind each expression of genre, challenges the founding notion of identity on which autobiography depends. To some extent, this questioning of identity (through gender and genre as they are represented in autobiography) goes beyond questions about autobiography's referentiality to challenge how we understand autobiography. I grant that autobiography's task is always to strive to produce "truth" and that cultures code this truth production through discourses that can be judged as truthful. If so, gender would be a technology of truth that is policed, regulated, enforced. And genre, too, insofar as I take autobiography to have a history as a genre— hence an effective legacy of determining which texts are and are not · autobiographical—is a technology that is read for truthfulness. We can use the notion of technology to focus on the discursivity of "identity," that is, on identity as a network of representational practices in which the production of truth is everywhere on trial.

Here I would assert with Foucault that "what is at issue" in autobiography, broadly, is the overall "discursive fact" (*History of Sexuality* 1:11), and what is at stake is the relation between discourses of power and identity. For the autobiographers I study here, whose subjectivities and truths reveal the limits of dominant notions of identity, the "discursive fact" of being interpellated or not interpellated as a subject had (and continues to have) a rippling effect throughout the historically varied technologies of autobiography. That these autobiographers' identities could not be inscribed in relation to dominant forms of truth telling—or, when they were, were not interpreted so— broadens our notion of "discursive fact" to include the material consequences that precede, coincide with, and follow self-representation. In order to emphasize this discursivity and its effect on the interpretation of autobiography, one could pursue Foucault's strategy of "locat[ing] the forms of power, the channels it takes, and the discourses it permeates . . . in short, the 'polymorphous techniques of power'" (11). For de Lauretis, whose work both challenges and extends Foucault's "technological" inquiry into the category of gender, power is exercised over and through representations of gender. One critical aspect of de Lauretis's method is an understanding of gender as (self-) representation, drawn from Louis Althusser's influential theory of ideological interpellation.[5] De Lauretis wishes to theorize a "female-

[5] Louis Althusser, "Ideology and Ideological State Apparatuses," trans. Ben Brewster, in *Critical Theory since 1965*, ed. Hazard Adams and Leroy Searle (Tallahassee: Florida State University Press, 1986), 239–50.

gendered subject" who is positioned both inside and outside the ideology of gender; a subject interpellàted as a "woman" who recognizes and knows herself, to some extent, through her culture's gender codes but who can also critique this coding and read gender as a construction. De Lauretis presses this argument less as a way of further alienating women from the dominant cultural codes of gender (though this is certainly one of its effects), than as a conceptual framework through which to reconceive the subject as a site of excessive and oppositional solicitations and markings. Her feminist theory of gender views female-gendered and feminist subjects as discursive products of the technologies of gender. For de Lauretis, the recognition of gender as a construction follows the logic of consciousness raising: it politicizes the subject.

To pursue the Althusserian connection, both the state ideological apparatuses and the micropolitical and sociocultural technologies of gender overwhelm the subject. They disallow its "coherence." The subject is crisscrossed by a multiplicity of "discourses, positions and meanings" (de Lauretis, *Technologies*, x), none of which totalizes the subject. Thus, the "feminine" subject immersed in the ideology of gender is not the only gendered construction available to women. Indeed, the various positionings of women within and against constructions of gender provides a powerful illustration for claims against the "naturalness" of gender. Throughout *The Technologies of Gender*, de Lauretis argues for a feminist subject and its "inscription in certain critical textual practices" (xi) as both a description of how gender construction functions and a prescription for how it can be made to "malfunction" through feminist intervention. I take genre to be one of the critical textual practices that de Lauretis's analysis can illuminate, especially as generic criticism deploys variously "gendered" rhetoric and criteria for evaluation. Given Althusser's insight about self-recognition as a feature of ideology—one is hailed as a subject and waves a hand of acknowledgment in return—we can hypothesize the significance of nonrecognition as an act of resistance, a refusal to speak when spoken to in the language of address. To refuse the location of subject, to speak ex cathedra, has been an underinspected mode of self-representation. For some autobiographers, when autobiography seems to collect under a single name the related ideologies of identity, power, and history, the refusal to identify self-representation with that name marks the site of resistance. Similarly, some autobiographers who, for a variety of reasons, do not recognize themselves within dominant representations and self-representations of gender refuse to represent themselves as "knowable" through gender. But the history of such refusals, a history indicated through absences in traditional studies of autobiography, is written against the grain of a powerful technology of identity.

The law of genre which defines much of traditional autobiography studies has been formulated in such a way as to exclude or make supplemental a discussion of gender.[6] The order of analysis has gone something like this: "First, we'll figure out what autobiography is; then we'll figure out what women's autobiography is." The appeal of such a method needs to be inspected immediately, especially since the metaphors of law on which it depends tend to generate critical narratives: once one has adopted figures such as "the law of genre" to describe cultural production, the oppositional figure of the outlaw—here, the woman writer as the protagonist of her own cultural narrative—must emerge, and isn't she all-too-familiar in this role? In

[6] What I am characterizing as traditional autobiography studies designates the pre-structuralist writing about autobiography which more or less ended its hegemony by the early 1970s. Its methods and premises have been recuperated by a number of critics who began publishing on autobiography in the 1970s. My use of the word "traditional," then, does not denote "past"; rather, it characterizes criticism that shares the humanist bent I outline. Specifically, "traditional" interpretations of autobiography take the self as a coherent and unified producer of truth and meaning and claim that this "self," as in Georges Gusdorf's significant article, is formed outside a community. See Gusdorf, "Conditions and Limits of Autobiography," trans. James Olney, in Olney, ed., *Autobiography: Essays Theoretical and Critical*, 28–49. One critical precursor of the renewed interest in autobiography is Roy Pascal, *Design and Truth in Autobiography* (London: Routledge, 1960). A survey of important work contributing to the transformation of autobiography studies would include Elizabeth W. Bruss, *Autobiographical Acts: The Changing Situation of a Literary Genre* (Baltimore: Johns Hopkins University Press, 1976); Spengemann, *Forms of Autobiography*, with a valuable bibliographical essay; James Olney, ed., *Autobiography: Essays Theoretical and Critical* (Princeton: Princeton University Press, 1980); a groundbreaking feminist anthology edited by Estelle C. Jelinek, *Women's Autobiography: Essays in Criticism* (Bloomington: Indiana University Press, 1980); followed by Domna Stanton's collection, *The Female Autograph* (1984; Chicago: University of Chicago Press, 1987); Karl Weintraub, *The Value of the Individual: Self and Circumstance in Autobiography* (Chicago: University of Chicago Press, 1978); and Paul John Eakin, *Fictions in Autobiography: Studies in the Art of Self-Invention* (Princeton: Princeton University Press, 1985). See Sidonie Smith, *A Poetics of Women's Autobiography*, for a lucid and learned analysis of this history and the impact it has for feminist criticism of autobiography.

Feminist criticism of autobiography uses gender as a category of analysis. Some excellent recent work includes Bella Brodzki and Celeste Schenck, eds., *Life/Lines: Theorizing Women's Autobiography* (Ithaca: Cornell University Press, 1988); Shari Benstock, ed., *The Private Self* (Chapel Hill: University of North Carolina Press, 1988); Nancy K. Miller, *Subject to Change: Reading Feminist Writing* (New York: Columbia University Press, 1988); Smith, *Poetics of Women's Autobiography*; Felicity Nussbaum, *The Autobiographical Subject: Gender and Ideology in Eighteenth-Century England* (Baltimore: Johns Hopkins University Press, 1989). New work is coming out even as I write these footnotes.

short, the law of genre creates outlaws. Although she was already lurking in the discourse of law and "crime," such a metaphor and its ensuing narratives efface other analyses. Primarily, the outlaw image immediately obscures how women's fairly visible and sometimes highly visible cultural contributions were marginalized, as well as how real cultural struggles of regulation and control force some texts and persons to the margins. Struggles for interpretive power are waged not only *by* noncanonical genres and marginalized writers but *with* the very contexts that make such struggles possible and necessary. Indeed, as I will show in a later chapter on the mystics, women's self-representation cannot strictly be considered as an outlaw or marginal discourse, because of its shaping influence on how the church came to know, interpret, and regulate religious experience through the confession. As a figure for an interpretive strategy, the law-outlaw metaphor is useful; yet, as a metaphor for women's writing, it tends to reinforce the conception that women are always already banished to the margins, and it may naturalize the practices that construct margin and center and then relegate some women to those margins.[7] Many women autobiographers, wary of the problem to varying degrees, have produced within the dominant mode an alternative autobiographicality that attests to the entrenched patriarchal view, reinforced by traditional studies of autobiography, that powerful cultural institutions and the very possibilities of self-representation are interpreted as the same discourses.

The renewed interest in autobiography has been energized by various contemporary interests in the subject, language, and history. I agree with the critical insight that texts perform a complex kind of cultural work—never more so than when they seek to represent the

[7] For two different views on marginalization, see bell hooks, *Feminist Theory: From Margin to Center* (Boston: South End, 1984); and Alicia Ostriker, *Stealing the Language: The Emergence of Women's Poetry in America* (Boston: Beacon, 1986). Important work that explores these cultural dynamics and constructs a context in which to read African-American, Chicano, and Native American autobiography includes William Andrews, *To Tell a Free Story: The First Century of African-American Autobiography, 1760–1865* (Urbana: University of Illinois Press, 1986); Arnold Krupat, *For Those Who Come After: A Study of Native American Autobiography* (Berkeley: University of California Press, 1985); Françoise Lionnet, *Autobiographical Voices: Race, Gender, Self-Portraiture* (Ithaca: Cornell University Press, 1989); Ramón Saldívar, *Chicano Narratives: The Dialectics of Difference* (Madison: University of Wisconsin Press, 1990); Valerie Smith, *Self-Discovery and Authority in African-American Narratives* (Cambridge: Harvard University Press, 1987); Robert Steptoe, *From behind the Veil: A Study of African-American Narrative* (Urbana: University of Illinois Press, 1979); Hertha Dawn Wong, *Sending My Heart Back across the Years: Tradition and Innovation in Native American Autobiography* (New York: Oxford University Press, 1992).

"self." Insofar as a text forms a specific discursive instance of more generalized and determining modes of production, the text and its readers participate in the modes of production. Part of the work of any text is the reproduction of ideology. I continue to use Althusser's definition of ideology here to describe "the imaginary relationship of individuals to their real conditions of existence" (241).

But how does one identify? With what, precisely? And how does this sense of identification signify in autobiography? A text momentarily stabilizes ideology for a reader, allows her to identify with or against the persons and situations represented, to imagine the scene, and, in so doing, creates the conditions in which ideology is reproduced. Yet, I would argue that this identification is not the result of a face-to-face encounter between reader and autobiographer in which the text is the mediator. Rather, the identification of the reader's text with the writer's text results from their triangulation with ideology. The reader sees not so much herself in the autobiography as the representation of her position in relation to other familiar positions within cultural scripts. Put another way, readers read texts ideologically, but the critical effects of that reading are obliterated through the mechanism of identification.

In autobiography, identification entails reproducing the complex ideology of "identity," variously inflected in the categories of "personhood," "citizenship," "women," and so on. By identifying with an autobiography, the reader constructs an "imaginary relation" to the situation the text depicts. Autobiography as unproblematized "realism" licenses this seeming referentiality between the text and real life. Identification as a primary mode of reading, then, is precritical and reinforces the value-laden sorting of autobiographers into "same as" or "different from" the reading *I*. To read an autobiography in this way, then, is to participate in a "truth"-structuring discourse, to affirm the reality of the autobiography, to naturalize ideology, and to stabilize "truth" as if all these simply pointed to the "real conditions of existence." Given this strong statement, however, it is important to clarify the differing politics of identification as a reading strategy, particularly in this respect: With what ideology is the reader identifying? Dominant ideology is reproduced through the precritical reading practice of identification. The reader projects into the text and extrapolates from the text an imaginary relation to, on the one hand, another imaginary relation (the domain of the text) and, on the other, material reality. In so doing, in the case of autobiography, the reader remakes the subject of autobiography into an extension of reading practices and confers upon that subject the status of an object.

Readers at odds with the dominant ideology may use identification as a critical reading strategy, but the theory of this practice works differently. Clearly, for many readers the possibility of seeing not only some aspect of their lives but a member of their community represented in print may decisively alter their notions of what counts culturally, of what is possible. Hence, the representational politics of identification are not used only to maintain restrictive ideological values. For many gay and lesbian readers, for example, the pleasures of identification are considerable, especially in a representational and legal culture of constraint, and many of the autobiographers I consider have been read to those productive ends. Imagine a reading practice that listens for another's voice, sees another's face even where sameness is sought, and searches not for the universal but for the specific, the unexchangeable. Identification, then, is contoured along the lines of the politics and possibilities in the cultural unfolding of self-representational writing.

As an example of reading strategies that can be usefully applied to autobiography, de Lauretis gains considerable theoretical leverage by situating the subject in relation to interimplicated networks and by theorizing the contradictory and opposing grounds on which (self-) representation must occur. She defines the subject as "en-gendered in the experiencing of race and class, as well as sexual, relations; a subject, therefore, not unified but rather multiple, and not so much divided as contradicted" (*Technologies*, 2). Gender, as de Lauretis has shown, should not be conceptualized as sexual difference, which boils down to woman's difference from man, but as both "representation and as self representation, . . . the product of various social technologies . . . and of institutionalized discourses, epistemologies, and critical practices, as well as practices of daily life" (2). Gender is not a static category, nor—and this is crucial—does it attach only to women. An analysis of the technologies of autobiography also allows for a focus on the formation and expression of race, ethnicity, sexual orientation, and class—in short, all aspects of identity which are represented, in varying degrees, through and in relation to the discourses of gender. Gender as the category that seems to sum women up, indeed, legitimates and necessitates the very category of women, can be further externalized and inspected by an analysis of the category of "women." As Denise Riley argues ("*Am I That Name*"), "women" is not as stable, as inevitable (let alone natural) a category as it seems. Indeed, according to Riley's historically oriented argument, it never has been. The political uses to which such constructions have been put is based less on "nature" than on arguments that claim a natural right. These same contradictions in the single subject "woman" and the plural subject "women" to a large degree structure what I take to be the technologies of autobiography.

To apply de Lauretis's formulation concerning gender and representation to autobiography, we can say that the autobiographical subject is a representation and its representation *is* its construction. The autobiographical subject is produced not by experience but by autobiography. This specification does not diminish the autobiographer; rather, it situates her or him as an agent in autobiographical production. For the discourses of truth and identity are varied and complex and when an autobiographer wishes, for example, to represent herself in opposition to a certain standard of "truth," I would argue that she knows what she's doing *rhetorically* and is not merely telling what happened. An emphasis on the rhetorical dimension of autobiography indicates its performative agency. Agency, as performance (that is, as discourse), has been identified as the action of the subject. How might autobiographical agency, identified in the rhetoric of truth telling, recast the autobiographical subject?

Autobiographical identity and truth are produced in relation to, if not precisely through, a subject I may now describe as "contradictory." That is, the subject is not simply what autobiography seeks to represent, as if it existed prior to the text. In saying this I am not invoking the specific arguments that drive philosophical discussions about perception and knowledge, namely, that the differences between persons and texts, between language and reality, are constitutive and not secondary. Nor am I suggesting that the *person* who writes an autobiography is *created* by discourse. Rather, I locate the subject of autobiography in relation to discourses of identity and truth. For that reason, I do not understand autobiography to be any experientially truer than other representations of the self or to offer an identity any less constructed than that produced by other forms of representation simply because the autobiographer intends the subject to correspond to herself or himself.

Much autobiography criticism acknowledges an interpretive division between those who take autobiography as a factual document and those who view it as much more closely, and less damningly, aligned with fiction. This very division, however, results from premises about autobiography's relation to "truth" in conjunction with premises about the "truthful" and "authentic" subject position that autobiography itself constructs. The ethical and political meanings of this subject position contain powerful contradictions: whereas "truth" is the neutral term toward which all persons strive (this is, by humanist definitions, our task and our reward), some are already farther ahead in the climb and stand to reap more massive material rewards for their efforts, while others may climb a bit behind or to the side of those persons who are privileged through their proximity to the alignment of "truth" with race, class, gender, and sexual orientation. Some stories are criminalized from the start when the amount of "truth" one can claim devolves from the amount of cultural authority already attached, within a terrain of dominance, to the person speaking and the place from which s/he speaks. This cultural terrain, in which truth represents both a place where some may not stand and a language that some are not authorized to speak, is mapped onto the practice and study of autobiography through publishing practices, college curricula, community reading programs, and a range of practices through which we are interpellated as readers and writers of autobiography.[8]

Thus it is inadequate to understand the contradictions generated by the demands of "truth" production through the deceptively neat binary of truth/falsehood or to explain that subject's authority through this implicitly juridical grid. Feminist theories of self-representation and subjectivity offer more shaded and internally differential interpretations as well as a way to explore what happens formally when the instabilities in gender represented by the category "women" and the instabilities in genre manifest in the category "autobiography" converge. Frequently, as in Audre Lorde's *Zami: A New Spelling of My Name* (1983), the search for a way to represent this instability forms the grounds of autobiographical experimentation. In *Zami*, Lorde sketches her parents' immigrant history in Harlem and traces her own growing up from early childhood to adulthood in the late 1950s. Arriving in New York from the West Indies in 1924, her mother and father fashion a home from the practices, memories, and rituals they bring with them. Trips to the market for the familiar fruits and spices of what is increasingly presented as the mother's home, become an

---

[8] In 1989, as part of a Maine Humanities Council grant that helped to fund a conference on autobiography at the University of Southern Maine, I designed a reading series for public libraries in New England. The person in charge of those programs in Maine resisted the inclusion of Carolyn Kay Steedman's *Landscape for a Good Woman* because of Steedman's analysis of class, asserting that this emphasis, while important to British readers, would be lost on Maine readers because the United States is not a class-stratified society. The book stayed in the series, and I elaborated the significance of Steedman's critique of class, though I cannot say that either the inclusion of the book or my description of it was successful in framing the issue of class. The institutional assumption governing the reading series was that readers prefer "good, easy" reads that reproduce rather than challenge ideology.

exercise in nostalgia for a distant island that Audre the child knows as little and with as much longing as she knows her mother's body. Reinventing the island home, a "home" Lorde never knew, becomes a central feature of her mythmaking project in which what is not yet visible propels the autobiographer into a textuality of invention as well as documentation. The *topos* of autobiography—self/life/ writing—is exchanged for the terrain of *biomythography*, Lorde's name for her form of writing. In a self-representational text subtitled *A New Spelling of My Name* Lorde's renaming of her text and her self creates a representational space where homes, identities, and names have mythic qualities.

In her foreword to *Wild Women in the Whirlwind*, and in reference to the systematic devaluation and erasure of black women's cultural contributions, Lorde writes: "It's not that we haven't always been here, since there was a here. It is that the letters of our names have been scrambled when they were not totally erased, and our finger-prints upon the handles of history have been called the random brushings of birds."[9] I want to use Lorde's interpretation of the histor-ical silencing of black women's writing as a way to contextualize her emphasis on renaming and new spellings. If, as Lorde suggests, the problem is not with the presence of black women but with their visi-bility, not with writing but with the means of cultural expressivity, not, in short, with production but with power, then what is needed is a form of interpretation that rereads the misspellings, misnamings, and mistreatment of black women as oppression rather than as simple omission. In terms of autobiography, what does it mean always to have been here, "since there was a here," only to be constructed as nowhere or elsewhere by autobiography studies? And more to the point, how do we re-member—which I take to imply both the act of memory and the restoration of erased persons and texts as bodies of evidence—that place, that "here"? As Lorde defines this project in *Zami*, it requires us to "[move] history beyond nightmare into struc-tures for the future."[10] Lorde re-members as myth a history that has been forgotten and destroyed.

In the transposition of autobiography to biomythography, the self,

[9] Audre Lorde, Foreword to *Wild Women in the Whirlwind: Afra-American Culture and the Contemporary Literary Renaissance*, ed. Joanne M. Braxton and Andrée Nicola (New Brunswick, N.J.: Rutgers University Press, 1990), xi. For a discussion that situates Lorde's project in relation to an overall black diaspora, see Chinosole, "Audre Lorde and the Matrilineal Diaspora," in *Wild Women*, 379–94.

[10] Audre Lorde, *Zami: A New Spelling of My Name* (Trumansburg, N.Y.: Crossing, 1983), acknowledgments.

"auto," is renamed "myth" and shifted from the beginning to the center of the "new spelling." Lorde's mythmaking attaches less, then, to the life she retells than to the self who can tell it. Central to this mythic self is her place in a history where she can feel at home, in particular ways, with women. The emotional and representational focus lies between the hunger for language, for adequate meaning, expressed in a phrase that could well function as a signature clause for the book, "but my heart ached and ached for something I could not name" (85), and the desire for a place replete with the mythic qualities of home: "But underneath it all as I was growing up, *home* was still a sweet place somewhere else which they had not managed to capture yet on paper, nor to throttle and bind up between the pages of a schoolbook" (14). Between the hunger for language and the desire for home, Lorde builds a mythic image of herself in relation to mythic, historical, and potential lesbians: "When I was growing up, *powerful woman* equaled something else quite different from ordinary woman, from simply 'woman.' It certainly did not, on the other hand, equal 'man.' What then? What was the third designation? . . . I believe that there have always been Black dykes around—in the sense of powerful and women-oriented women—who would rather have died than use that name for themselves. And that includes my momma" (15). Lorde is concerned throughout *Zami* with finding an adequate form to represent herself in relation to her mother and other women, a form that will claim the designation "lesbian" for the power women possess.

Lorde's first act of renaming involves a simply orthographical operation: "I did not like the tail of the Y hanging down below the line in Audrey, and would always forget to put it on, which used to disturb my mother greatly" (24). Such a decisive removal of what hangs down, the unattractively phallic *y*, prefigures a more comprehensive renaming. Lorde renames her biomythographical subject and herself "Zami. A Carriacou name for women who work together as friends and lovers" (255). Because Lorde works to rename the signing self, the *auto*graphical aspect of autobiography, and not to discover its origin, her self-representation is antidevelopmental and even, in the context of traditional autobiography, antiontological. For her identity derives through the challenges to incorporate the nonidentical, other woman. Lorde writes in the epilogue: "Every woman I have ever loved has left her print upon me, where I loved some invaluable piece of myself apart from me—so different that I had to stretch and grow in order to recognize her. And in that growing, we came to separation, that place where work begins. Another meeting" (255). "That

place where work begins," with its historical and mythical reso-
nances, is figured as the mother's West Indian birthplace: Carriacou.
It is an especially difficult place to locate. In a footnote to a discussion
of the sounds, smells, sights, and meanings of Carriacou, Lorde
writes: "Years later, as partial requirement for a degree in library
science, I did a detailed comparison of atlases, their merits and particular strengths. I used, as one of the foci of my project, the isle of
Carriacou. It appeared only once, in the *Atlas of the Encyclopedia Britan-
nica*, which has always prided itself upon the accurate cartology of its
colonies. I was twenty-six years old before I found Carriacou upon a
map" (14).

Zami pulls at the coherence of autobiography, refuses the identity of
its name, constructs and claims a subject position that renders genre
and gender codes unintelligible by looking to other textual forms for
self-representation and other geographies for identity. The traditional
development of the male autobiographical self begins in relationship
(to a person, a family, a place) but develops into an understanding of
his separateness from others, the nonidentical correspondence of relationship, the self-identical foundation of the proper name. Thus the
autobiographical self closes the hermeneutic circle on others and rests
on the mimesis of the self as self-naming and self-named, where
identity has its meaning in the identical relationship between self and
name. In contrast, the ontological status of the autobiographical self is
everywhere questioned and, ultimately, nowhere bound for too long
in *Zami*.

Lorde begins using destabilization and the mobility it produces in
the prologue, a half-page italicized speculation on family, sexuality,
and identity, which explores graphically what in Adrienne Rich's
terms is the "geography closest in—the body." Lorde begins: "I have
always wanted to be both man and woman, to incorporate the strongest and richest parts of my mother and father within/into me—to
share valleys and mountains upon my body the way the earth does in
hills and peaks" (7). The imagined geography that links land to body
also links parents to child. The image is clearly incorporative, but
instead of offering a single metaphor or emblem that Lorde will pursue through a recounting of her history, the image sets the stage for
further subject positioning. In the second sentence of the "biomythography," Lorde replaces a focus on landscape with the dynamic
of desire that will refigure the familial and the communal she has just
posited: "I would like to enter a woman the way any man can, and to
be entered—to leave and to be left—to be hot and hard and soft all at
the same time in the cause of our loving." In this image of identity as

penetrative sexuality, Lorde presents a series of mobile fantasy positions in which subject and object interchange, "to enter . . . and to be entered—to leave and to be left," which demonstrate how she might incorporate, make bodily, "mother and father within/into me." For Lorde, the fantasy of mobility is revealed as a politics as the eroticism becomes "the cause of our loving."

The sequence of subject positions shifts again in the prologue when the autobiographer as musing masturbator draws toward the "geography closest in": "When I sit and play in the waters of my bath I love to feel the deep inside parts of me, sliding and folded and tender and deep" (7). From the subject position of masturbation, Lorde reimagines the legacy of sexual difference so that it does not translate into heterosexuality: "I have always wanted to be both man and woman, to incorporate the strongest and richest parts of my mother and father within/into me." She also links autoeroticism to autobiography as a way to reposition and rethink the sources of eroticism and biography. What is previously unthought becomes centrally imagined. The body's geography is redrawn against the formalist gender logic I described as a domino theory of desire in which the sex one can *see* becomes the gender one must *be* and is, consequently, the setup of heterosexuality. The remapped geography of the body abandons the prescribed development of sex, gender, and desire as Lorde denaturalizes gender through an analogical slide to nature: "to incorporate the strongest and richest parts of my mother and father within/into me—to share valleys and mountains upon my body the way the earth does in hills and peaks."

Such a revised embodiment reorients the meaning of identity from ontology through epistemology, imagination, and desire, all of which become politicized in the "cause" of love: "I would like to enter a woman the way any man can, and to be entered—to leave and to be left—to be hot and hard and soft all at the same time in the cause of our loving." By touching herself and constructing sexuality as the focal point of her identity, Lorde can see her family and, most important, her mother differently. No longer the role model for normative heterosexual development, the mother affords the daughter a way to experience herself in relation to other women, a shift in perspective which Lorde figures as a change in identity: "I have felt the age-old triangle of mother father and child, with the 'I' at its eternal core, elongate and flatten out into the elegantly strong triad of grandmother mother daughter, with the 'I' moving back and forth flowing in either or both directions as needed." Lorde refuses to write autobiography because it represents and solidifies identity in "the age-old triangle of mother father and child." In order to represent identity in mobility, Lorde finds self-representation at the limit of autobiography and refashions form into "biomythography."

Framing her autobiographical act with concerns about beginnings and endings similar to Johnson's in *Minor Characters*, Lorde builds the beginning and end of her book into spaces in which she can feel at home. Such a textual site is often at odds with the limited safety and familiarity the world would offer. Yet, the sort of "home" traditional autobiography offers would domesticate Lorde's experimentation, and she rejects it as a textual site of sustenance and meaning. If, as I am suggesting, her refusal to spell the self-representational form "a-u-t-o-b-i-o-g-r-a-p-h-y" is an act of resistance, a refusal to recognize herself within the gender and genre boundaries delimited by that spelling, Lorde's biomythography raises two questions: What does it mean to refuse the name of autobiography and to "spell" or name self-representation through different categories of identity and writing? What political possibilities are generated through the visibility this new spelling commands?

Lorde's text has many of the "classic" features of autobiography: it concerns the author's self-development and struggle to become a writer, and its organization depends on certain narrative continuities in time, place, and person. Yet the eurocentrism and heterosexism that define that "classicism" lead Lorde to conclude that "autobiography" itself combines a political law of the subject within its formal law of genre. In wishing to write a coming-out narrative and to represent the mutual complexities of race and sexual orientation within identity, Lorde discovers she has no models and renames her text a "biomythography." When Lorde confronts the law of gender and genre, a "law" that Derrida has rather ironically elaborated as two versions of the same old structure, she brings the genre to crisis, generates an excess that demands repression—or interpretation.[11] By taking on the problematic of self-representation, Lorde confronts gender as an internalized and naturalized "condition" deriving from history and experience and, through writing, externalizes gender as a construction. Writing her life offers a different perspective on her estrangement from the codes of gender and positions her as a feminist subject (that is, both inside and outside the ideology of gender). From the black, lesbian, feminist subject position that Lorde carves out, then,

[11]Jacques Derrida, "The Law of Genre," trans. Avital Ronell, *Glyph* 7 (Spring 1980), rpt. *Critical Inquiry* 7 (Autumn 1980): 55–81. See also Derrida, *The Ear of the Other: Otobiography, Transference, Translation*, trans. Peggy Kamuf (New York: Schocken, 1985).

the effects of gender can be accounted for, even argued against, rather than simply represented as the experience that follows naturally from a bodily condition. Gender, race, and sexual orientation, quite to the contrary, must always be enforced and policed, their codes scrupulously monitored and attended, and their challengers, like Lorde, must continually find strategies of (self-) representational resistance.

As a subject, Lorde is complexly positioned. Literary tradition and aesthetic categories alone do not fully describe her situation, although she defines herself as a literary subject who knows herself as a developing writer. So, too, Lorde moves both within and against political ideologies that take the subject to have a single, primary identity: either lesbian *or* black *or* working class. I take the problem of Lorde's subject positions to be central to autobiography's law of the subject. While subjects are doubtless complex, our ideologies of personhood reduce this complexity for political ends. One is permitted to be a member of *a* group; indeed, the force with which we are named and contained therein testifies to the compulsory nature of group identification. But the more politically troublesome challenges to such ideologies of the person are precisely those that cannot be contained by a single group identification.

The absence of autobiographical categories to mirror the complexity of human life reveals, of course, autobiography's sustaining role in hegemony. Where, for example, is the narrative of development that constitutes political identification as an irreducible, fully embodied "identity"? Where is the ideology of identity that collects sexual orientation, class, and race and represents them together in the fullness of lived experience? Where are the interpretive devices, so crucial for political and self-representation, that make us knowable in our complexities to ourselves and to others for the purposes of social change, cultural analysis, imaginative transformation, and political activism? The reduction of identity to a one-to-one correspondence between *the* group and *the* individual is reinforced in studies of autobiography which value a single representation of subjectivity and therefore suppress the range of subjectivities written in relation to, and often in complicated interaction with, one another. Lorde's subjectivities have different representational trajectories: narratives of coming out as a lesbian, of struggling with levels of racism, of leaving home and returning, of becoming educated, and of becoming a writer overlap in *Zami* and would, within traditional autobiography studies, be outside the categories of analysis. But Lorde's multicultural autobiography is a contemporary example of the rhetorical strategies shared by many women writers who have already crossed a boundary of the dominant representations of identity by resisting the codes of gender in a particular culture; by inhabiting the sexual body as a lesbian, bisexual, or celibate; by crossing class or achieving a rebellious class consciousness; or by seizing upon self-representation as a strategy to change the story of one's life.

The law of genre contravened by Lorde's biomythography, like the law of gender, stipulates that genres are not to be mixed. At its base, the law of genre stakes its claims through a rhetoric of purity and contamination. Generic criticism thus installed as a border guard defends against the threat of mixed forms. If we shift our attention from the law of genre to the vigorously enforced law of gender, the politics of this rhetoric becomes clearer. The law of gender erects an enforceable border between the selfsame and the other, for it stipulates that there are two genders and that we know which two they are. This rhetoric reveals its internal strains when homosexuality is described as the third sex. The law of gender marks out two and only two domains of sexed identity and requires that persons mix sexually across that border and not within the domain of the selfsame. The compelling attractions of the selfsame, however, while impermissible for genders, are fully expected of genres. The relationship, then, between gender and genre operates through the logic of the chiasmus, but where do the twisting complications of gender and genre intersect with each other?

Lorde indicates that the translation of gendered identity into heterosexual identity intersects with the translation of self-representation into the recognizable genre of autobiography. For Lorde, then, this is the intersection at which *Zami* is situated, a sexual and textual crossroads where she determines to follow what we could call, following Jonathan Dollimore's suggestion, a "perverse dynamic." The division between genders is maintained up to the point of sexuality and then a swift but sure crossing of the gendered border into heterosexuality is required, a crossing made possible through the seeming stability of that border. The schematic simplicity of this arrangement is imposed, however, as Freud acknowledged, on a considerably more complicated field of desire. As Dollimore has cogently argued, although the definition of homosexuality as "perversion" implies a swerving away from this static field, in fact, according to Augustine, Shakespeare, Freud and others, it is precisely "perversion" that is structured into our early and late modern notions as the developing self. It is precisely the "perverse" desires, Freud theorized, that must be sublimated or repressed and the "mastering" of them is what we are thought to share: they constitute our social interests. For Dollimore, then, "one does not become a pervert but remains one; it is sexual perversion, not sexual 'normality', which is the given in human nature. . . . The clear implication is that civilization actually depends upon that which is usually thought to be incompatible with it."[12] The division among genres speaks of a polymorphously perverse textuality that must be regulated at many different borders. In autobiography, then, "perversion" underlies and threatens the laws of gender and genre, fractures the spatial logic of separate (and separable) spheres, and emerges in Lorde through her choices not to reproduce legalized sexual and textual identities.

In autobiography, the law of genre has not been as uniformly codified as those concerning gender; indeed, as one of its most influential critics observes: "Everyone knows what an autobiography is, but no two observers, no matter how assured they may be, are in agreement."[13] The familiarity of this formulation identifies a dangerously commonsensical appeal. It is the same nonargument that elides seeing and knowing and thereby makes interpretation superfluous and somehow indulgent in the face of the obvious. It is manifestly difficult to steer out of the definitional ruts of common sense. The statement, however, goes to the problem of defining autobiography, for autobiography is the point where the unknowns that haunt questions of self and identity seem written in the form of a single equation: How is the self in the text constituted? How is the self in "real life" constituted? The incommensurability of those two questions has until recently formed a stumbling block to the development of theories of autobiography, for the differences between and within the selves in question constitute the production of autobiographical identity. That is, the questions are irreducible to a single answer: those multiple levels of self-representation, in fact, help to define autobiography. Still, the perceived form of autobiography's equation has persisted. It offers the assurance that could we answer either question successfully, the whole of the self would then appear, miraculously summoned from the page. While "no two observers" might agree on how to characterize the unknowns of autobiography, its promise appears as the coincidence of incommensurables, the single equation "everyone knows" must exist. The ontological being is manifest in the author's signature.

[12] Jonathan Dollimore, "The Cultural Politics of Perversion: Augustine, Shakespeare, Freud, Foucault," in *Sexual Sameness: Textual Differences in Lesbian and Gay Writing*, ed. Joseph Bristow (New York: Routledge, 1992), 9.

[13] James Olney, "Autobiography and the Cultural Moment" in *Autobiography*, ed. Olney, 7.

In this circular referentiality, the constitutive differences among and within a historical self, a fictive self, and the writing self in the process of constructing an autobiographical text disappear into the signature's guarantee of anchoring textual and temporal concerns.

Questions of genre immediately pose the problem of boundaries, of determining limits. In genre studies autobiography has been located almost wholly within the realm of nonfiction. A further discrimination may be made: in a hierarchy of generic distinctions, autobiography carves out a niche within categories that are already divided (nonfiction/fiction, poetry/prose, books/letters, memoirs, diaries); thus its status as a border discourse can easily be put in the service of discrediting a text (as in "*only* an autobiography"). Popular and critical attention has focused almost exclusively on the person as "real individual in history," even as opposed to "author," rather than on the text. Thus the answer to Foucault's question "What is an author?"—or as we may currently be inclined to ask, "What was an author?"—when applied to autobiography seems glaringly obvious to many. What is an autobiographer? The person who writes an autobiography. For autobiography has been interpreted as the arena in which the self speaks itself without the artifice of fiction, where language is in some nonmysterious way a pure mirror of the writer's life, where Walt Whitman, for example, can assert along with Rousseau and Montaigne that the proper name conjoins the text and the self. "Who touches this," proclaims Whitman, "touches a man."[14] Yet, for all its variations, the autobiographical self emerges in these interpretations as a creation somehow independent of the pressures of writing in a way that implicitly privileges history and sameness over language and difference. And nowhere is the reliance on naive autobiographical realism more evident than in the conflation of "book" and "man" on the grounds that they share the same proper name.

The definitional locus of any generic category provides a clue as to what can and cannot be represented through any further analysis or elaboration of the category. In autobiography, that locus is formed by the narrativization of the self and history. In traditional studies of autobiography, both the self and history are overdetermined as "male." From the intractability of Augustine's *Confessions* as a point of generic origin to the formal limits such a precursor sets, traditional studies of autobiography repeat the founding, gendered premise of

[14] Walt Whitman, "So Long," *Leaves of Grass*, ed. David McKay (Philadelphia: Sherman & Company, 1900), 345.

autobiographical subjectivity and authority. A stable and fixed perspective (Augustine's) conjoins time, space, and identity in a signifier of commanding proportions: the autobiographical *I*. The mutually reinforcing networks of value which credit some and not others as authors, as persons having a story worth telling—that is, of possessing a life worth remembering and of being sufficiently representative to have their texts matter—has tended to seek a definition of autobiography in a very narrow sample: those that can be represented as identical with the unified *I*.

The sufficiency of autobiography's definition is interrogated by a feminist subject in *Landscape for a Good Woman: A Story of Two Lives* (1987), a text in which the analysis of class figures prominently in a way that it does not in "classic" autobiographies with their elitist or upwardly mobile or assimilationist politics. In it, Carolyn Kay Steedman challenges the sufficiency of two identity-authorizing discourses, psychoanalysis and Marxist class critique, to describe women's lives, here, hers and her mother's. Steedman, a scholar who has written working-class history in other forms, triangulates these two powerful theories of real life with her own history. Working within and against both discourses, Steedman confronts the centrality of stories drawn from a variety of sources in the constitution and interpretation of identity. Identity, in her view, is always multitextual, riddled with the discontinuities of each story, its embeddedness in other stories, and its competing interpretations. *Landscape for a Good Woman*, she writes, "has a childhood at its centre—my childhood, a personal past—and it is about the disruption of that fifties childhood by the one my mother had lived out before me, and the stories she told about it."[15]

In an effort to stretch what can be represented through autobiography, Steedman gives her book a painterly title, meant to evoke a place and the people who live there. A landscape is a representation, the painter's interpretation, and not, as we all know but habitually forget, the thing itself. This forgetting is so common that it constitutes a significant feature of aesthetics. We try to understand reality through our interpretations, through the stories we raise to significance, and through the meaning those stories make in the rest of our lives. It is also a feature of traditional autobiography. Stories told by others become part of our experience, as "real" as any house, school, or person in their ability to shape our lives. Steedman describes stories as "inter-

---

[15] Carolyn Kay Steedman, *Landscape for a Good Woman: A Story of Two Lives* (New Brunswick, N.J.: Rutgers University Press, 1987), 5.

pretative devices." Working within the methods of psychoanalysis, she agrees that the child prefers stories that resonate with some feature of her or his experience. If the adult can then interpret the stories, s/he can see into the developing world view of the child. Anyone who has watched a child become attached to a particular story, request it night after night, enact its narrative in play, and identify with a particular character has observed the child developing an emotional landscape. Whether it will be characterized by poverty or plenty has to do both with material and imaginative conditions.

Steedman's mother's life was shaped by loss and longing. She surveyed the difficulty of her working-class life and wanted *things*. Her interpretation of life never admitted any possibilities but those of grinding struggle, with the myth of her own good motherhood at the center of her daughters' lives. How did Steedman know she had a good mother? Her mother repeatedly told her so. Within the mother's self-representation emerged, in fact, a familiar enough working-class myth of the enduring mother, which, as Steedman understands, is perceived differently by boys and girls:

> Mothers were those who told you how hard it was to have you, how long they were in labour with you ('twenty hours with you', my mother frequently reminded me) and who told you to accept the impossible contradiction of being both desired and a burden; and not to complain. This ungiving endurance is admired by working-class boys who grow up to write about their mother's flinty courage. But the daughter's silence on the matter is a measure of the price you pay for survival. I don't think the baggage will ever lighten, for me or my sister. We were born, and had no choice in the matter; but we were burdens, expensive, never grateful enough. There was nothing we could do to pay back the debt of our existence. 'Never have children, dear,' she said; 'they ruin your life.' Shock moves swiftly across the faces of women to whom I tell this story. But it is *ordinary* not to want your children, I silently assert; normal to find them a nuisance. (16–17)

But it is not the mother's self-naming as a "good mother" that titles this text; rather, the title echoes the father's simultaneous defense of the mother and his flight from domestic conflict when he answers all challenges to the mother's authority with the disclaimer "She's a good woman."

The mother's interpretive legacy for her daughters, "the impossible contradiction of being both desired and a burden," reproduces the "impossible contradiction" that founds their family. Steedman's parents never married. Steedman pieces together the family secret of illegitimacy and the interpretation that she and her sister were inducements to marriage and the better life it signified to her mother. Mostly, the father enters the narrative through his effective absence. Describing the monumentality of his inconsequence in their lives, Steedman writes of her father's death in a logic of longing and unmet need which is strikingly like that which she attributes to her mother:

> When he died I spent days foolishly hoping that there would be something for me. I desperately wanted him to give me something. The woman he'd been living with handed over two bottles of elderberry wine that they'd made together out of fruit gathered from the side of the ring road where her flat was. I drank one of them and it gave me the worst hangover of my life.
>
> He left us without anything, never gave us a thing. In the fairy-stories the daughters love their fathers because they are mighty princes, great rulers, and because such absolute power seduces. The modern psychoanalytic myths posit the same plot, old tales are made manifest: secret longings, doors closing along the corridors of the bourgeois household. But daddy, you never knew me like this; you didn't really care, or weren't allowed to care, it comes to the same thing in the end. You shouldn't have left us there, you should have taken me with you. You left me alone; you never laid a hand on me: the iron didn't enter into the soul. You never gave me anything: the lineaments of an unused freedom. (61)

As the Lacanian law of the father prescribes, the father need not be present as the one to make good on the threat "Wait till your father gets home." In this passage Steedman addresses the dynamics sustained by this heavy absence. Her complaint turns swiftly from how she did not know him, through material or imaginative means, to how he did not know her: "you never knew me like this." Their mutual unknowability prevents other forms of self-knowledge, Steedman argues, as it is reinforced by what she cites as the dominant aspects of psychoanalysis and class critique. Neither adequately addresses how the daughter remains unknown.

Steedman refuses to be read and to read her family's life in the master narratives of class critique and psychoanalysis. Taken independently, neither master narratives nor stories (our imaginative lives) nor material reality (our social and economic conditions) can fully account for the meaning of a life, for it is a person's capacity to interpret which centrally concerns Steedman. From a feminist subject position she recognizes how she has been interpellated by both psychoanalysis and Marxist class critique to know herself as a woman. Steedman finds herself on a landscape, the landscape for a good woman, and does not recognize two prominent features (psychoanalysis and class critique) in relation to which she can plot a course. She does not trust the map to represent where she is; therefore, she becomes exemplary of the subject who must find her way by making a map for getting lost. She follows a route of persistent estrangement from master narratives, all the while homing in on the relationship of mother and daughter, the relationship insufficiently interpreted by the dominant theories of human development and social theory, but whose irreducibility and aching specificity run through so many self-representational texts by women. It is a relationship for both Steedman and Lorde in which the limitations of traditional notions of gender and sexuality are especially glaring.

What emerges from the self-representational strategies of Lorde and Steedman is not only a new way to understand the autobiographical agent but, in fact, a kind of autobiographical writing that breaks with monocultural imperatives of being.[16] No longer exclusively an object in the discourses of gender and identity, the differently positioned subject and the rhetorical and political strategies upon which this positioning depends lead us to examine not what autobiography is but what it does. In *Landscape for a Good Woman*, Steedman cautions about the irresistibility of narrative, of the way it seems synonymous with identity, when she writes of her own efforts to make the stories of working-class autobiographers comprehensible:

> I know that the compulsions of narrative are almost irresistible: having found a psychology where once there was only the assumption of pathology or false consciousness to be seen, the tendency is to celebrate this psychology, to seek entry for it to a wider world of literary and cultural reference; and the enterprise of working-class autobiography was designed to make this at least a feasible project. But to do this is to miss the irreducible nature of all our lost childhoods: what has been made has been made out on the borderlands. I must make the final gesture of defiance, and refuse to let this be absorbed by the central story. (144)

Although *a* stable autobiographical form against which women

[16] In the conclusion to her excellent book, *Subjectivities: A History of Self-Representation in Britain, 1832–1920* (Oxford: Oxford University Press, 1991), Regenia Gagnier asserts that "multicultural autobiographies" such as Lorde's *Zami* and Steedman's *Landscape* are "new narratives of social justice" (278). The texts she cites as examples are all by women, though Gagnier does not analyze this feature of her list.

have written about their lives does not exist, an evolving notion of what autobiography is has *not* been deduced from texts women did write, or from texts that problematize autobiography (or have been seen as problematical in themselves) or challenge the genre's formation, limits, and illusion of stability. Narrative, it was once agreed, was better suited to self-disclosure and historical writing than verse or drama, but when critics began to analyze autobiography in relation to representation, they found examples of self-reflexive writing in other genres. Yet, while autobiography began increasingly to mark a point of generic instability, autobiography criticism preserved the gender hierarchy within which that instability could be recontained. Hence even across recognizable changes in generic definition, women's autobiographical writing remains anomalous. Even when some critics open the canon—unformed as it may be in autobiography—to admit such "untraditional" works as Whitman's *Song of Myself*, Wordsworth's *Prelude*, or Joyce's *Portrait of the Artist as a Young Man*, they do not so much open the field for women's writing as expand it to include more men's writing.

Women's self-representational writing, bracketed from the defining discussions of genre, has both escaped and never been offered the fate of being defined as a genre of its own. Of course, the lack of generic definition poses particular problems. It seems to me that many women autobiographers, approaching autobiography from a profusion of positions, recognize the textuality of autobiographical identity; indeed, they insist upon it. The autobiographer is tethered, even if by the most slender of lines, to a discourse of self-remembering in which identity is preserved. Nor is this preservation the mark of unsophistication, a failure to grasp the poststructuralist lesson that identity has always already been created and dissolved in textuality. The recurring mark in the women's autobiographies I study here can be found in the shared sense that a written record, a testimonial, or a confessional document can represent a person, can stand in her absence for her truth, can re-member her life.[17] Indeed, even in the narrowest and most ambivalent sense, writing an autobiography can be a political act because it asserts a right to speak rather than to be spoken for. Such a claim is often made quite narrowly; that is, the writer may stand to gain little leverage against a particular institution or condition. It may be enough to refigure the grounds of contention as ideological.

[17] See especially, Doris Sommer, " 'Not Just a Personal Story': Women's *Testimonios* and the Plural Self," in *Life/Lines*, 107–30.

Interruptions

J/e is the symbol of the lived, rending experience which is m/y
writing, of this cutting in two which throughout literature is the
exercise of a language which does not constitute m/e as subject.
                    —Monique Wittig, *The Lesbian Body*

No longer understood mainly as the most available and uncompli-
cated kind of writing imaginable, "the story of my life" has been
framed within increasingly sophisticated critical discourses on the
shifting displacements of "identity" within language itself and on the
possibility of political opposition based on testimonial and confessional writing as forms of resistance. The construction of autobiography as a simple form of nonfictional prose is based in the notion that
it is closer to reporting than, say, to the realist novel. That is, the
organizational work is solved by chronology, the challenge of characterization is removed by what people really said and did, and invention is displaced by recalcitrant reality. What has been stabilized as
"autobiography," however, is more accurately described as a collection of the discourses and practices individuals have used to represent themselves in relation to cultural modes of truth and identity
production. The "subject of autobiography" emerges within these
practices, although that subject is unevenly authorized by the varying
modes of dominant ideology. As Lorde and Steedman demonstrate,
the perception of autobiography as a generically unified set of texts
does not appeal to all writers. It neither composes an enabling tradition nor offers an adequate access to "truth." The self-representational texts within this network of identity and identification are
less characterizable, therefore, as autobiograph*ies* when they do not
reproduce dominant ideologies of subjectivity.

According to Althusser, "All ideology has the function (which defines it) of 'constituting' concrete individuals as subjects" ("Ideology,"
244). In this sense, the subject of autobiography has been interpellated by a host of institutions and discourses which have effectively
privileged certain men. The subject of autobiography has come to
designate a stable *I* anchored within a relatively stable genre, though
this definition has come at the cost of dramatically narrowing the field
of self-representation. It is important to claim autobiography as a kind
of writing and not a genre per se in order to emphasize further the
extent to which women's autobiography invades, permeates, and also
is invaded by canonical genres. Erupting in texts where it is not
licensed, women's self-representation has frequently been silenced or

marginalized because it has not been interpreted/named/authorized as such.

I offer the term *autobiographics* to describe those elements of self-representation which are not bound by a philosophical definition of the self derived from Augustine, not content with the literary history of autobiography, those elements that instead mark a location in a text where self-invention, self-discovery, and self-representation emerge within the technologies of autobiography—namely, those legalistic, literary, social, and ecclesiastical discourses of truth and identity through which the subject of autobiography is produced. Autobiographics, as a description of self-representation and as a reading practice, is concerned with interruptions and eruptions, with resistance and contradiction as strategies of self-representation.

A text's autobiographics consist in the following elements in self-representational writing, or writing that emphasizes the autobiographical *I*: an emphasis on writing itself as constitutive of autobiographical identity, discursive contradictions in the representation of identity (rather than unity), the name as a potential site of experimentation rather than contractual sign of identity, and the effects of the gendered connection of word and body. Autobiographics gives initial conceptual precedence to positioning the subject, to recognizing the shifting sands of identity on which theories of autobiography build, and to describing "identity" and the networks of identification. An exploration of a text's autobiographics allows us to recognize that the *I* is multiply coded in a range of discourses: it is the site of multiple solicitations, multiple markings of "identity," multiple figurations of agency. Thus, autobiographics avoids the terminal questions of genre and close delimitation and offers a way, instead, to ask: Where is the autobiographical?[18] What constitutes its representation? The *I*, then, does not disappear into an identity-less textual universe. Rather, the autobiographicality of the *I* in a variety of discourses is emphasized as a point of resistance in self-representation.

I think of autobiographics operating within texts that have not been seen as autobiographies and occurring in the margins of hegemonic discourses within cultural texts, in the social spaces carved in the interstices of institutions, and so it is there that the terms of a different reading and retextualization of the subject of autobiography must be located. It is there also that we may begin to think about agency. Thus, the traditional construction of autobiography may be pressured

---

[18] See Celeste Schenck, "All of a Piece: Women's Autobiography and Poetry," in *Life/Lines,* 281–305.

further by my refusal to produce a critical study that differs from its predecessors and contemporaries in content only. A study of auto-biographics allows for removing the following writers, among others, from interpretive contexts in which their works are canonized, though not as autobiography: Julian of Norwich, Gertrude Stein, Monique Wittig, and Minnie Bruce Pratt. These writers removed themselves in material and psychological ways from a social economy in which they would function as objects of exchange through self-representational practices and social and political acts and choices, and they represented their identities through an emphasis on the *I* that contrasts with the *I* in the traditional forms or epistemologies they restructure.[19]

Steedman, for example, retains the argumentative and intellectual emphases of scholarship, though with an autobiographical *I* as the speaker. She resists, too, the chronological and developmental em-phases associated with the autobiographical *I* and produces a social study of the politics of childhood fantasy and everyday life. Similarly, Lorde, writing from the multiply marked subject position of poet and essayist uses an autobiographical *I* through which to represent the

[19] I use the phrase "objects of exchange" in reference to Claude Lévi-Strauss's claim that the exchange of women fundamentally underlies and perpetuates culture. See *The Elementary Structure of Kinship* (Boston: Beacon Press, 1969). As a repeated and distinc-tive feature of kinship structures and as a code that articulates male bonding and authority, the cultural definition of women as objects of exchange is inscribed within language, history, economics, the family, and all other mutually constitutive systems that produce us as gendered beings. Lévi-Strauss does not conclude that women are only objects, though his theoretical failure to account for gender leads him to conclude, basically, that man is the universal human. Women share in this humanity as subjects when they are coded as men. As Gayle Rubin notes, "'Exchange of women' is a shorthand for expressing that the social relations of a kinship system specify that men have certain rights in their female kin, and that women do not have the same rights either to themselves or to their male kin" ("The Traffic in Women: Notes on the 'Political Economy' of Sex," in *Toward an Anthropology of Women*, ed. Rayna R. Reiter [New York: Monthly Review Press, 1975], 177). If the "exchange of women" is an aspect of the myth that produces man as a coherent subject capable of sustaining ties with others through the shared, almost unconscious reliance on variously integrated systems, then women are external to the language of myth. Myth as it reproduces culture encodes women as objects of exchange whose words and bodies function for the use of others: "Women do not have the same rights . . . to themselves." Yet there is an opening in the objectifica-tion of women, for in the realm of myth women function both as signs and as ex-changers of signs, as both objects and subjects. "Woman's" condition as a dweller on this borderline suggests for Lévi-Strauss a time in which all objects were endowed with subjectivity. For women writers, the legacy cuts the other way; women can and do remember how subjects are subjected and reduced to the status of objects. And insofar as women can produce representational and semiotic practices that confound "ex-change," the genres in which we read their autobiographics broadens.

histories of communities of women, and thereby dislocates the single-
ness of the autobiographical subject through her depiction of female
influence and desire. In the context these readings create, we see
how, as an interpretive project, finding a text's autobiographics initially depends on a revised reading of the autobiographical *I* and
depends as well on a critique of contractual metaphors that represent
identity as what one solely owns by virtue of signing the representational contract in the appropriate language and form of autobiography.

Emile Benveniste's essay on the nature of pronouns can serve as a
beginning:

> What then is the reality to which *I* or *you* refers? It is solely a "reality of
> discourse," and this is a very strange thing. *I* cannot be defined except in
> terms of "locution," not in terms of objects as a nominal sign is. *I* signi-
> fies "the person who is uttering the present instance of the discourse
> containing *I*." This instance is unique by definition and has validity only
> in its uniqueness.[20]

As in language more generally, selves in autobiography seem to pro-
liferate and are ambiguously tethered to the overdetermined autobiographical *I*, a linguistic "shifter" that does not properly refer.
Many critics of autobiography have sought to insulate autobiography's truth claim from the radical impossibility of sustaining this
claim. The autobiographical code of referentiality deploys the illusion
that there is a single *I*, sufficiently distinct from the *I* it narrates to
know it and to see it from the vantage of experience and still, more
problematically, to be that *I*. All of this depends on not looking too
closely at the profound shakiness caused by the motion of these *I*'s.
They not only redouble their path through the looking glass of time
and space but press against the constraints of linguistic reference
through an overdetermined dependence on the "shifter," *I*. The shifting levels of textual identity in autobiography construct its characteristic rhetorical instability as well as the illusion, often put to political
ends, of its stability. This is the problem of referentiality established
through the complicated and specific dynamics of the autobiographical *I*.

I want to demonstrate here how to read for a text's autobiographics,

[20] Emile Benveniste, *Problems in General Linguistics* (Coral Gables: University of Miami
Press, 1971), 218. For an excellent feminist discussion of the autobiographical *I*, see
Brodzki and Schenck, Introduction, and Brodzki, "Mothers, Displacement, and Lan-
guage in the Autobiographies of Nathalie Sarraute and Christa Wolf," in *Life/Lines*.

that is, how to discern in the discourses of truth and identity those textual places where women's self-representation interrupts (or is interrupted by) the regulatory laws of gender and genre. But first a methodological concern: I need to insist that my own analysis of texts as "interrupted" does not lead me, in a final move, to unify them through my readings, to discover among the fragments the true voice of a woman speaking. Nor do I find that women's self-representation shatters discourses that were previously whole. Masculinist discourses of identity are themselves already built up through repressions and silences, chief among them the cultural imposition of silence on women. Rather, my inspection of discontinuities in the technologies of autobiography leads to a focus on how women negotiate the interrupted discourses of self-representation. Certainly, other approaches to these texts are possible, useful, and illuminating of other interpretive and theoretical claims. I wish, however, to underscore that the technologies of autobiography are conflictual through and through, derived as they are in relation to discourses of identity and truth which are themselves held together by means of some rhetorical violence.[21] Even in their surface presentation of unity and linear development, autobiographies pull together such a variety of kinds of writing (history, memoir, confession, even parody) that the "unifying" *I* at their "center" is already fractured by its place in varying discourses (political, philosophical, psychological, aesthetic), and what frequently fractures such totalizing theories of identity is gender. Thus, my own argumentative teleology can only be a structural substitute for the coherence I find neither in the technologies of autobiography nor in the agent that pieces and is pieced together through them. Considering the history of autobiography and its study, the recognition of what is provisional in a theory of self-representation may be rather welcome.

If Augustine's question "How can the self know itself?" has a corollary in the history of women's self-representation, perhaps it would be Margaret Cavendish's gritty appropriation of the question she knew would be turned against her: "Why hath this lady writ her own life?" In her *True Relation of My Birth, Breeding, and Life* (first published in 1656), the duchess of Newcastle addresses the ways in which her culture codes women's texts as marginal, marks women's self-representation a priori as an act that will require defending. Cavendish's comment reveals an attention to an interlocutor or a witness to whom autobiographies of the marginalized are frequently addressed.

[21] Teresa de Lauretis, "The Violence of Rhetoric," in *Technologies of Gender*, 31–50.

How does this incorporation or intertextualization of an audience differ from other autobiographical positionings of writer and audience? Augustine, for example, presents the *Confessions* as a discourse of the relation of the self to itself. He defines his project as a dialogue that takes a split self as speaker/knower of identity. This closed circuit of self-referentiality obscures the tautological nature of his autobiographical act: the self knows itself as a self knowing itself. Autobiographies that present God as an ultimate reader tend to isolate the autobiographer from human communities. That Cavendish poses autobiography as an activity to defend relocates human agency in a broader discursive context: she is addressing other interlocutors than the self/God of the *Confessions*. Her enemy is not as metaphysical as Augustine's. Whereas writing the *Confessions* certainly offered Augustine the opportunity to represent his crisis of legitimation and identity as a cosmic struggle between good and evil over the fate of his soul, the duchess of Newcastle's antagonists were closer to home and less susceptible to metaphysicalization. Even in her grander autobiographical moments, when she appears to be writing about the soul—an effect after which autobiographers only infrequently strive, despite what taking the *Confessions* as a paradigm would suggest— she continually calls the reader's attention to the technologies of autobiographical production: What are the culture's views of truth, of personhood, and hence, of appropriate autobiographical representation? How can she position herself within these discourses in order to be read as she wishes?

Cavendish's opening query indicates her awareness that her position as a woman requires some further effort on her part to justify seizing the authority of autobiography. She realizes also that the gender and genre codes are at odds in the project of self-representation, and she looks to the points of rupture in both. Yet even when self-consciousness about the technologies of autobiography goes unspoken or unwritten, concealed as it is within the daily functioning of ideology, evidence of this awareness persists. Women have frequently been compelled to adopt defensive postures in autobiography and to argue for some claim to the discourses of truth telling it deploys. The shared argumentative strategies of Cavendish and other marginalized authors reveal the extent to which the technologies of autobiography involve political agendas that specify who is authorized to tell and judge the truth in a culture, as well as the historical persistence of this nonetheless shifting structure of authorization.

I want to show how these technologies can be interrupted, first, by describing a grid for theorizing how the temporal instability of auto-

biographical self-representation constitutes a persistent form of interruption and makes rupture a feature of self-representation and,
second, by focusing on how rupture works internally and externally
through a discussion of four kinds of interruption. Then I want to
question the autobiographical agent's role in the appropriation of rupture for feminist ends.

One's relation to the discourses of truth and identity is always historically specific and determined: this claim has relevance to the synchronic and diachronic axes of historical meaning, and we can describe
the intersection of these lines as the point at which the autobiographer
appears as author of her text. This intersection can be described as a
map of tradition in which neither the diachronic continuum—what we
can call the history of women's self-representation—nor the synchronic slice of life—what we can call the network representing a
specific autobiography's relation to the technologies of its production
at any point in time—is a sufficiently isolable axis for the interpretation
of an autobiography. Neither history nor a specific text can sufficiently
explain autobiographical production or the complicated claims made
on art and life through these technologies, because each must be
grasped in its relation to the other. We can see how the X that marks the
spot of autobiography, sketched as the relation between the synchronic
and the diachronic, really involves at least four terms rather than two:
any intersection does, although we customarily understand a straight
line as a single identity (and the intersection of any two lines as a point
of convergence between the two).

I would like to call attention to the four vectors that move through
and away from the intersection. The meaning of this intersection—a
point reread as the convergence of four terms—places us beyond the
initial triangulation of autobiographical selves with which I began,
where the autobiographical *I* simultaneously named the historical
person, the textual construction, and the author—all of which describe different functions in the autobiographical act. I pointed first to
the intersection itself in order to indicate the place where meaning
both escapes and returns via four vectors. What can be gained by
reference to autobiography's location at the temporal crossroads—
past/future as horizontal axis and thick present as vertical axis—is a
recognition that the subject of autobiography is stretched out in time
in a way that the problem with pronouns, the autobiographical *I*,
obscures. The *I* refers to all the "times" of the person (the appearance
of temporal coherence across past, present, and implied future),
which are subordinated to the process of naming. The coincidence
between the historical person and the autobiographical representa-

tion of that person by her- or himself is enabled by the noncoincidence of discourses that create this effect. Thus it is crucial to examine this X (perhaps it designates the signature of those who cannot sign the autobiographical pact) as a key feature of autobiographics: it allows us to focus both on the autobiographical I's temporal locations and on the autobiographical I as an agent of dislocation and disruption in history and in the text. This agent is represented by the figure of the signature—autobiography's X-factor, the referential anchor that will not hold—as a site of dissimulation, a site where identity is produced through the technologies of autobiography and is not unproblematically *there*.

I do not mean that autobiographers have not claimed the certainty of identity, have not obscured the problems of its production. In fact, it may be important here to acknowledge that the fiction of identity has been especially significant for feminist criticism and theory. Some feminists will surely question whether my focus on the duplicity of autobiographical writing disallows a focus on political agency for women autobiographers, taking duplicity as dissolving the representation of women's experience into another rewriting of the logic of the chiasmus.[22] To that challenge, I would respond that autobiographical identity and agency are not identical to identity and agency in "real life"; rather, they are its representation, and that representation, as I argued above, is its construction. To confer upon the autobiography the authority of a person and to read her or his agency as inevitably the same thing is to repeat the referential fallacy that consigns all autobiographies and their authors to the same space in history. I see this strategy as profoundly limiting to a feminist study of autobiography and women's self-representation. Autobiographical identity and agency are historically dynamic. There is no single transhistorical identity that all autobiographers invariantly produce or strive to produce. To thematize "a" question or "a" goal toward which all autobiographers tend is to privilege the constructed continuity of literary and historical tradition over the discontinuity of self-representation and the insights we can derive from that discontinuity, a history of Truth over a history of "truth" *telling*. Moreover, the technologies of autobiography—the discourses of truth and identity available at a particular time—will vary for autobiographers positioned differently within those discourses because of gender, race, class, sexual orientation, religion, and so on. Thus, a series of intersections and the axes

[22] See Alice Jardine, *Gynesis* (Ithaca: Cornell University Press, 1985), for an extended analysis of the chiasmus and of the multiple effects of putting "woman" into discourse.

that determine them may allow us more flexibility in locating women's autobiographicality in texts that do not and, indeed, cannot sign the autobiographical pact, and thus may open up an inquiry into self-representational texts previously sealed by critical practices.

To return to the main analysis, then, the X as a sign of illegibility, as well as the space where the signature belongs, can be used to illustrate another feature of the technologies of autobiography: interruption. Interruption is a discursive effect of gender politics and self-representation and evidences the possibilities of and limitations on women's self-representation. Each text is itself an instance of how women's agency and efforts at self-representation exist in complicated relation to each other and to the texts in which we read them.

The tradition of women's autobiography is an interrupted one. Margaret Cavendish's challenging question indicates that she knew she would have to turn the question around within discourses inhospitable to her presence. In order to develop a way of reading women's autobiography, we need to look beyond criticism that would legitimate mainly "the lives of famous men" as bona fide autobiography. Further, if any text with a more or less legible title page is in some ways autobiographical, such a text may record the interrupted autobiography of more than one person. A broader view of what constitutes textual self-representation may allow us to see how genres other than autobiography are already ruptured by autobiographics. How, then, does such rupture work? Internally, it erodes the illusion of textual coherence, not just thematic or even formal coherence, for what is being interrupted in autobiography is the more entrenched coherence of "subjectivity," on one hand, and, on the other, the cultural production of "writing" through the silencing of women. Externally, rupture works against hegemonic discourses of identity, whether they are psychological or political. I will examine four instances that constitute interruptions of the autobiographical: the "preparation" of women's writing for publication, the censuring responses of readers and reviewers, the subtler infiltrations of texts by women, and the appropriation of women's narratives by men.

The fate of Sarah Knowles Bolton's autobiography is a representative case of the first form of interruption. Bolton, an animal rights activist living in Boston in the early twentieth century, kept volumes of diaries, which she collected into an autobiography. Her son "edited" the text and published it privately as *Autobiography for My Son* in 1915. The unedited version—that is, Bolton's own manuscript—dwells at length on her advocacy of animal rights; her focus on what she clearly viewed as her life's work is as prominent as her discourse on her family. Integrating her political activism with family and social life shapes her autobiography and characterizes the major interests of her middle and later years. She was unafraid of personal criticism, which she withstood, and while she justified her activism as ultimately in harmony with the Christian ideal of stewardship, Bolton was no fanatic. Some of the most humorous passages tease out the dilemma of political consciousness at odds with social obligations and pleasures. For example, Bolton had both a long-standing friendship with the Rockefellers and an intractable disagreement concerning the insufficient care of some cats living in their barn. Bolton fed the cats and found them homes while the Rockefellers remained oblivious of the shrinking and growing feline population Bolton scrupulously monitored. Nor did she conceal her management of the situation. On the day of an elegant luncheon at the Rockefeller mansion, Bolton details the sumptuous menu and describes the guests with obvious delight. She concludes the narration with witty understatement: "Didn't feed the cats today."[23]

Much of her autobiography catalogs scenes of cruelty to animals. While her commitment is strengthened and renewed by successes and Bolton is sustained by the daily work of caring for animals, images of abuse dominate the text and renew her sense of her life's work. When her son prepared the text for publication, he seems to have found those images redundant or perhaps superfluous to his sense of her life's work: being his mother. So the document she prepared to stand, at least in part, as a record of her effort to end animal abuse, becomes the story of a woman's place in relation to her family. The virtues of patience and endurance are channeled into their "normal" expression of motherhood and wifely and neighborly service. Bolton's son acted against Bolton's sense of her identity and attempted to refashion her as a more appropriate woman. He thereby, in a sense, denied her ownership of her self, editing her back into the confines of her role as he conceived it. When the liberal autobiographical pact, modeled on the liberal social contract, can be so easily and so violently disregarded by a helpful son, how sufficient is it to an exploration of women's self-representation? But perhaps this question implies that the autobiographical pact is fine in itself, and we need only ensure that it be extended to all. The liberal position here needs a critique in terms other than its own, for the unequal positioning of persons in relation to the autobiographical pact, to self-

---

[23] Sarah Knowles Bolton, "Autobiography," unpublished manuscript, Schlesinger Library, Radcliffe College, not numbered.

ownership, reveals its complicity in social structures of hierarchy. Although a radical and a socialist feminist critique would differ, they agree in their mutual refusal of the pact's seeming fairness, its seductive packaging of the self as a commodity that it already owns and whose circulation it controls.

Even in those instances when the autobiography is published without such editing, censure frequently follows in the form of public disapproval, a form of interruption so loud that many authors cannot be heard over the clamor. Indeed, the socially constructed silence of women suggests how highly endangered the autobiographical act can be. One has to claim, with authority, the very grounds of identity that patriarchal ideology has denied women: a self worth its history, a life worth remembering, a story worth writing and publishing. When Hannah Tillich, who fled from Germany to the United States as Hitler was gathering ground, published *From Time to Time* in 1974, she was roundly criticized for having wasted the reader's time by telling the story of her own life when she could have written about her husband. The transgression was clear: she had valued her story rather than history. Her autobiographical recollections of marriage to theologian Paul Tillich were scandalous in what they revealed of his private life. The multiple infidelities, his habit of hiding pornographic photos in theology books, and the generally shabby treatment Hannah Tillich struggled through were equally represented alongside his better-known activities. These revelations were unexpected and perhaps inexplicable because they got at the complexity of a particular marriage in a way that rendered bitterness and savagery with tenderness and forgiveness. The autobiography is never simply focused on Paul Tillich, never, that is, a biography. And Hannah Tillich's denial of the form she was expected to produce prompted severe scrutiny of her character rather than her husband's.

Significantly, she began her autobiographical project dutifully enough: she would focus on the story of their life together as a way to deepen the historical record of Paul Tillich's contributions to the spiritual life of the twentieth century. But she failed to write this hagio/biography when, in the process of writing, she discovered her subject: "From those [stories about Paul Tillich] the tale of *my* life unrolled in an attempt to understand and clarify my own self."[24] The emphasis on her self brings about "the triumphant return of the 'I'" that had been lost through a lifetime of learning to listen to and tell

[24] Hannah Tillich, Interview in *Contemporary Authors*, vol. 73–76 (Detroit: Gale Research, 1978), 610.

the "proper" story. Refusing a master narrative that prescribes silence
and submission for women becomes a defiant act, along the lines of
Steedman's refusal, which wins back for Tillich the self she felt she
had lost to a husband, a social circle, a religion, and two cultures
(German and American) that owned the Truth.

As Bolton and Tillich's autobiographies demonstrate, what one
might think the most available subject matter, one's own life, is not
equally available to all persons at all times and in all places. Significantly, during periods of prolific publication for men's autobiography,
women's autobiography virtually disappears, goes unnoticed or unpublished.[25] Times of sparse publication for men (e.g., during wars)
witness the proportional flowering of women's texts. The possibilities
and politics of self-representation for women in a literary and historical tradition that works to exclude them focus some of the persistent
conflicts many women writers experience. When the identity of real
women is figured as the "dark continent" of femininity and their
literary tradition is covered over and obscured deep in the heart of
nowhere, what may a woman see of herself or other women in conditions of self-effacement and estrangement? What identity must she
construct when the rules of sexual identity and aesthetic reception,
indeed, of the hermeneutic act itself, are mapped onto a phal-
lomorphic order?

The difficulties of construction are demonstrated by a third instance
of interruption: the one-sided, fragmentary correspondence that in-
trudes onto the landscape of William Carlos Williams's *Paterson*. In
books 1 and 2 of this epic about the monolithic and representative
Man/City, a frustrated poet, Cress, simultaneously rebukes the mas-
ter/male poet for his lack of response and pleads with him for admission to the company of poets. Cress writes:

> Despite my having said that I'd never write to you again, I do so now
> because I find, with the passing of time, that the outcome of my failure
> with you has been the complete damming up of all my creative capaci-
> ties in a particularly disastrous manner such as I have never before
> experienced.
>
> For a great many weeks now (whenever I've tried to write poetry)
> every thought I've had, even every feeling, has been struck off some
> surface crust of myself which began gathering when I first sensed that
> you were ignoring the real contents of my last letters to you, and which
> finally congealed into some impenetrable substance when you asked me
> to quit corresponding with you altogether without even an explanation.

[25] Estelle Jelinek, Introduction to *Women's Autobiography*. See also Gerda Lerner, *The
Female Experience* (Indianapolis: Bobbs-Merrill, 1977).

That kind of blockage, exiling one's self from one's self—have you ever experienced it? I dare say you have, at moments; and if so, you can well understand what a serious psychological injury it amounts to when turned into a permanent day-to-day condition.[26]

According to Williams, the letters from Cress are drawn from his own correspondence with Marcia Nardi, whom he does not name in the poem. The woman poet in the world and the one in this poem speak in the same voice about the same sense of exile. The fragment's double voice—Cress is a woman poet both in Williams's poem and in the world—dramatizes the necessity and the consequences of trying to speak/write oneself into a tradition that excludes women poets. Cress has devoted her energy to a patriarchal poetic men's club that cannot admit her. When she attempts to break into voice, to disrupt the silence threatening her, her depths are denied, and she becomes "some surface crust of myself," which nothing can penetrate and from which nothing can issue. This impenetrability signals a fatal rupture of identity, "a blockage, exiling one's self from one's self." The silence of the male and his refusal to acknowledge her act as a divisive force, which Cress internalizes as an opaque surface incapable of reflecting her self: her surface has "congealed" into undesired, ambiguously protective armor. If Cress looks to the man as gatekeeper, she will find no sympathy, no possibility of identification or engagement. Indeed, beyond the gate he is identical with the city itself.

Insofar as they are denied an active role in the city, women are identified with nature in the poem. The Woman/Nature construct functions as both the condition and the boundary of the story inscribed in *Paterson*; she is the threatening and desired wilderness that the Man/City must conquer and defend himself against. Similar interpretations advanced by recent feminist theory allow us to raise the stakes and claim that *Paterson* here stands in for Western metaphysics. Within the confines of both cities, women—or, Woman, as symbolized here—cannot think or be thought, nor can they speak for themselves. On their silence depends the flourishing of an empire. Were they to speak, these walls might come tumbling down. No chance of that in this poem, though, because Cress lacks the keys both to the city and to language. "Paterson/Williams" knows very well the importance of precursors. "There's nothing sentimental about the technique of writing," he advises an aspiring male poet. "It can't be learned, you'll say, by a fool. But any young man with a mind burst-

---

[26] William Carlos Williams, *Paterson* (New York: New Directions, 1963), 45.

ing to get out, to get down on a page even a clean sentence—gets courage from an old man who stands ready to help him—to talk to" (231).

In a kind of gloss on Cress's self-representation as exile, Virginia Woolf describes two forms the exile of women writers takes. In *A Room of One's Own*, the *I*-as-outsider describes an externally prohibitive version of exile: "He was a Beadle; I was a woman. This was the turf; there was the path."[27] The second form suggests the internalization of exile, in which the *I*-as-mirror "possess[es] the magic and delicious power of reflecting the figure of man at twice its natural size" (35). Commenting on both exiles, Woolf concludes that the former is less deeply damaging: "I thought how unpleasant it is to be locked out; and I thought how it is worse perhaps to be locked in" (24). In *Paterson*, Cress is reduced to this looking-glass function. She briefly reflects the passage of those for whom the city's maze of poetic influence is comparatively clearly mapped. The male poet looks at her and sees nothing, that is, nothing other than a magnified version of himself. She looks at him and sees, simply and devastatingly, nothing. He will not hold her gaze, and the dynamic of beholding and begetting is destroyed in this refusal.[28] Female speech as transgression and poetic tradition as male bonding are so deeply inscribed in this poem that Cress cannot steer herself out of its ruts. She vanishes into silence.

When Bolton's son tampers with the text, he changes his mother's autobiography and reveals something of himself and his culture's assumptions about what is "interesting." Similarly, by refusing to acknowledge a woman's life as sufficiently worth writing about when that woman has a famous husband, Tillich's audience recreates the ideological silencing of women. And when William Carlos Williams refuses to help "Cress" publish her poetry under her own name but includes her letters in his epic, then silencing women becomes more than a thematic coincidence or an accident of personal history.[29] In-

[27] Virginia Woolf, *A Room of One's Own* (New York: Harcourt, Brace, 1929), 6.

[28] For an extended analysis of this dynamic, see my article "The Gaze of the Other Woman: Beholding and Begetting in Dickinson, Moore, and Rich," in *Engendering the Word*, ed. Temma Berg et al. (Urbana: University of Illinois Press, 1989), 81–102.

[29] Sandra Gilbert and Susan Gubar argue that Williams uses the strategy of hiding things in the open to deflect negative reaction: "Noting that to hide her words 'would be a confession of weakness,' this man of letters who was later to tell Nardi her poems were so good 'that I feel ashamed for my sex' adopts instead the brilliant strategy of the hero of Poe's 'The Purloined Letter,' concealing the threat implied by the dangerous letters he has purloined by placing them in the open that no one would suspect their power" (*No Man's Land*, vol. 1: *The War of the Words* [New Haven: Yale University Press, 1988], 153). See also Sandra Gilbert, "Purloined Letters: William Carlos Williams and 'Cress,'" *William Carlos Williams Review* 10.2 (Fall 1985): 5–15.

deed, these three forms of interruption indicate the ways in which narratives of development lack a point of entry for women: the signature or autograph does not fit the narrative. Steedman's and Lorde's own use of autobiographics, I believe, indicate the extent to which they comprehend and refuse the self-representational limitations required of Bolton, Tillich, and Nardi. As the historical specificities of each of these instances make clear, Steedman and Lorde draw upon two solid decades of feminist work to stake their self-representational projects in different terms.

For a fourth form of interruption, let us turn to a text that feminist critics have been reinterpreting from a variety of perspectives: Freud's *Dora: An Analysis of a Case of Hysteria*. The talking cure has been used by some critics as a metaphor for the autobiographical process of forming the chaotic elements of life into a narrative that replaces and transcends those experiences in a healing and restorative way.[30] Autobiography scholars who take this view would agree with Freud that the events themselves are subordinated in analysis (as in autobiography) to the process of forming a therapeutic narrative. In other words, the subject moves, via autobiography, from *hysteria* to *historia*. Insofar as Freud presents his views on Dora's progress toward achieving this curative end, and inasmuch as Freud's version of Dora's story represents his desire to found a psychoanalytic method through the talking cure and, hence, a major phase in his life, perhaps *Dora*, though not the "proper" autobiography of either Freud or "Dora," is the autobiographical fragment of both.

Some aspects of Dora's case are well known.[31] Like Cress, Dora is a code name: the woman's name was Ida Bauer.[32] She was a young woman, Freud tells us, suffering from hysteria that resulted from her love for her father's acquaintance, Herr K., who attempted to seduce her. Although she desired this seduction, she could not admit her desire, and developed the syndrome of somatic effects named hysteria. According to Freud, Dora is, in almost schematic clarity, a picture

---

[30] Paul Jay, *Being in the Text: Self-Representation from Wordsworth to Roland Barthes* (Ithaca: Cornell University Press, 1984).

[31] Among the many critical anthologies and articles, see Charles Bernheimer and Claire Kahane, eds., *In Dora's Case: Freud—Hysteria—Feminism* (1985; New York: Columbia University Press, 1990); Monique David-Ménard, *Hysteria from Freud to Lacan: Body and Language in Psychoanalysis*, trans. Catherine Porter (Ithaca: Cornell University Press, 1989); Dianne Hunter, ed., *Seduction and Theory: Readings of Gender, Representation, and Rhetoric* (Urbana: University of Illinois Press, 1989); Sarah Kofman, *The Enigma of Woman: Woman in Freud's Writings*, trans. Catherine Porter (Ithaca: Cornell University Press, 1985); Biddy Martin, *Women and Modernity: The (Life)Styles of Lou Andreas-Salomé* (Ithaca: Cornell University Press, 1991).

[32] Ida Bauer's name was not revealed until 1978 by Arnold A. Rogow.

of repression. In order to succeed in analysis, Dora must craft a narrative that would restore her to bodily and psychic health, a narrative with a purpose, which would enable her to exchange the narrative in which she is ill for the narrative that will make her well. While there is considerable discussion about how Dora structures and insists upon her own hysterical narrative, Freud's writing is charged with a more pressing concern: his search for a narrative form that will found his new discipline.

In his "prefatory remarks," Freud indicates that the development of a new narrative technique to reproduce the analytical scene of the talking cure will mark the founding of a new science. He writes that "the presentation of *my* case histories remains a problem which is hard for me to solve."[33] The task, as he sees it, is representational. It involves the production of a narrative based on Dora's narrative that recasts her as a character in his narrative rather than as the speaking subject of her own. In his prolepsis, he justifies his revelation of Dora's case: "Whereas before I was accused of giving no information about my patients, now I shall be accused of giving information about my patients which ought not to be given" (21). He has changed names and locales to throw even the shrewdest of bloodhounds off the trail: "I have allowed no name to stand which could put a non-medical reader upon the scent" (23). Freud wishes to protect Dora from nonmedical readers, from "enquiring minds," although the purely professional guidelines for such confidentiality seem fuzzy to him and his remarks about them are fraught with defensiveness.

As the prefatory remarks presently reveal, Freud is obliquely addressing Dora. He counsels her from beyond the couch when he suggests how she should interpret his publication of her case history: "I naturally cannot prevent the patient herself from being pained if *her own case history* should accidentally fall into her hands. But she will learn nothing from it she does not already know; and she may ask herself who besides her could discover from it that she is the subject of this paper" (23, emphasis added). Who, indeed, is the subject of this paper? His phrase—"if her own case history should accidentally fall into her hands"—reveals Freud's ownership of this narrative. Freud moves from issues of confidentiality to the border of confession, a border that is structured like a fault line through the politics of representation: What is it proper to say? Necessary to say? For whom do I speak? About what should I remain silent? The anxiety is occa-

[33] Sigmund Freud, *Dora: An Analysis of a Case of Hysteria* (New York: Collier, 1963), 22, emphasis added.

sioned by an absence of clear rules; that is, the formal demands of this confessional narrative are unclear to Freud because it involves an appropriation of Dora's confession as a means to make his own. Thus, Freud maneuvers his interpretation to the fore as he reconstructs Dora's history, narrative, and interpretation as the ground from which *he* works. By taking for himself the place of confessing subject, he, rather than Dora, becomes the autobiographical subject. Freud compels Dora to confess to and through him, then offers her account as the basis for his own, as an autobiographical pre-text.

How were the grounds of Freud's authorization constituted? Dora was taken to Freud by her father after she attempted suicide at age eighteen. Her father wanted her out of the way; Freud wanted to test psychoanalysis. The bargain in which they exchanged Dora included making her well. The issue of exchange comes up in Dora's analysis: "When she was feeling embittered she used to be overcome by the idea that she had been handed over to Herr K. as the price of his tolerating the relations between her father and his wife; and her rage at her father's making such a use of her was visible behind her affection for him" (50). We do not know what Dora wanted once the bargain between her father and Freud was struck, whether she embraced the idea of analysis, whether she welcomed time away from her father, whether she sensed that she was passing again from one man to another. We know what she wanted before the exchange, namely, for her parents to believe her story about what Herr K. wanted when he propositioned her by the lake. They didn't. If they were mistaken, as Dora insists they were, Freudian psychoanalysis builds from interpretive error toward claims of interpretive insight. Following her parents' discrediting of her story, Ida/Dora wrote a suicide note and, after arguing with her father and fainting, was taken to Freud. Throughout the analysis, and beyond, Dora persists in her desire to have her narrative believed. Freud was supposed to persuade Dora to collude in the bourgeois family silence surrounding sex and power. In fact, he wanted her to talk about it, but her inability to be heard in her own language and her inability or unwillingness to "tell the truth" in Freud's language undo her. She loses her voice.

Hysteria, as a pathology, is the gaping hole in the seamless fiction of bourgeois family unity borne in the bodies of women, experienced as somatic reality, as truth become burden, as medical identity, and as a lie. A densely encoded body language, hysteria signifies a disease in the body of the family expressed through symptoms in the hysteric's body, in this case, through her loss of voice. Dora returned to Freud fifteen months after breaking off the analysis to corroborate her side of the story and also, I think, for revenge. Herr K. had admitted his sexual proposition and Frau K. had admitted her affair with Dora's father. Dora returned to the family as the place of absolution and to Freud's office for the same purpose: she has been wrongly accused, tried, and treated, and she wants her interlocutor to concede her truth. It seems to me that rather than consider the accuracy of Freud's interpretation or the literal and legal elements of this dilemma, it is possible to aim athwart the story, to come at it from an oblique angle, as Jacques Lacan advised, and see Dora's desires, her questions, her departures, and returns in the context of self-representation, most acutely in its possibilities and politics.

When Dora poses identity questions, she seems always to run into trouble: the answers she works out to questions of family identity, sexual identity, and gender identity are fraught with silencing fathers, complicitous mothers, and never the right lovers. That the urge toward detective work which Freud installs in the prefatory remarks continues to compel many critics of Dora's case indicates that psychoanalysis is a powerful technology of autobiography, interested in the subject's identity, in the narrative dimension of case history, and in the "truth," even when it constructs it as an intrusion.

Freud places a knot of desire at the center of his analysis; yet, he swerves from what he calls the "strongest unconscious current in [Dora's] mental life," her desire for women. Freud considered her homosexuality to be the perversion she had repressed even further than her desire for Herr K., for Dora was in love with the unwelcome seducer's wife, Frau K., the woman who was also her father's lover. Woven throughout Dora's narrative of the trauma that propelled her into troubled unhappiness is a narrative of more successful attachments to women. The world of women to which Dora was attracted forms the mere backdrop for Freud's analysis. Of course, Dora's lesbianism was not the kind of choice Freud could facilitate; one can imagine a very different story unfolding, though not through Freudian psychoanalysis, in which Dora's narrative of lesbian sexuality was achieved and deemed therapeutic. Yet if Freudian therapeutic narratives are more or less exchangeable (within the limitations of the political unconscious, to use Fredric Jameson's term), if the final truth is untethered to facts, then why are the healing narratives the ones that fold the female patient into Freud's discourse of "normal" womanhood? As one of the major truth- and identity-producing discourses of the twentieth century, Freudian psychoanalysis depends for its "success" on a definition of women as deformed and deficient men. Such is the production of women's authority in a discourse that

Foucault has described as "yet another round of whispering on a bed" (*History of Sexuality* 1: 5). Thus while I would agree that the "talking cure" offers a significant metaphor for thinking about autobiography, any restoration it offers must concede that, for Freud, women's constitutive lack of a penis can never be restored and women are trained by means of Freudian psychoanalysis to accept this totalizing premise.

In this context, several features of Dora's story are important. First, Dora was an intelligent storyteller. Freud found himself compelled enough by her stories virtually to invent psychoanalysis as a codification of and tribute to her hysterical talent. Imagine the hours Freud spent listening to Ida talk herself into his own dreams, creating the occasion for his interpretive talents to flower, becoming "Dora." Their interplay forms the subtext of Freud's *Analysis of a Case of Hysteria* and is the story he in some ways represses. Second, Dora controls more of the situation than Freud would admit; no doubt such admissions are not necessary to the *Analysis*, but I think we see something of the artist in Dora when she abruptly cuts off the analysis, with dramatic flair, on the final day of the year 1900. When Freud wakes up in the twentieth century, the analysis of her dreams will carry psychoanalysis forward. She is also an active and competent collaborator in their analysis of her dreams. Freud comments: "She had already had some training in dream interpretation from having previously analysed a few minor specimens" (82). Third, her absence and silence mark Freud's theory as a discourse of loss that attempts to recuperate "the hysteric" as it fails to recuperate Dora's voice.

Some more specific attention to Dora's most troubling symptom, her loss of voice, can be given here in the context of Freud's objective which he articulates in the prefatory remarks: "My object in this case history was to demonstrate the intimate structure of a neurotic disorder and the determination of its symptoms" (27). Dora's voice appears in Freud's text as reported discourse, fragmented, illustrative, a symptom of illness. There is the comment on Frau K.'s "adorable white body" (79); we hear "her usual reply: 'I don't remember that'" (74), and Dora's skilled, though still harmful repression, at which Freud marvels. He notes an example:

> "I can think of nothing else," she complained again and again. "I know my brother says we children have no right to criticize this behaviour of our father's. He declares that we ought not to trouble ourselves about it, and ought even to be glad, perhaps, that he has found a woman he can love, since mother understands him so little. I can quite see that, and I

should like to think the same as my brother, but I can't. I can't forgive him for it." (71–72)

Her interpretations contribute to her illness, according to Freud. They may be ingenious, affecting, even "right" in some way, but inasmuch as they have not cured her, they must be resisted. The psychoanalytic process turns on the subject's formulation of her past into a narrative, not on the recovery—through unblocking memory—of the past itself. The past has no existence outside this formulation; the talking cure's power lies in this transformation. In this context, it is also important to point out that the claim of psychoanalysis to disinterest in the literal truth is somewhat disingenuous or at least overstated. After all, Freud believed in lies. Memories could be falsified, obscured, repressed; indeed, the analyst's skill at dislodging the truth from the cover of protective memory is always being tested. Could Freud have been so certain that Dora was lying if he did not concede the centrality of something functioning as "truth" which he controlled? The point is, the relative relevance of "truth" is decided by those who can determine who is lying, and make their judgment count. Dora's words refuse to yield to Freud's discourse of health. Required to exchange her words and interpretations for the doctor's—and how to measure the degree of coercion involved?— Dora becomes silent. Freud's analysis of this symptom is consistent with the sexualizing of all physical, hysterical symptoms. But her loss of voice, her refusal to participate either in her illness or in Freud's transformation of it, is consistent with Cress's sense of self-exile. Cress's armored body is as impenetrable a mystery in Williams's *Paterson* as Dora's silence and disappearance is to Freud. Both represent the difficulty of locating the autobiographical site, the engendering *I*, within a discourse—poetic or psychoanalytic—in which authority is so heavily weighted, even beyond the authorizing signature, toward the masculine.

Freud located the sources of identity and desire in a sexualized economy based, for women, on scarcity and noncoincidence. Women's constitutive lack determines inferiority and projects hysteria as a plausible resistance to this flawed body. Male identity and desire circulate within a self-referential economy of met needs. Such a system cannot contain female desire and identity as "fullness"; thus, the excess or plenitude represented by rapture and ecstasy, to which I shall turn in Chapters 3 and 4, fractures this model of exchange. It is not so much that women's desire cannot be measured by the patriarchal model, rather that the measure of desire is reduced to women's desire for the phallus. Especially in this context of representation, an economy of scarcity as opposed to an economy of plenitude is operating implicitly in the way a culture values the currency of women's lives.

The first form of interruption—the posthumous editing and private publication of Bolton's manuscript as *Autobiography for My Son*—concerns public reputation; the autobiography addressed to "others" about one's life and career is a common form of men's autobiography. Thus, I would conclude that Bolton's "signature" to such a document was illegible and that the discourse of public reputation in early twentieth-century America, despite the careers of many women, was masculinist. Even when Bolton was quite possibly attempting to present her career in animal rights activism in relation to this discourse, there was one significant reader who refused this (self-) representation. It is rather more likely that her son saw this compassion for animals as a "feminine" virtue, though Bolton's activism certainly clashed with the rules for female comportment.

In Tillich's case, I think it is possible to see further how women are refused the self-authorizing function that some critics have suggested resides in autobiography. What criteria about the value of women's lives are operating when Tillich can be criticized for choosing the wrong "subject" for her autobiography? I do not mean to let these texts stand as different examples of the more or less monolithic oppression of women; instead, I am trying to underline the "policing" of the autobiographical pact which goes on through a variety of regulations and regulators. The role of those who may judge the truth, who may appropriate women's self-representation as "inspiration" or more "raw material" for men's theories and representations of the self, make codes of reading sensitive to the disruption of the discourse of self-identity critical to a study of women's self-representation.

In neither *Paterson* nor *Dora* are the women's real names used. The women stand in these texts as figures: in Cress's case, of poetic talent thwarted and turned against itself; in Dora's case, of sexually repressed and self-deluding hysteria. They function, too, as the narrative voices enclosed within structures (poetic and scientific) of Williams's and Freud's devising and as such reveal how the self-representational desire *of* female subjects can become figures for desire *in* narrative. Like psychoanalysis and the city of Paterson, autobiography is a practice of language, a signifying system charged with the representation (and construction) of identity through the organizing modes of gender and genre. In autobiography, Woman as a figure of the desire the Other possesses and may exchange, rails against her enforced silence, writes hard and indicting letters, or falls silent and disappears from the narrative structure designed to record her diminishment.[34] The figure of Woman as ground of representation and object of capture is implicated in autobiography's dream of identity. Once Cress and Dora are captured within a narrative that reworks their self-representational desires for agency and subjectivity into the demands of Williams's and Freud's texts, their identity is no longer coincident with the form in which they speak. They are at odds with the narrative structure; they speak against themselves. If we continue to romanticize identity, on one hand, as it is represented by the signature, then we necessarily conclude that Williams and Freud have artfully shaped the real voices of women and deserve themselves to be "authorized." If, on the other hand, we agree to read against the authority of the signature in these cases and instead to press this claim to its limits and read for self-representation at odds with the masculinist discourses that frame them, then we have interrupted Freud's and Williams's texts, denied them at least for the space of this reading the univocal voice of their authorship, and reread Cress's and Dora's signatures through and against their coding *as* illegibility.

Currently, there are at least two ways to interpret rupture within feminist theory: one perspective would align rupture with rapture, with feminine *jouissance*, and claim, as Hélène Cixous does, that women are *figures* of rupture, those wild women, sorceresses, and conjurers who threaten phallogocentrism with their witchy words and ways. Another perspective would argue that women are *agents* of rupture whose actions in the world, including writing, are appropriated by masculinist institutions that women can, nevertheless, resist. Figures of the feminine who disrupt patriarchal language or real women who are oppressed by and resist patriarchal institutions? Both have been used in feminist arguments and have been used to rally feminist actions inside and outside the academy. Both analyses help to frame the problems I have associated with authorization in self-representation. And while these two views are incompatible, depending as they do on definitions of "women" which are themselves

[34] I am reminded here of Teresa de Lauretis's, description of Zobeide, the imaginary city in Italo Calvino's *Invisible Cities*, as "a city built from a dream of woman [which] must be constantly rebuilt to keep woman captive. . . . [T]he woman is at once the dream's object of desire and the reason for its objectification: the construction of the city. She is both the source of the drive to represent and its ultimate, unattainable goal. Thus the city, which is built to capture men's dream, finally only inscribes woman's absence" (*Alice Doesn't: Feminism, Semiotics, and Cinema* [Bloomington: Indiana University Press, 1984], 12–13).

unstable, both reveal the problem of grounding feminist analysis in the identity of women.[35]

Many women writers, even when they are on the apparently common ground of language and literature, experience their desire to write as trespassing. Virginia Woolf couches her ambivalence in the metaphor of property: "Literature is no one's private ground; literature is common ground. . . . Let us trespass freely and fearlessly and find our own way for ourselves."[36] Woolf associates writing with a transgression of the patriarchal privilege and indicates that the illusion of ownership which accompanies writing has been viewed as a male right to property in which a woman's access to property through the legitimate mechanisms of inheritance and ownership are denied. Similarly, Hélène Cixous claims, "It is no accident: women take after birds and robbers just as robbers take after women and birds. They [*illes*] go by, fly the coop, take pleasure in jumbling the order of space, in disorienting it, in changing around the furniture, dislocating things and values, breaking them all up, emptying structures, and turning propriety upside down."[37]

In the context of these important feminist insights, we could argue that first-person, nonfictional narrative offers voice to historically silenced and marginalized persons who penetrate the labyrinths of history and language to possess, often by stealth, theft, or what they perceive as trespass, the engendering matrix of textual selfhood: the autobiographical *I*. Such "theft," however, belongs to a language of proper, legal ownership and is therefore problematical in the resisting reading I offer of the autobiographical pact. I would conclude by suggesting that the violence described through my use of "interruption" and "autobiographics" does not necessarily denote the liberation of a female speaking subject. Rather, it seeks to be attentive to the cultural specificities of self-representational experimentation by women. Such violence may not so much mark a breakdown in the functioning of the masculinist discourses of truth and identity as evidence

[35] For other discussions of the constitutive incompatibility between and among feminist positions, see, for example, Michèle Barrett, "Some Different Meanings of the Concept of 'Difference': Feminist Theory and the Concept of Ideology," in *The Difference Within*, ed. Elizabeth Meese and Alice Parker (Amsterdam: John Benjamins, 1989), 37–48; and Riley, "*Am I That Name?*"

[36] Virginia Woolf, "The Leaning Tower," quoted in Elizabeth Meese, *Crossing the Double-Cross: The Practice of Feminist Criticism* (Chapel Hill: University of North Carolina Press, 1986), 4.

[37] Hélène Cixous, "The Laugh of the Medusa," trans. Keith Cohen and Paula Cohen, *Signs* 1 (1976): 873–93. "Illes" is Cixous's third-person, plural neologism combining "elles" and "ils."

how they can be mobilized to maintain their power. Yet, feminist criticism can intervene in those practices and does interrupt those discourses, at least here and at least now, where the axis of theories of traditional autobiography and the texts they describe intersects the axis of feminist theory and women's self-representation, which is where we are. X.

2

Technologies of Autobiography

Figuring (Out) Identity: Representing "Realism"

The real does not efface itself in favor of the imaginary; it effaces
itself in favor of the more real than real: the hyperreal. The truer
than true: this is simulation.
                                    —Jean Baudrillard, *Fatal Strategies*

The relationship between representation and the real concerns
many critics of autobiography, as well as many autobiographers. At
stake is the relationship between autobiography's privileged signifier
of identity, the name, and autobiography's simulation of real life. In
autobiography, the name has several functions: it identifies a person
within a historical context of place and patrilineage, and focuses
attention on the solid corporeality to which it refers. Ultimately, it
seems to mark a ground zero of representational veracity: "Who *is* the
autobiographer?" can be answered by a simple cross-check and verification of the author's name against the main character identified in
the text. If the names are the same, you have autobiography. But the
case for the name as a simple referential anchor that holds the world
to the text through the name of the autobiographer denies the specificity of autobiography even as it advances its argument. Such a claim
depends upon taking autobiography's "realisms," its *representations* of
identity and the real, as identity and the real *themselves*.

In the first part of this chapter I examine critical texts that focus on
the name as a privileged signifier of identity to explore their claims
about autobiography's relation to the real through a discussion of
metaphor and metonymy. These texts come from the "new wave" of
autobiography studies in the 1970s whose assumptions about autobiographical power and value continue to inform contemporary criticism: Paul de Man's "Autobiography as De-facement" (1979), James
Olney's *Metaphors of Self* (1972), and Philippe Lejeune's notion of the

autobiographical pact (1975).[1] I consider the critical figuring out of identity (through a variety of tropes) and situate autobiography criticism within the technologies of autobiography—those discourses and practices that construct truth and identity—in order to challenge the sufficiency of these formulations for the study of women's self-representational writing. I conclude by discussing a group of contemporary self-representational texts that take the name as the site and not the limit of experimentation, focusing especially on Sandra Cisneros's *House on Mango Street* (1991) and Jamaica Kincaid's *Annie John* (1986).[2] The general issues of autobiography's privileged relation to the real and the function of the name as a magical signifier of identity underwrite this inquiry.

If the coincidence of the signature on the title page and the name of the main character provide the proof of autobiographical identity, the even more coincidental autobiographical *I*, which we could call the autobiographical signature, does less to bolster claims that a clear and solid ID has been made than to call it into question. Coming at the project of self-representation from different angles, Adrienne Rich and Roland Barthes pose illuminating questions about the autobiographical *I*. Barthes is concerned with the nexus of identity and representation which underlies autobiography as an act: "I cannot *write myself*. What, after all, is this 'I' who would write himself?"[3] Rich questions the transformation of life into words and the identity conferred in that activity: "What kind of beast would turn its life into words? / What atonement is this all about? /—and yet, writing words like these, I'm also living."[4] Not only does autobiographical writing split (or double) the *I* into "myself" and "herself" (or "himself") for both writers, but the ways of understanding that differentiation are closely bound up in political and aesthetic discourses interested in nothing less than truth and identity. Rich's and Barthes's questions

[1] Paul de Man, "Autobiography as De-facement," *Modern Language Notes* 94 (1979): 919–30. My thanks to Richard Machin for illuminating conversations about de Man. Philippe Lejeune, *Le Pacte autobiographique* (Paris: Seuil, 1975). Lejeune has revised his emphasis on the pact in more recent work, though his early formulation marks a critical turn in the study of autobiography. James Olney, *Metaphors of Self: The Meaning of Autobiography* (Princeton: Princeton University Press, 1972).

[2] Sandra Cisneros, *The House on Mango Street* (New York: Vintage, 1991, first published in slightly different form by Arte Público Press 1984 and revised in 1989); Jamaica Kincaid, *Annie John* (New York: Farrar, Straus and Giroux; first Plume Printing, 1986; first published in slightly different form in the *New Yorker*, 1983).

[3] Roland Barthes, *A Lover's Discourse: Fragments* (New York: Hill and Wang, 1978), 98.

[4] Adrienne Rich, "Twenty-One Love Poems," in *The Dream of a Common Language: Poems, 1974–1977* (New York: Norton, 1978), 28.

are central to the concerns of autobiography criticism insofar as they raise the issues of who speaks for and as the autobiographical *I*, how that identity exceeds its representation, and how the violence of that splitting makes possible both alienation and nostalgia for the fictional unity of an *I*.

The crucial figure of the *I* is one of autobiographical identity's names. It marks a place in self-representational writing where someone *is*. From this location, the autobiographer brings forward self-evidence. The autobiographical *I*, however, is only deceptively self-authorizing, if, as I have been arguing, not all autobiographers may write with equal authority from this location.[5] Wherein, we may ask, lies autobiography's authority if not primarily in the self-authorizing *I*? I have advanced several contexts of authority that privilege an auto-biographical *I*: hegemonic traditions linking human value to race, gender, class, and sexual orientation; certain historical situations for certain persons; and discourses of individualism. To pursue a formal location further, autobiography's power has been especially identified in the realism of nonfictional narrative, in critical essays, and in mani-festoes. In sum, the authority of the autobiographical *I* coincides with other forms of authority. Autobiographical authority may be attri-buted to human agents but also to genre(s) of self-representation (especially, autobiography itself).

The autobiographical subject represents the real person not only as a metaphor of self, as Olney has described, wherein the self in the text transcends its materiality and becomes an emblem for a person's striving. In this view, autobiography can be seen to exploit the meta-phorical resonance of *reality*, a metaphor that functions as a trope of truth beyond argument, of identity beyond proof, of what simply is. Much thinking about autobiography is antirepresentational in precise-ly this sense, for it neglects the narrative dimension of the text, ne-glects autobiography's textuality as anything other than a transparent view onto reality. This is an interpretation of autobiographical reality as a metaphor for the unambiguous real. It is an imaginary real, to be sure, and all the more powerful for being drenched in this desire. Yet, insofar as autobiography represents the real, it does so through metonymy, that is, through the claims of contiguity wherein the per-son who writes is the same as the self in the writing; one extends the other, puts her in another place. By my use of the real, here, I mean

[5] For two excellent discussions of authority in autobiography, see Thomas Couser, *Altered Egos: Authority in American Autobiography* (New York: Oxford University Press, 1989); and Saldívar, *Chicano Narratives*, esp. the chapter on autobiography.

material reality and its meaning for persons; thus, I do not exclude the Lacanian notion of the unconscious real, for the unconscious speaks from a real place, as Lacan has shown, through metonymy (as desire) and metaphor (bodily symptoms). Fredric Jameson's reformulation of the real as that which hurts is useful here, too, for autobiographers frequently wish to reposition themselves in narratives of their own authoring for cathartic, confessional, or therapeutic ends. Autobiography has a privileged relation to the unproblematized real, as in the "real life" whose existence seems so obvious that it barely deserves further explanation. For autobiography, then, the real is what is given, the ontology upon which autobiography is firmly grounded. Autobiography represents the real through extended figurations of continuums, through chronology and the implied continuities in places and persons. The real clings to metonymy; metaphor shakes off the real and transcends materiality. While I would agree that autobiographies are filled with metaphors for writing and for the self and that these metaphors are a crucial part of autobiography's rhetoric, it is autobiography's metonymies that seem to ground it in real life. Thus, as I will argue, it is within the structure of metonymy that autobiographical metaphors have meaning.

Analyses that focus on tropes have shaped the study of autobiography in crucial and surprising ways: on a theoretical level, such a focus can be used either to dissolve autobiography as a genre or to locate its meaning in schemes more grand than genre, where language itself is the system of meaning. On a thematic level, such discussions tend toward representations of life and death. On a political level, liberal and radical ideologies focus on the rhetoric of individualism. Perhaps it will seem to readers of contemporary theory that the figures of metonymy and metaphor offer a too-familiar organization, yet this organization has a history in the study of autobiography that I wish to indicate here in order to demonstrate how feminist criticism and its preference for metonymy can be contextualized.[6] Metaphor depends

---

[6] As an organizing binary, metaphor and metonymy offer a revealing example of how binary thinking, which disguises its hierarchical structure, furthers hierarchy in oblique ways. Where, we might ask, is the comparable literature on metonymy to balance the bulk of writing on metaphor? Metaphor has a more secure and lengthy place in the study of poetry, while metonymy lacks an equally prominent place in the study of prose. How, in the face of such non-equivalence, does the binary hold? Metaphor has essential components that must be present for us to recognize it as such; metonymy, conversely, has no set of formal features except its contiguity to metaphor. Roland Barthes indicates one reason for the persistence of their attachment, a reason that indicates only a changed attitude toward the persistence of this organizational logic: "For a certain time, he went into raptures over binarism; binarism became for him a

for meaning upon a relation of identity, and although it may be sustained in a text, the rightness of that relation depends upon its being grasped in an instant. Metonymy, however, depends upon a sustained patterning for meaning and therefore extends temporally in a way metaphor does not. The king, in other words, must wear the crown often enough for the crown to stand in metonymic relation to the king and kingship. Workers must regularly be associated with the labor of their hands in order to be known metonymically as "hands." Metonymy stabilizes certain forms (whether they are habits of reference or rituals of the state) and renders them recognizable through time. Thus when autobiography studies focus on metaphor as the defining trope, they participate in the production of identity as identity; that is, as a one-to-one mirroring of an essential sameness (the self) in different forms (real life and autobiography). When autobiography studies focus on metonymy, they recognize the continual production of identity as a kind of patterning sustained through time by the modes of production that create it. As ways to reproduce ideology, then, metaphor and metonymy, though linked in a rather deceptive binary relationship, have profoundly different forms. As I will show, the name is one example of their mutual implication and necessary dissimilarity.

Both Paul de Man and James Olney have profoundly influenced the study of autobiography, both share an interest in differentiating the self represented in the text from the self represented in history, and both suggest that the referential gaps characterizing autobiography are bridged tropologically. For both the autobiographical self is constituted linguistically—for Olney in *Metaphors of Self* via metaphor, for de Man in "Autobiography as De-facement" via a specific rhetorical figure, prosopopoeia—but they describe the effects of that self's relation to language in strikingly different ways. For de Man, the autobiographical self is both enabled and constrained by its mode of representation; specifically, the fiction of self-presence is simultaneously offered and denied by the language of self and self-identity that creates it. For Olney, the autobiographer takes on the role of God and creates, out of the language of autobiography, a metaphor of self capable of generating a new textual order. When both de Man and Olney arrive at a discussion of death and language, their different

---

kind of erotic object. This idea seemed to him inexhaustible, he could never exploit it enough. That one might say everything *with only one difference* produced a kind of joy in him, a continuous astonishment. Since intellectual things resemble erotic ones, in binarism what delighted him was a figure." See *Roland Barthes by Roland Barthes*, trans. Richard Howard (New York: Hill and Wang, 1977), 51–52.

models of identity and representation are most clearly revealed. Olney writes his way out of death by granting the "successful" autobiographer virtually divine status. De Man finds no way out, for if there is any system that totalizes the production of autobiographical identity, that system must be language. Both deploy figural readings from wholly different critical and, one could say, ideological positions. While this paraphrase certainly indicates the different conclusions a deconstructionist and a liberal humanist reading would reach, I hope to use it to illuminate how both critical and ideological positions attach to autobiography and how critical positions toward self-representation participate in the technologies of autobiography.

De Man, one of the first deconstructionists to turn his attention to autobiography, finds in it what he finds in most texts. That is, his concern is "no longer the meaning and the value [of texts] but the modalities of production and reception of meaning and value prior to their establishment." De Man balks at the specific effort to establish autobiography "among the canonical hierarchies of the major literary genres," an exercise that disappoints because of the apparent incommensurability of autobiography's divided status as historical document, on the one hand, and aesthetic artifact, on the other. Classification tends to run aground in this view especially as historical concepts of the self are matched up against literary representations. For this reason, de Man designates as "pointless and unanswerable" questions of genre that seek autobiography's origins in specific periods or discourses. Autobiography more accurately represents the collection of rules offered by and produced in language that prefigures and even determines the historical modes of expression. In other words, in choosing autobiography, a writer is both enabled and constrained by the rhetoric of its style. Writing autobiography produces its own constitutive difficulties, particularly as it constructs subjectivity. These complexities, therefore, are not external to autobiography; they define it.

De Man focuses the relation between metaphor and metonymy through a reading of Proust. When we read autobiography, de Man explains, in order to believe our newfound knowledge concerning the subject, in this case Proust, we have to read narrated events that happened to him and situations in which he is described metaphorically. The subject cannot simply and unambiguously "be there" in the text. We construct him as we read; narrated events shape his representation and appear necessary (inescapably and irrevocably) in reproducing "Proust." They totalize his character for us. Moreover, events must be presented within "narrative"; the revelation of character depends on a temporal distribution of narrated acts. Thus, narrative creates character through metonymy, and identity in the text emerges through contiguity. Catachrestically, de Man asks which is the cause and which the effect: metonymic narrative process or the metaphorical definitions it produces? Where do we place autobiography: in the realm of fiction or biographical fact? This is not, of course, one of the "pointless and unanswerable" questions; rather, "the distinction between fiction and autobiography is not an either/or polarity . . . it is undecidable" (921).

Autobiography emerges as a special case in the definition of subjectivity because it interiorizes the specular play between the producer/producing and the produced. De Man indicates that the same difficulty arises whenever a text is said to be *about* anything or even *by* anyone. Thus, he begins to undermine claims to authority that are based on privileging self-referential power (in the form of understanding and knowledge) and authority (the source of power). Autobiography unfolds as a special case because of the reading situation it creates. Certain conventions of reading reinforce the production of subjectivity in autobiography: the reader polices the writing, makes sure the rules are followed, judges the authenticity of the name on the title page, and certifies whether or not the truth, the whole truth, and nothing but the truth is told. Yet, de Man does not locate these expectations in history; for him, they are, fundamentally, manifestations of a linguistic structure. Explanations that resist autobiography as a linguistic phenomenon and try to locate its authority in history will inevitably be undone by the instability inherent in the failure to grasp the referent in the text: "The specular moment that is part of all understanding reveals the tropological structure that underlies all cognitions, including knowledge of self" (922). De Man begins to describe the specularity in autobiography as it enacts the relationship between fiction and fact, metaphor and metonymy, through a reading of the dynamics of undecidability.

Autobiography is improperly understood as a genre or a mode, then, for the "autobiographic moment" is constituted by the specularity of authors and readers staged in the text, and this phenomenon primarily describes a figure of reading. The oscillation that occurs between readers and subjects depends on a structure that contains both their differences and their similarities and enables their "mutual reflexive substitution." The self implicit in this theory of language is clearly a linguistic structure; it differs from the historical self and inhabits the text as a trope. The historical self, the "real" self of the signature, would be a trope passing itself off as the truth. The truth of such a duplicitous self (that is, doubled, irreducible to and incommensurable with historical reality) is both offered up and recedes into the language that seems to contain it. Tropes beguile us into thinking we have nontropological knowledge, especially in autobiography. The desire to locate the real self in autobiography is a consequence of its rhetoric; the self and language are privative, for they generate and deny the very thing they cannot render.

For de Man, autobiography *is* prosopopoeia, which he defines as apostrophe, a call to an absent, dead, or inanimate object. Talking to the dead or the inaccessible establishes a strong movement of control: you not only assume the ability to address rocks, waterfalls, absent loved ones, and yourself, you confer upon the Other the ability to respond. De Man presents this "speak when spoken to" function visually: faces speak; so prosopopoeia is the rendering visible and invisible of faces, and because a voice speaks from this face, prosopopoeia also involves giving and taking away voice. Figuration becomes disfiguration as autobiography de-faces the subject: "The restoration of mortality by autobiography (the prosopopeia of the voice and the name) deprives and disfigures to the precise extent that it restores. Autobiography veils a defacement of the mind of which it is itself the cause" (930). The specularity and substitution we have seen earlier makes this move dangerous because making the dead speak also risks rendering the speaking subject speechless. Through deconstruction, de Man's discussion of voice in autobiography arrives at a site of cultural anxiety sometimes represented through the figure of the zombie. I use this image to dislodge the considerable horror that runs through de Man's anxiety about voice. This anxiety is associated with the animation, or reanimation, of the dead, with their strangeness, to be sure, but more eerily, with their uncompromising familiarity. The zombie is an extension of another's will; it rises only to do another's bidding. Thus autobiography offers an object summoned by an Other and not a self-summoning subject. For autobiography then, as de Man so rightly perceives, the problem is less with the jolt of recognition provided by the zombie than with agency. The question de Man poses concerns authority and identity; it is the same one posed in different terms by Barthes and by Rich, who preserves the monstrous element: In whose voice can the subject of autobiography speak? Its own multivocality becomes fraught with potential silences. De Man's argument produces a classic (or death-bound) point about a self constructed within a language of privation, within a tropological system: "Death is a displaced name for a linguistic predicament" (930).

De Man's exemplary text is Wordsworth's "Essays on Epitaphs," which thematizes the tension between what language appears to promise and what it cannot produce. Though one is born into language, one cannot die out of it. The dead seem to haunt language (prosopopoeia evidences that they do) as figures of identity haunt texts (the "autobiographic moment" evidences that they do) when the moment of self-knowledge or identity appears to have been achieved. De Man chooses a passage in which Wordsworth attacks language as the "clothing" of thought, rather than thought itself: language is deceptive in that it leads us away from true thought, which it only represents. The language so violently denounced, however, is the language of metaphor, of prosopopoeia; that is, the very thing that makes the unknown knowable. The language we depend upon to produce things for us—the subject of autobiography, for example, by way of prosopopoeia—is silent. It cannot itself speak, nor is it the thing itself; yet it generates for us the thing in-and-for-itself while radically excluding us from it. To the extent that we depend upon such processes of representation, or of production, we are "eternally deprived of voice and condemned to muteness" (930). Intending to represent life, the autobiographer maps loss and transgression. According to de Man, this is not a falling away from the task; it defines, rather, the task's requisite turning away from (or de-facement), represented as nostalgia. Autobiography's escape into nostalgia is its concession to loss. For de Man, this is the lingering effect of language's systematic self-enactment through prosopopoeia. Loss and transgression—of face, of voice—are part of language, part of autobiography.[7]

While autobiography might offer de Man a metaphor of death in the trope of prosopopoeia, for Olney metaphors of self convey life. Olney focuses in *Metaphors of Self* on questions aimed at accounting for the universality of autobiography's appeal: "Behind the question 'What is man?' lies another, more insistent question—the ulti-

---

[7] See Mary Jacobus, *Romanticism, Writing, and Sexual Difference: Essays on "The Prelude"* (Oxford: Clarendon Press, 1989), for a discussion of autobiography and the Romantic Sublime in which she focuses on a confrontation that seemingly threatens to negate the very possibility of autobiography. The Sublime encounter is imperiling because it is always associated with the extinction of consciousness, and consciousness—or self-presence—is precisely what autobiography seems to ground itself in. In book 6, Wordsworth describes crossing the Alps and subsequently descending into the Vale of Gondo. Jacobus reads this central passage as "a symbolic representation of another crossing—that of the autobiographical poem's turning on itself at its midpoint to reflect on the peculiar status of autobiographical inscription, and, in so doing, on the impossibility of autobiographical self-encounter" (6). For Jacobus's reading of Wordsworthian autobiography, "any inscription—spells the death of the writer" (7).

mate and most important question, I should think, for every man: 'How shall I live?'" (xi). Autobiography is a monument to the self it constructs and that constructs it, and it results from the "natural" impulse to order. Olney claims that order is the primary urge characterizing all human behavior, and autobiography proves this contention as well as any other artifact. Metaphor stands in the gap described by prosopopoeia, but in Olney's interpretation it stands ready to deliver the goods from the "out there" of history to the "in here" of the text. The model of the self and the theory of language which enable this conception depend on an a priori assumption that language can render the self whole, can perform a curative function as it heals the chaos of life, can, in expressing the truest parts of one man, represent the truest parts of us all: "One cannot write an autobiography without being alive and without proving the quality of that life in the created metaphor; for to exercise memory, to be conscious and to increase consciousness, to make one's metaphor, is to live" (331).

Because, in Olney's analysis, metaphors of self function for the writer in a primarily epistemological way and provide "essentially a way of knowing" (31), the system of referentiality is totalized by unreflecting reflexivity and thereby achieves nearly perfect closure. This argument is at least implied by an epigraph from Ludwig Wittgenstein which Olney does not explicate: "Here we see that solipsism strictly carried out coincides with pure realism. The *I* in solipsism shrinks to an extensionless point and there remains the reality co-ordinated with it." Olney's language of presence presumes that at the very least the self can be fully present to itself, present enough to represent itself for the benefit of others. The self controls language's effects and is the shaping agent of representation, for the achievement of self-presence occurs prior to writing, prior to language. Autobiography is merely and magnificently the literary reflection of the realized self. Olney's argument, however, refutes its own claims because it is metaphor that permits the knowing of the unknown.

Olney suggests that metaphor has extralinguistic properties and can thus correlate pre- or nonlinguistic experience with knowledge: "It is only metaphor that thus mediates between the internal and the external, between your experience and my experience, between the artist and us, between conscious mind and total being, between a past and a present self, between, one might say, ourselves formed and ourselves becoming" (35). He requires a particular kind of work of metaphor in which the "betweens" become capable of nearly endless multiplication; eventually, he requires metaphor to do the patterning work of metonymy. The crucial substitution autobiography finally effects, through the metonymic action of what Olney continues to call metaphor, is an exchange of the author's self-knowledge for the reader's self-knowledge. De Man, conversely, dimisses this possibility early on: "The interest of autobiography, then, is not that it reveals reliable self-knowledge—it does not—but that it demonstrates in a striking way the impossibility of closure and of totalization (that is the impossibility of coming into being) of all textual systems made up of tropological substitutions" (922).

I have posed de Man and Olney as influential commentators on autobiography because their arguments in many ways define the boundary between humanism and feminism, in Olney's case, and deconstruction and feminism, in de Man's case—for all three discourses value autobiography highly. The political ideology of individualism so defining of our understanding of autobiography has been complicit with the oppression of women. Metaphors of self available through the discourse of identity focus on hierarchy, on status and privilege, on rising and standing above. Whereas de Man's language of privation goes beyond a description of autobiography's linguistics and thematics to a theory of language as constitutively privative, such a theory does not offer a self fully present, at least to itself, wholly representative and representable, waiting to leap into or out of the text. This autobiographical identity is a metaphor for the discourses of truth and identity; itself a representative symptom, this version of the autobiographer leads us into the metonymic structure of individualism. Through the political discourse of individualism, the privileged *I* stands in for you and for me so many times that its interests and trajectory in the social world represent our desire. Olney's expressivist theory of language depends on this assumption, which frames the metaphoricity of presence he finds in autobiography. That is, his reliance on metaphor as a trope of substitution beguiles him (de Man might say) into thinking he can move between the text and the world. The fluidity of access to language and history which Olney envisions characterizes gender-, class-, and race-bound privilege in both structures. Both analyses have different limitations for feminist theories. It has been a crucial insight of many feminisms that it is a good deal easier to abandon yourself to disappearance and Nietzschean death if you already dominate all you survey. Indeed, many women autobiographers tend to attribute to speech, presence, political enfranchisement, and cultural authority the same tonic effects contemporary critics associate with the (more or less) free play of signifiers.[8]

Another "father figure" in autobiography studies is Philippe Le-

---

[8] See especially Nancy K. Miller's "Changing the Subject: Authorship, Writing, and the Reader," in *Subject to Change*, 102–21.

jeune whose early formulation of autobiography's contractual basis focused on the guarantee offered by the signature. For Lejeune, the title page functioned as a signed document attesting to the historically truthful representation of the coherent self of an actual person. The "autobiographical pact," as Lejeune described it, maintains a powerful hold on discussions of meaning in autobiography in large part because the terms on which such a contract depends—reality, experience, truth—surely constitute what it is most crucial to theorize in autobiography. The "pact," however, presents reality and the truth one might tell about it as simply *there*; it names the autobiographical real. Not only are the constructive and even more generally narrative dimensions of autobiography undervalued, but the cultural and political realities of who writes and who reads lie outside the gaze of Lejeune's truth-seeking reader. While the signature confers legal authority and obligations upon the text, the text itself is meaningful for what it may confirm about the world. Although Lejeune's system cannot interpret autobiography except as part of the record of what really happened, neither can he distinguish it from fiction. The only characteristic that defines autobiography's specificity is the identity of the one who signs and the one who narrates the text. Although Lejeune begins by discussing the name as a trope for identity, he moves quickly to confer upon the proper name or signature—terms he uses interchangeably—the contractual indebtedness of speech acts. Autobiography's testimonial nature authorizes critics to police its claims; therefore, the specificity of autobiography lies in what it licenses its readers to do with the information it presents.

De Man and, more recently, Michael Ryan have offered critiques of this view. Ryan challenges Lejeune on explicitly ideological grounds and combines deconstructionist interest in rhetoric with a Marxist analysis of political rhetoric.[9] By focusing on the political ideology informing Lejeune's rhetoric, Ryan construes his notion of the autobiographical subject's ownership of identity, its contractual entitlement to self-representation, as a feature of the liberal humanist ideology of personhood. In Lejeune's autobiographical pact, the signature underwrites the coherence of the self suddenly made specular; that is, the writing self and the written self (the *I* who writes *I*) do not properly refer to each other, and therefore they make invisible precisely what de Man clarifies. De Man faults Lejeune for shuttling within a system of theoretical substitutions erected around the lack of

[9] Michael Ryan, *Politics and Culture: Working Hypotheses for a Post-Revolutionary Society* (Baltimore: Johns Hopkins University Press, 1989).

differentiation between the proper name and the legal signature: "For just as it is impossible for him to stay within the tropological system of the name and just as he has to move from ontological identity to contractual promise, as soon as the performative function is asserted, it is at once reinscribed within cognitive restraints" (922–23). Lejeune's substitutions involve moving around the locus of "transcendental authority" in the text: it remains in play and can be appropriated by any of autobiography's subjects; that is, the reader can revoke the author's contract if veracity has been violated. Thus, Lejeune asserts that it is precisely the ability to decide autobiography's authenticity that defines its contractual nature. Readers and authors enact this structure, and for Lejeune, it is sufficient that the substitutions happen.

In autobiography, what de Man calls specularity, Ryan sees as that feature of liberalism whereby the self can be said to own itself as property, to be endowed with certain capacities and rights that it alone may lay claim to. In Lejeune's model, this entitlement takes a defensive edge and comes encoded in the language of contracts and obligations. The autobiographer's name makes contractually binding what autobiographical textuality represents as an impossibility: the coherence of textual identity, the ownership of one's self as property based on models of patrimony and paternity, and the stability of identity as an entity that exists unproblematically outside—rather than in relation to—the discourses of identity through which it is produced alongside the discourses of truth which authenticate it. Claims to the ownership of identity and to its singularity can be confounded by the temporal deferral of autobiographical self-representation, that is, by the absence of any fixed moment when the self *is* itself, when it can be said to speak from a place in which it already has told the whole truth. No wonder Lejeune focuses on the title page. Its legibility as a contract condenses identity to a proper name and requires that name to refer to its owner (as self and as property). To read beyond the name is already to subject that contract to review, to seek its "truth" even as its textuality displaces any moment where one stands with conviction in its presence.

In contrast to Olney's and de Man's quite different emphases on metaphor as a way to understand self-representational figuration, some feminist critics find female self-representation to be figured metonymically in autobiography where women represent the self in relation to others. The inference some feminist critics have drawn— that metaphor is a favored trope for male self-representation and metonymy is a favored trope for female self-representation—can be understood at least partly through its politics. To prefer a trope of contiguity and relation (metonymy) to a trope of hierarchy and identity (metaphor) is to do something other than simply discern rhetorical style. If ideology, as Althusser argues, operates rhetorically to promote dominant systems (and systems of domination), then precisely how one figures identity as well as how one describes that figuration can be a site of reproduction or resistance. Metaphor is based on identity, and metaphors as durable as those attached to the "individual" in Western culture depend upon a world outside the changing contingencies of time and space.

Ryan explores conservative and progressive uses of figural language in a political reading of metaphor and metonymy.[10] Acknowledging that there is no inherent political meaning in a trope and that other interpretations of metaphor and metonymy are certainly possible, Ryan nevertheless argues that the difference between social arrangements preferred by conservatives and progressives gets "configured rhetorically as the difference between the metaphoric axis and the metonymic" (116). Ryan specifies:

> The conservative use of rhetoric can be described as being aligned with the vertical pole of linguistics, which is usually associated with metaphor, substitution and the paradigmatic register (sets of terms that, though different from each other, serve an identical function or fit into the same slot in a sentence), while the progressive use of rhetoric can be described as more in line with the horizontal axis, which is associated with metonymy, displacement and the syntagmatic register (which concerns the serial order of terms in relation to each other in sentences). (116)

Metaphor aligns along the vertical axis of meaning, metonymy along the horizontal. To prefer one figure to another in a discourse of identity is to represent the place of the self in the world differently: a metonym has meaning in context, as when feminists contend that women autobiographers represent the self in relation to others. A metaphor does not depend on a real situation for meaning; rather, it isolates an ideal and draws an analogy between essences, as when the early autobiography scholar Georges Gusdorf claimed that the autobiographical self derives its meaning outside the community and in

---

[10] For feminist views of deconstruction which elaborate this notion, though not specifically with regard to autobiography, see also Barbara Johnson, *The Critical Difference: Essays in the Contemporary Rhetoric of Reading* (Baltimore: Johns Hopkins University Press, 1981); Meese, *Crossing the Double-Cross;* and Meese, *(Ex) Tensions: Re-Figuring Feminist Criticism* (Urbana: University of Illinois Press, 1990).

relation to a higher self. A metaphor has one "proper" interpretation; a metonym allows for a variety of arrangements and indeed resists the way in which metaphors mean. Thus in my own description of metonymy as the trope through which autobiography figures the real, I run against the grain of interpretations that focus on the stability of material reality. The real—whether construed as the naturalness of gender identity or the inevitability of racist oppression—must be repeated by force of imposition and force of habit to become "real." Certainly, I would agree with Ryan that neither metaphor nor metonymy is inherently patriarchal or feminist. One could imagine reversing those positions, but the point here is that critical choices structure the way we talk about and understand identity and when autobiography criticism does that it becomes another discourse of identity and, therefore, implicated as a technology of autobiography.

Self-representation has been "naturalized" through a rhetoric of unproblematized realism which depends upon the distinction between fact and fiction in determining autobiographical authenticity and which consolidates as diverse a textual field as self-representation into the genre of autobiography. Indeed, in this interpretive context, we can see that metaphor's idealism has been coded as realism. At this point, Adrienne Rich's sense of curiosity and skepticism are welcome: Is autobiography a monstrous document produced by a subject become beastly through the act of writing?[11] Although autobiography has rarely been considered in this way, Rich suggests the transgressive aspect of its alchemy of turning life into words, rather than its ameliorative effects, and provides a hedge against the notion that autobiography is somehow closer to real life than any other kind of writing presumably because one need neither imagine nor invent it. It lies there, intractably real: it happened. "Realism," then, refers not only to a textual production but to a cultural practice, one that allows us to think of our lives as more rather than less coherent, linear, and plausible. Yet it is precisely Rich's focus on the constructive dimension of writing which breaks from the notion that autobiography is a genre with formal characteristics and turns toward an inspection of the technologies on which such an idea depends.

If subjectivity, figured by the autobiographical *I*, is produced in relation to discourses and institutions, then autobiography, the "genre" most explicitly identified with self-representation, can be

---

[11] Barbara Johnson explores monstrosity and female autobiography in "My Monster/ My Self," in *A World of Difference* (Baltimore: Johns Hopkins University Press, 1987), 144–54.

taken as a participant in that production. If we then also regard auto-biography more broadly as part of a historically and formally chang-ing discourse of self-representation, it is possible to interpret it as a political site on which human agency is negotiated within and against institutions on the grounds of truth. If this is so, then autobiography may also be a site of resistance, especially as it engages the politics of looking back and challenges the politics of how the past and present may be known in relation to a particular version of history. The aes-thetics and politics of autobiography always operate in relation to what its producers and consumers understand as authenticity, wheth-er they name it "truth" or "history." Criticism, then, that takes an unproblematized authenticity as a register of value follows one of the coldest trails of meaning in autobiography studies. Issues of value take hold at a fairly recalcitrant level in these discussions: the worth of the text turns on the worth of the autobiographer's "truth." Autobiog-raphy's proximity to discourses that construct the mutuality of truth and identity, such as the confession, however, evidence the cultural density of its authority. Our notion of the autobiographical is bound up in our notions of authenticity and the real, of confession and testimony, of the power and necessity to speak, and of the institution-al bases of power which impose silence. The significance of the auto-biographical "subject" emerges, in all its historical variability, through the networks that produce it—intimate and institutional—and these networks constitute the technologies of autobiography. Insofar as au-tobiography criticism, as I have maintained, determines the "value" of any autobiographer's "truth," it participates in the political produc-tion and maintenance of the category of "identity." "Bad" autobiogra-phers are rarely aesthetic criminals. They are more usually repre-sented as "bad" persons. And it is precisely this elision of political and aesthetic value to which autobiography has been especially sus-ceptible.

Autobiography criticism has made the subject of autobiography "knowable" in particular ways. This much can be claimed about any literary criticism. But the study of women's self-representational writ-ing suggests a counterhegemonic if not definitionally incoherent pro-ject. It is counterhegemonic to the extent that such study depends on a critique of the generic grounds of autobiography itself, especially the key figures that underwrite the genre: the self and history. It is incoherent to the extent that this terminology has, in many ways, "created" the autobiographical subject. Traditional studies of auto-biography have focused on patterns of coherence among texts rather than on points of incoherence in the discourses of truth, gender, power, and identity. Much of this approach is entailed in the texts that have come to form the history of autobiography. By placing the project of defining the subject of women's autobiography within a feminist theory of autobiographical production, I take this incoherence as significant. Moreover, I believe the appeal of incoherence lies in its conceptual affiliation with many contemporary feminist theories that stress the historical instability and political volatility of "women" and "identity" and also in its refusal of some of the most compelling models of identity rationalist and humanist thought have offered. Gayatri Spivak's description of the ongoing tension generated by cultural critique applies here, for the reader/critic of autobiography is being asked to engage in "the persistent critique of what one cannot not want," the critique of a genre that, in effect, constructs a self with a story to tell.[12]

If we look at the history of the signature in some women's writing, we must make a very different case from Lejeune's. For men, the mythology of the signature involves either the empowerment or the anxiety of influence: tradition, genealogy, and the legacy of naming constitute a mutual heritage. For women, the title page is frequently the site of a necessary evasion. One reads here not the signature but the pseudonym, not the family name but "Anon." The title page of women's writing presents itself not as a fact but as an extension of the fiction of identity, and it is frequently more comprehensible as a corollary to laws regarding women's noninheritance of property.[13] For women, the fiction that our names signify our true identities obscures the extent to which our names are thought of not as our own but as the legal signifier of a man's property. The name has a less lofty and romantic tradition for women in Western culture: it signifies ownership, to be sure, but not of ourselves as our property. To call women objects of property and marriage contracts bills of sale works only

[12] Gayatri Spivak, comments at the conference "Nationalisms and Sexualities," Harvard University, June 1989.

[13] A feminist debate about the signature was staged in the pages of *Diacritics* between Peggy Kamuf and Nancy K. Miller. Kamuf argued that to assign a gendered identity to the signature was to foreclose the play of that signifier and limit its meaning to referentiality and intentionality. Miller argued that the gendered identity of the signature mattered politically and historically and that instead of foreclosing the full meaning of the signature, an absence of attention toward the gender of the signature recapitulated the cultural erasure of women. In this debate, Miller saw an equivalence between signature and person, whereas Kamuf situated the signature in relation to other signifying practices of identity in language. I think the debate setting quite possibly obscured Miller's and Kamuf's considerable political agreements. See Peggy Kamuf, "Replacing Feminist Criticism," and Nancy K. Miller, "The Text's Heroine: A Feminist Critic and Her Fictions" in *Diacritics* 12 (Summer 1982).

partially as an analogy; however, it does indicate how the laws of property and ownership are immediately present, if obscured, in the metaphysics and mythologies of the name.

Scholars of autobiography, until influenced by structuralist and poststructuralist revisions of subjectivity, sought patterns of continuity and unity in self-representation in ways that uphold claims of the universality of the self. Yet, the history of autobiography reveals that the self is not a transcendent construct that is recorded in its essential continuity by generation after generation of autobiographers. Indeed, one might well look to autobiography as a place to begin interrogating the value-laden assumption of the immutability and deep-down sameness of selves, for one finds in autobiography a virtuoso display of the complexities and difference within gender, place, time, religious practice, the aesthetic, the family, work, as well as the experiences of class, race, and ethnicity which self-reflexive narratives must manage. The ontological "irreducibility" of the self as reducible, across temporal and textual boundaries, to a unified and unifiable category of being and knowing is a representational fiction produced by the mapping of patriarchal ideology onto the subject it inscribes, the relentless objectification of persons. The fictions of identity staged and witnessed by many male autobiographers and critics mirror and recapitulate desires that become values in an economy invested in reproducing this dynamic.

The models of identity I have outlined are aligned with theories of language. For example, the unified self is capable of expressing itself in words that reflect the world. This self is inviolate, prior to language, and is the manipulator of language's secondary effects rather than, as we are perhaps more apt to see it now via poststructuralism, itself language's most splendid effect. Thus theories of language inevitably project and operate in the service of an implicit model of social relations since they deploy conceptions of identity and the nature of its authority and meaning. As Raymond Williams explains, "a definition of language is always, implicitly or explicitly, a definition of human beings in the world. The received major categories—'world,' 'reality,' 'nature,' 'human'—may be counterposed or related to the category 'language.' "[14] Self-representation can perhaps be most fruitfully understood for autobiography as the mutual interdependence between discourse and identity rather than a priority of discourse over identity, as, that is, a discourse of identity. A theory of language

[14] Raymond Williams, *Marxism and Literature* (Oxford: Oxford University Press, 1977), 21.

allied with what can be described as a gendered object entails a complementary version of literature and its interpretation. In this context autobiography comes to bear the burden of logocentric authority, for the proper name unites author and authority in an exercise in truth telling: the name of the father reproduces the law of the father.[15] This generalization can be particularized by looking at the assumptions traditional critics of autobiography share with male autobiographers vis-à-vis epistemology and value, self-knowledge and self-expression, for it is an act of interpretation to read the history of autobiography as identical to the progress of men through public, political, and military history. According to this interpretation, the male autobiographer represents the self who is the subject of a master narrative. Traditional critics of autobiography have found (made and placed) "him" everywhere.

For example, William Spengemann declares: "St. Augustine set the problem for all subsequent autobiography: How can the self know itself?" (*Forms of Autobiography*, 32). Spengemann concurs with Augustine's implicit evaluation of self-knowledge as the grounds of autobiography and consequently establishes self-representation as a more or less fixed exercise. Where the goal is static, the self that undertakes this search must be similarly stable, for how else might it transcend those differences that would obscure its unity with the dominant pattern? Spengemann's interpretation suppresses the possible arena of difference—representation—by describing it as contingent, secondary, and more or less formulaic: there are "three methods of self-knowledge" accompanied by "three autobiographical forms." Spengemann undervalues the place of self-representation and the cultural contexts that generate and shape it because his model of the self depends on a language that could answer Augustine's enduring question. For Spengemann, the self is synonymous with mind or consciousness. Self-representation seeks to reveal the mind in the act of knowing itself.

It is striking that the self appearing in autobiography studies is presumed to exclude the body. The mind/body split is reproduced through the public/private, outside/inside, male/female categories that order perception and experience and is derived from a way of

---

[15] See Jacques Lacan, *Écrits: A Selection*, trans. Alan Sheridan (New York: Norton, 1977), and the following critics of Lacan: Shoshana Felman, *Jacques Lacan and the Adventure of Insight: Psychoanalysis in Contemporary Culture* (Cambridge: Harvard University Press, 1987); Jane Gallop, *Reading Lacan* (Ithaca: Cornell University Press, 1985); and Juliet Mitchell, *Psychoanalysis and Feminism* (New York: Pantheon, 1974).

knowing which cannot account for the knowledge of the body. Indeed, until feminist criticism, predominant ways of knowing defined the body's knowledge as that which is unknowable. The self has functioned as a metaphor for soul, consciousness, intellect, and imagination, but never for body. Karl Weintraub presents "a major component of modern man's self-conception: the belief that, whatever else he is, he is a unique individuality, whose life task is to be true to his very own personality" (*Value of the Individual*, xi). Self-conception is formed without a body. The "search for conditions of self-conscious individuality" (1), as Weintraub conceives it, excludes those conditions entailed by having a body. Many women autobiographers, however, have found the body to provide rich grounds for thinking through the relationship between identity and representation.

By exploring the technologies of autobiography, we see that autobiographical identity is always constructed through the changing and contradictory exigencies of the specific and that the autobiographer's reinscription of and resistance to a model of selfhood is a dialectic that shapes self-representation. The identity an autobiography inscribes is something more like a process that variously synthesizes or is fragmented by these discourses. The contradictory and fragmented, though resilient subject of autobiography structures narrative and its effects and is a fictive and textual construct. The interdependence and mutuality of the relationship creates autobiographical identity: as I have said, its representation *is* its construction. This analysis, then, arrives at the relation of truth production and identity production (the technologies of autobiography) to metonymy. When I described gender as a kind of patterning in which the female subject is produced as an object by the practices and discourses of femininity, I did so through the logic of metonymy and not metaphor. Women are not identical in some especially metaphorical way to the gendered constructions we perform. Identity is not the explanation for gender. Rather, gender performance/existence, like metonymy, succeeds through repetition. In this way, the representation *is* the construction.

In the context of autobiography studies, metaphor has been an underlying organizational logic for understanding the self and its relation to autobiographical representation. The ways in which autobiography itself patterns a recognizable autobiographical subject may well have more to do with metonymy, however. The truth any autobiography produces is always necessarily a truth restructured and revised in its telling, a mixture of past and present, a process of self-invention in which the content of a life—the very subject of autobiography—is not impassive but mutable. Autobiography is characterized by a particular act of interpretation: lived experience is shaped, revised, constrained, and transformed by representation. In telling the story of the self, the writer imposes order where there is chaos, structural coherence where there is memory and chronology, voice where there is silence. Yet this process is no simple mimesis shaped by the internal coherence of life and text. When we take representation into account, we move closer to seeing how the characteristic translation autobiography enacts (that is, how the self becomes the subject of its own story and the repetition this transformation entails) is obscured.

Autobiography describes the textual space wherein the culturally constructed and historically changing epistemology of the self finds particular expression. Pressured all around by textuality, the autobiographical self owes its existence to the system of representation in which it evolves and finds expression. "Being" in the text thus requires the ontological differentiation that would break the tautological hold of referentiality, for the autobiographical *I* "becomes" a self, spins out the poetics of its identity, in a way that may thematize the chronology of birth, life, and death, but which enacts it textually. Autobiography provides a stage where women writers, born again in the act of writing, may experiment with reconstructing the various discourses—of representation, of ideology—in which their subjectivity has been formed. Thus, the subject of autobiography is not a single entity but a network of differences within which the subject is inscribed. The subject is already multiple, heterogeneous, even conflicted, and these contradictions expose the technologies of autobiography. While the historical self may be the autobiographer's explicit subject—the story of her life with self-development as the structure of the text—this subject is distributed across the historical self and the textual self, both of which are versions of the self who writes.

The relationship between truth telling and referentiality upon which traditional autobiography studies depended can be seen as a discursive process rather than an essential mirroring. The neglected aspect of this analysis is the writing self. While the author as the person in the world and the author as the person in the text are the two representations of identity addressed by both truth telling and referentiality, the author as the person who writes (the *I* who writes *I*) is left precariously unaddressed. We have a hazy view of this self's structure and thus allow for a similar vagueness in definitions of autobiography. We are able to tolerate such startling incoherence in the subject in question when we refer all questions of difference to the author's name as the final unity that represents the levels of selfhood. Yet the differences between the self as historical and as narrative subject construct the intersubjectivity that defines the autobiographical form. Only in a first moment may the coincidence of persons, places, and events in both structures be glimpsed as unproblematic. Simultaneously, repetition and coincidence create verisimilitude. It is autobiography's particular burden and appeal—that is, these "problems" constitute its rhetoric—to produce this coincidence textually.

Autobiography demonstrates that we can never recover the past, only represent it; yet, it encodes the possibility of recovery as desire and the possibility of representation as its mode of production. The autobiographical *I* is at home in both history and narrative because it is produced by the action that draws those fields together. To conflate these structures of subjectivity and to misread their interaction as the mirroring of essentially the same subject is to reveal the very scene in language we recognize as autobiography. The reading effect whereby we construe the *I* as everywhere referring to a stable presence outside the text characterizes a typical response to autobiography. This dynamic of production and reception structures the invisibility of the *I* whose identity is "I am writing."

Autobiographics and Naming

Naming is a difficult and time-consuming process; it concerns essences, and it means power.
    —Jeanette Winterson, *Oranges Are Not the Only Fruit*

Anybody saying how do you do to you and knowing your name may be upsetting but on the whole it is natural enough but to suddenly see your name is always upsetting. Of course it has happened to me pretty often and I like it to happen just as often but always it does give me a little shock of recognition and non-recognition. It is one of the things most worrying in the subject of identity.
    —Gertrude Stein, *Everybody's Autobiography*

To write often means remembering what has never existed. How shall I succeed in knowing what I do not know? Like so: as if I were to remember. By an effort of "memory" as if I had never been born. I have never been born. I have never lived. But I remember, and that memory is in living flesh.
    —Clarice Lispector, *The Foreign Legion*

"The problems common to all proper names," Foucault wrote, "are that they establish relationships between and among things that are not identical."[16] Thus, even if we hope a name gives us some owner-ship by designating an identity, place, and function, that hope is withheld by the structure that generates it. Whereas names perform a host of functions, only one is properly referential, and it is impossible to distinguish that function—in a word—from the others that bear its name. For example, "Augustine" refers to the author of the text, to the subject of the story, to the church father: in other words, one can multiply functions to show how the proper name involves much more than a case of pure and simple reference. But even when the writing subject disappears into the seams created by names running parallel to functions, the autobiography itself keeps representing that subject as if it were abundantly possible for it to spring up every-where. This shifting absence, played out as presence, also character-izes autobiography's use of the personal pronoun.

In his discussion of the figural couple "the author and his work," Foucault has described a relationship on which readers, writers, and critics of autobiography depend. One of the proofs that such a rela-tionship defines and precedes autobiography is that even when the writing self disappears (which is the philosophical problem, or tradi-tion, of the death of the author) the proper name continues to dis-guise the disappearance because that name refers to all the levels of subjectivity autobiography puts into play. Where the author, the text, and the protagonist share the same name, the author's disappearance is almost superfluous for *he* is always already overrepresented. Prop-er names assert an identity and continuity between the self and lan-guage, between signifier and signified, and cover over the differences produced by discourse. The talismanic power of the name depends on a logocentric commitment to the *propre*, or selfsame, which one might associate with autobiography. Yet this assertion of a singular voice and subject, of a unique and unified self, contravenes the very dynamic that enables the autobiographical act and its characteristic play of identity in language. Further, such an investment in sameness follows from and is complicitous with a hierarchical model of the self, of language, and of social relations which would modulate difference—specifically, sexual difference as the site of gender's ar-ticulation in culture and the selves and stories that define this difference—with the soothing, silencing balm of sameness.

Foucault describes writing as a game "that invariably goes beyond its own rules and transgresses its limits" (102). In writing, the point is not to manifest or exalt the act of writing, nor is it to pin down a

---

[16] Michel Foucault, "What Is an Author?" trans. Josué Harari, in *The Foucault Reader*, ed. Paul Rabinow (New York: Pantheon, 1984), 105.

subject within language; it is rather a question of "creating a space into which the writing subject constantly disappears" (102). The disappearing act performed by the writing subject contributes to the problem of reference in autobiography. Indeed, for some, autobiography pulls this trick off so neatly that the effect defines the problem. When the direct referent of "the subject of autobiography" is the writing subject, that *I* disappears and makes possible the emergence of other *I*'s. In autobiography, the levels of subjectivity signified by the author's name are substitutable at every turn within the text's production by *I*.

The problem with the personal pronoun is further compounded by its relation to the proper name. When one of the major cultural and economic institutions of our free-market economy—the bank—wants to know a secret about you, something only you could reasonably be expected to know, something that someone attempting to pass her- or himself off as you wouldn't know, you are asked for your mother's maiden name. This is your password. How does your mother's maiden name come to be the guarded secret that U.S. banks believe it to be? The patronym represents public identity, bankable in more obvious ways but without any intimate authority: one is publicly known by this name, but one intimately knows (or is intimately known by) the mother's maiden name. The "name of the father" and the mother's maiden name represent different orders of knowledge and explain the cultural ambivalence many women feel about our own names. Such binary distinctions are definitional strategies, part of the production and maintenance of the technologies of truth and linked to their hierarchizing organizations of knowledge—here, the gendered distinction between secret and legal (private and public). This play on authority, staged through the recoding of the mother's maiden name as "secret" in order to enforce the "public" authority of the name of the father, reveals a structuring antithesis in names.

To elaborate the authority of names and signatures in autobiography, we can think of autobiography for a moment as a framing device, rather like the swinging door between street and saloon in a movie western. The world of the street and the world of the saloon communicate through an unstable portal. Never closed, the doorway frames the action in both arenas as it includes each as background and foreground. The swinging door further obscures the distance between street and saloon because each can be seen from a position within the other. There is, however, a world of symbolic difference between the two and the way each frames action (hence, agency) and knowledge. In more courtly westerns, antagonists offer to take conflict "outside."

In others, the refusal to admit distinctions between inner and outer locations, between more privatized spaces (because owned) and public space, is symbolized by the Clint Eastwood character who will kill anywhere and who is powerful through an ability to absorb difference. This character is unruly, disobedient, dangerous, and ready to exploit the swinging door that distinguishes street from saloon.

The trick that defines this characterization lies in the interpretation that Eastwood *is* the character in the movie (it works best when the character in the movie is unnamed, free to roam the imaginative landscape as "Eastwood"). Whether he plays Dirty Harry, or "Blondie" (the man with no name), or the mayor of Carmel, audiences cheer Clint Eastwood. The coherence of the symbolic function of his name obscures the differences between street and saloon, between lived experience and autobiography, precisely by insisting that whatever the differences may be, their significance fails before the fallacy of autobiographical reference: the person in both is the same. Correspondingly, in this limited view, autobiography is the textual equivalent of the action adventure movie with a star/hero in which celebrity simply *is* identity rather than a representational effect. The autobiographer and the hero are cheered not for an ability to enable you to suspend disbelief but for their success in subsuming signification and interpretation to the name. Significantly, this conflation is viewed as the expansion of Eastwood, or the autobiographer, as the ground of identification and not as the reduction of interpretive pleasure.

We substitute protagonist for author in order to grasp the "real" self in history. As Foucault pointed out, writing creates and disguises a particular kind of invisibility, and we have been unaccustomed to "seeing" this in autobiography because of the multiple I's we assume share the same referent and our anxiety about imperiling the coherent self it designates. The text interiorizes this substitution by a series of gliding adjustments. "Historical," "textual," and "writing" selves do not announce their role in constructing the poetics of identity, for it is their irreducibility that underpins the privileged "fullness" and "presence" offered by the autobiographer's signature. The *I*, then, is filled up in the text as naturally as it is filled in everyday life; it refers to a person in both instances, not to a "narrator." The tension between ordinary and literary language is evident here, for the artlessness of autobiography, its way of seeming uncomposed, results from the assumption that the *I*'s coherence operates in autobiography as it does in ordinary discourse and not as it does in fiction. Plot is inherited, determined by memory and circumstance; personae are extrinsic to autobiographical discourse. The autobiographer simulates nonliterary conditions and suppresses the art in the venture by appearing to inhabit the *I* as simply as in daily life. The autobiographical *I* appears to erase the conditions of fictionality as it creates a textual identity commensurate with a historical reality, although this *I* is already a fiction produced by the tropological nature of language.

Might this dance of *I*'s displace autobiography's authority—that is, as a social practice autobiography promises to expose the self and to tell the truth—as it edges toward a potentially annihilating narcissism? If we accept Foucault's agenda and shift our curiosity from author to discourse, from self-contained to culturally interactive ways of interpreting texts, we would appear to be a short step away from watching contemporary theories of language disallow autobiography. I would like to use the insights produced by poststructuralist theories of language to call attention to two questions posed from the outset of my inquiry: What might a dissolution of belief in the self that has always been the subject of traditional autobiography permit us to see first in women's autobiography? What can a feminist theory of autobiographical production enable us to understand about the categories that have defined our knowledge of autobiography, the self and history? In other words, to push further how we ground answers to the question "What is this 'autobiography' that everyone knows and on what does it depend?" we need to ask how the claim that women autobiographers construct a space from which they can speak differs from Foucault's sense that all writers inevitably construct a space into which they disappear. Autobiographics is distinct from Foucault's questions of authorship here, in that it interprets women's self-representational writing as a discourse of re-membering and self-restoration written against the language of privation *as* the language of presence that assures their absence as it appropriates them historically and linguistically.

I have been describing the technologies of autobiography as the space into which the writing subject disappears. The structure of that space is organized through the discourses of truth and identity, and what is left behind there is the artifact of autobiographical identity. The space is constructed in such a way that it records this disappearance and makes it meaningful. What disappears here is what has always been disappearing, namely, the male author who leaves a monument to his absence, an epitaph in the form of autobiography that memorializes his passing. This disappearance is patterned metonymically through discourses of identity laden with nostalgia and mourning but also through political rhetorics of presence that project the representative man as a metaphor for democracy. The

woman autobiographer, however, caught in the act of self-representation, disappears without a trace, for her passing has not been patterned into these discourses. Thus the difference between these dis-
appearances is necessarily a product of how the space into which men
and women disappear as writing subjects is gendered.

Foucault identified the problem by posing the question "What is an
author?" Nevertheless, the problem persists. Taken seriously,
Foucault's essay signaled the end of simple biographical and inten-
tionalist readings of authorship and made the "author" into the constructed space of its own disappearance. What remains as autobiographical identity has been structured through the technologies of
autobiography and authorized through its power mode of truth telling. Women have not been seen as telling the truth, as leaving behind
a name worthy of an epitaph, nor have their autobiographical or
authorial identities been sufficiently recognizable within those technologies to register. This space has been organized to catch the same
things in its sieve of truth and therefore must be reorganized through
discursive practices that change the modes of truth telling, for it is
precisely this space that women's self-representational writing inhabits differently. Unless the space is changed, the newly re-membered
subject will disappear as usual.

Foucault held out the possibility of new modes of discourse, and
thus of authorship, but they would necessarily restructure the space
to which he drew our attention. Through autobiographics, this space
may record what it has always failed to notice: women's self-
representation. I believe that a discourse of re-membering and self-
restoration organized differently through metaphor and metonymy
around the name is currently being written. It restructures the space
the writing subject occupies in the discourses of truth and identity. A
discourse of re-membering, then, leaves behind something other than
the epitaph that marks the author's disappearance for Foucault, the
prosopopoeiac zombie of de Man, and "the real truth" of Lejeune.
None of these critics is sufficiently attentive to women's agency or the
fictions of identity in which women find themselves represented to
account for the kinds of contemporary writing represented by Sandra
Cisneros's *House on Mango Street* and Jamaica Kincaid's *Annie John*,
among others.[17]

The House on Mango Street, Sandra Cisneros's experiment in self-

---

[17] Another of the several texts that could be explored as part of this new discourse of
self-representation is Jeanette Winterson, *Oranges Are Not the Only Fruit* (New York:
Atlantic Monthly Press, 1987; first published by Pandora, London, 1985).

representation, calls into question the constructed line between autobiography and fiction.[18] Cisneros describes growing up poor in a
Hispanic neighborhood of Chicago through a series of forty-five vignettes, much like dramatic scenes with a single speaker, which present the neighborhood, family, assorted places, persons, and events,
and especially the girls and women of Mango Street through the eyes
and in the voice of Esperanza Cordero. Framing this text are telling
marginalia in the form of a concluding note about the author and a
prologue drawn from the book. Whereas the text within this frame
explores the limits of separating autobiography from fiction as distinct
modes of self-representation, the prologue and conclusion further
indicate how insufficient that distinction is to reading this text. In the
concluding biographical sketch, "About the Author," we read: "Sandra Cisneros was born in Chicago in 1954. . . . The daughter of a
Mexican father and a Mexican-American mother, and sister to six
brothers, she is nobody's mother and nobody's wife" (111). Although
most of this note is styled as a standard "bio," the final clause echoes
both Esperanza's language and her expressed concerns. In a frontispiece that functions as both advertising blurb and prologue and is
drawn from the section titled, "My Name," the language is all Esperanza's, but the "quoter" is unidentified:

"In English my name means hope. In Spanish it means too many
letters. It means sadness, it means waiting. It is like the number nine. A
muddy color. It is the Mexican records my father plays on Sunday morn-
ings when he is shaving, songs like sobbing.

"It was my great-grandmother's name and now it is mine. She was a
horse woman too, born like me in the Chinese year of the horse—which
is supposed to be bad luck if you're born female—but I think this is a
Chinese lie because the Chinese, like the Mexicans, don't like their
women strong. . . .

"At school they say my name funny as if the syllables were made out
of tin and hurt the roof of your mouth. But in Spanish my name is made
out of a softer something, like silver, not quite as thick as sister's name—
Magdalena—which is uglier than mine. Magdalena who at least can
come home and become Nenny. But I am always Esperanza.

"I would like to baptize myself under a new name, a name more like
the real me, the one nobody sees. Esperanza as Lisandra or Maritza or
Zeze the X. Yes. Something like Zeze the X will do."

[18] For a discussion of "autobiographical fiction" and French women's writing, see
Leah Hewitt, *Autobiographical Tightropes* (Lincoln: University of Nebraska Press, 1990).
Some work questions the constructed line between autobiography and criticism; for
examples of "personal criticism," see Rachel Blau DuPlessis, *The Pink Guitar: Writing as
Feminist Strategy* (New York: Routledge, 1990); Nancy K. Miller, *Getting Personal: Feminist
Occasions and Other Autobiographical Acts* (New York: Routledge, 1991).

The page on which this passage appears is headed "Sandra Cisneros's House on Mango Street" and the passage is surrounded by quotation marks. Through this intertextual reference, the issue of voice and autobiographical identity in self-representation is raised. Esperanza speaks elsewhere as the voice in the text without quotation marks; in the prologue, she speaks as the voice of the text, literally under the name of Cisneros. Esperanza is introduced in the act of introducing herself. In effect, Cisneros names herself Esperanza, and Esperanza, in the quoted vignette, considers renaming herself. In this exercise in naming, Cisneros offers Esperanza as an autobiographical identity that will register as a character in fiction, as a simulacrum of the author, and as a figure for a historically verifiable place and time that are not tied to the author for verifiability. In sum, she offers a self-representational text that includes a fictional and an autobiographical identity bordering the text. The deliberate staging of the book's interrogation of the line between autobiography and fiction, memory and fantasy, and event and interpretation allows the reader to face the three identities of autobiography: the *I* who lived, the *I* in the text, and the *I* who writes *I*.

As I described in Chapter 1, a text's autobiographics may consist in the following emphasized elements: writing itself as constitutive of autobiographical identity, discursive contradictions (rather than unity) in the representation of identity, the name as a potential site of experimentation rather than a contractual sign of identity, and the effects of the gendered connection of word and body. *The House on Mango Street* may be read through these elements in order to recognize the extent to which Cisneros's project is specifically self-representational. Moreover, in *The House on Mango Street*, the writing subject is re-membered in a form that contravenes the autobiographical limit. Esperanza desires a name beyond the name(s) of the father, a text that re-members her desire for both a house and a voice of her own, and increasingly, an autobiographical identity structured through this convergence of desire and representation. Throughout the shifting scenes of self-representation on and near Mango Street, Esperanza's desire is figured in her longing for a house of her own, in her dawning sexuality and skirmishes with sexualization, and in her wish to become a writer. Lacan's notion of desire is applicable here. In Lacan, desire follows from lack and takes the form of metonymy. What is absent, the gaping hole around which the subject constructs identity, is figured through the subject's desire, which, in its patterning of that lack into all subsequent actions, is expressed as metonymy. In this sense, Lacan's psychoanalytic theory can be substantiated by relating it to the experiencing of class and ethnicity within family relations and relations among women. Esperanza's poverty is patterned through the family's lack of a constant address; yet, that lack becomes desire only as it structures Esperanza's imaginary relations to her material existence.

As if each vignette were an already crowded frame, a dream too full of meaning, a dramatic moment without catharsis, Cisneros keeps Esperanza moving through the familiar on her way to some sort of difference. In this sense, the metonymic organization is clear, and Esperanza runs at an oblique angle to the scenes of female entrapment in order to repattern the desire that drives self-representation. The name is the nexus of repatterning: no longer, or not only, Cisneros, Esperanza as "hope" is both metaphor for the writerly ambitions, which are insepaprable from the desire for a house, and metonymy for identity. Insofar as "hope" names desire, it also describes an attitude toward action; thus, Esperanza is identical to what Cisneros wants (or "is") and what she does over and over in the scenes. The name structures the relationship between metaphor and metonymy in two languages: "In English my name means hope. In Spanish it means too many letters" (10). The name also belongs to her great-grandmother, and it is precisely the name's metonymic power that Esperanza fears: "She looked out the window her whole life, the way so many women sit their sadness on an elbow. I wonder if she made the best with what she got or was she sorry because she couldn't be all the things she wanted to be. Esperanza. I have inherited her name, but I don't want to inherit her place by the window" (11). Because a name can be repeated and thereby made to stand in for the person, the contract depends upon metonymy even as it insists that the relationship between name and person is metaphorical when it takes the name to represent the person faithfully. The person is not simply the referent but a ground of meaning accessed via metaphor and metonymy through the name. As if to elude the identifying and predictive power of naming, though evincing a belief in that power, Esperanza offers to name herself: "I would like to baptize myself under a new name, a name more like the real me, the one nobody sees. Esperanza as Lisandra or Maritza or Zeze the X. Yes. Something like Zeze the X will do" (11).

Esperanza's longing for "a name more like the real me" is similar to her longing for a house. While the structure of desire is metonymic, as Lacan has shown, it consists of metaphors; in this case, the house as a figure for a better life. In the title vignette, "The House on Mango Street," Cisneros describes her house as an improvement over the previous family rentals but decries its inadequacy to her wishes: "The house on Mango Street is ours, and we don't have to pay rent to anybody, or share the yard with the people downstairs, or be careful not to make too much noise, and there isn't a landlord banging on the ceiling with a broom. But even so, it's not the house we'd thought we'd get" (3). The family's shared fantasy—"the house we'd thought we'd get"—is a model of middle-class comfort viewed from the perspective of poverty: "And our house would have running water and pipes that worked. And inside it would have real stairs, not hallway stairs, but stairs inside like the houses on T.V. . . . This was the house Papa talked about when he held a lottery ticket and this was the house Mama dreamed up in the stories she told us before we went to bed" (4).

In a scene strikingly like one described by Carolyn Steedman which occurred in south London in the 1950s, Esperanza describes a galvanizing encounter with a nun in front of the family's apartment (before the move to Mango Street) in which Esperanza's lack and subsequent desire are named:

> Where do you live? she asked.
> There, I said pointing up to the third floor.
> You live *there?*
> *There.* . . . The way she said it made me feel like nothing. *There.* I lived *there.* . . . I knew then I had to have a house. (5)

In *Landscape for a Good Woman*, Steedman recalls an experience that helps to uncover how class and gender are linked in these felt attacks on domestic adequacy:

> Upstairs, a long time ago, [my mother] had cried, standing on the bare floorboards in the front bedroom just after we moved to this house in Streatham Hill in 1951, my baby sister in her carry-cot. We both watched the dumpy retreating figure of the health visitor through the curtainless windows. The woman had said: "This house isn't fit for a baby." And then she stopped crying, my mother, got by, the phrase that picks up after all difficulty (it says: it's like this; it shouldn't be like this; it's unfair; I'll manage): "Hard lines, eh, Kay?" (Kay was the name I was called at home, my middle name, one of my father's names). (1–2)

In both examples, the censorious word is delivered by a woman standing in for institutional authority; in both examples, the hearer formulates a desire, whether to get by or to get out; and in both examples, the identity of names hovers at the edges of a scene of judgment, calling into question the rightness of this identification of appearance with verdict, reality with name.

Esperanza rejects the family fantasy of the house and refuses the

Sunday drives to the homes where her father labors in the gardens of wealthy Chicago suburbanites. Her access to these homes appears no different to Esperanza on her father's day off from when he works there all week, and she begins to separate her family's unrealizable dream from her own desire: "I don't tell them I am ashamed—all of us staring out the window like the hungry. I am tired of looking at what we can't have. When we win the lottery . . . Mama begins, and then I stop listening. . . . One day I'll own my own house, but I won't forget who I am or where I came from" (86–87). The longing that pervades both Steedman's and Cisneros's narratives wells up from the experience of underprivilege, signifies lack in the economic sense that comes to structure desire, and is expressed by Steedman through a commitment to represent historical conditions and people's lives that have disappeared from the historical narratives and autobiography. "(The point is *not* to say that all working-class childhoods are the same, nor that experience of them produces unique psychic structures)," she insists; she tells her story "so that the people in exile, the inhabitants of the long street, may start to use the autobiographical 'I', and tell the stories of their life" (16). If, as I have been arguing, autobiography itself seems closed to women's self-representation, then women may choose forms other than straightforward, contractually verifiable autobiography for self-representation, as is the case with Steedman, Cisneros, and Audre Lorde. What is also the case for these writers is the fusion within that form of aesthetic and political interests. Steedman wishes to open self-representation up so that the "profoundly a-historical" landscape of each person's life can be found on the historical landscape. In the absence of a whole world of personal narratives, history dismembers rather than remembers the lives of those without the self-representational franchise. Cisneros recognizes the need to root a personal narrative in political commitments and historical specificity when she announces, even as she distinguishes her family's fantasy from her own, "I won't forget who I am or where I came from."

Of course, autobiographical fiction is situated at a boundary and calls attention to its hybrid form by lacking a distinct generic name: autobiographical fiction depends for its coherence on the license of fiction to underwrite the contract of autobiography. Cisneros calls attention to the boundary itself as shaping identity in a way that is similar to that employed by the Chicana writers Cherríe Moraga and Gloria Anzaldúa. For all three, multicultural communities shape "borderland" identities rather than the autonomous *I* represented in the dominant tradition of Anglo and European autobiography. Both Moraga and Anzaldúa blend Spanish and English and mix forms to radically challenge the meaning of "the book." Cisneros shares the search for form while retaining a single style. In what, then, consists her autobiographics? To begin, the definition of the bildungsroman, or novel of female development, explains the narrative content—the story of a girl who wishes to be a writer—but not the vignette form. The story of Esperanza does not unfold through plot development. The shifting scenes move us through episodes of male violence and its effects on women's lives, from the curtailed expectations of the great-grandmother who waits by the window to the brutalization in "Minerva Writes Poems," quoted here in full:

> Minerva is only a little bit older than me but already she has two kids and a husband who left. Her mother raised her kids alone and it looks like her daughters will go that way too. Minerva cries because her luck is unlucky. Every night and every day. And prays. But when the kids are asleep after she's fed them their pancake dinner, she writes poems on little pieces of paper . . . that smell like a dime.
>
> She lets me read her poems. I let her read mine. She is always sad like a house on fire—always something wrong. She has many troubles, but the big one is her husband who left and keeps leaving.
>
> One day she is through and lets him know enough is enough. Out the door he goes. Clothes, records, shoes. Out the window and the door locked. But that night he comes back and throws a big rock through the window. Then he is sorry and she opens the door again. Same story.
>
> Next week she comes over black and blue and asks what can she do? Minerva. I don't know which way she'll go. There is nothing I can do. (84–85)

Minerva represents the life Esperanza wishes to avoid: the woman writer trapped in the male violence of her community, pulled back into it by a deeply ambivalent response. Cisneros's formal use of vignettes is the textual equivalent of these abrupt ends and precipitous turns toward another life. In these moments, Esperanza wishes to defend women, her girlhood friends, from their propulsion into the violent world of heterosexuality. Whereas Minerva is already living out the familiar gender patterns when she enters the text, Sally, Esperanza, and her sister Nenny must cross a border into gender as a life sentence. In early vignettes, Esperanza and Sally, a character who dominates the concluding sections of the text, stage playful border skirmishes with incipient heterosexualization. Their forays are without consequence at first; the rituals of femininity are dress-up games, masquerade. Following these experiments with makeup and high

heels, the girls return to being "themselves." Although gender possesses a palpable inevitability, they do not know themselves exclusively through its demands.

In one of the longest vignettes, "The Monkey Garden," however, it
becomes clear that Sally wishes to cross this border sooner than does
Esperanza. When Sally flirts with some neighborhood boys who have
stolen her keys, Esperanza interprets this scene as an apocalypse. She
races from the Monkey Garden, once the site of idyllic play, to the
boys' mother to save the day. The mother's response comes as a
casual betrayal that initiates the shattering of Esperanza's world:
"What do you want me to do, she said, call the cops?" (97). Esperanza
had desired a rescue attempt equal to calling the cops; a girlfriend in
danger is worthy of nothing less. She returns to the Monkey Garden,
which has become a negative Eden of horrific sexuality, armed with
"three big sticks and a brick." In "Minerva Writes Poems," Esperanza
realizes the limits of rescue: "There is nothing *I* can do." With Sally,
however, she is driven by a colliding sense of power and powerlessness into swift and fateful action. Sally will not be saved, though, and
sends loyal Esperanza away. The betrayals of women by women and
the prospects of gendered and heterosexual identity cause such deep
trauma in Esperanza that she no longer recognizes herself from the
vantage point of this terrible knowledge: "I looked at my feet in their
white socks and ugly round shoes. They seemed far away. They
didn't seem to be my feet anymore. And the garden that had been
such a good place to play didn't seem mine either" (98).

Following this expulsion from girlhood, Esperanza is propelled in
the subsequent vignette into heterosexual violence, a revelation of
rape which builds upon the shattered narrative of female loyalty.
Esperanza declares: "Sally, you lied. It wasn't what you said at all.
What he did. Where he touched me. I didn't want it, Sally" (99). In
this scene, titled "Red Clowns," Esperanza has accompanied Sally to
the carnival. Despite her dislike for the atmosphere, its off-center
power represented through the tilt-a-whirl beside which she waits,
Esperanza luxuriates in Sally's company. On this night, however,
Sally has gone off with a boy, leaving Esperanza alone and waiting.
Esperanza is raped and in narrating the vignette addresses herself
again to Sally: "Sally, make him stop. I couldn't make them go away. I
couldn't do anything but cry. I don't remember. It was dark. I don't
remember. Please don't make me tell it all" (100). The real that hurts,
in Jameson's words, is the predictable violence of rape, horrific and
shattering as it is, coupled with the betrayal and abandonment by

women and the forceful expulsion from the world where women and girls have the power to "make it stop" into a heterosexual world of violence where it is let go.

The house as the scene of domestic violence looms large throughout, as does the fragility of female bonds forged outside the home's grim sentence. If she is to become a writer, Esperanza must build a new house as surely as she must resist the fate of gender when that means a life saturated with male violence and female acquiescence. The "Red Clowns" vignette comes close to the end of the book where Esperanza's desire for a house intersects with her aspiration to be a writer. Thus this vignette is critically placed. Rape is the experience and the cultural discourse that dismembers women. It robs Esperanza of voice, unmakes her through its violence into one without memory who will tell no more. In the context of women's self-representation, rape signifies the death of the author. Rape is the space into which women disappear, dis-membered and voiceless. Esperanza's repetition of the phrase "I don't remember" can be read as the fragmenting of identity: "I don't re-member," or, "I cannot be re-membered"—the absence of memorial.

In the vignette following "Red Clowns," Sally has married, predictably, a violent man and is immured in a house that offers her less than that achieved by the great-grandmother, who could at least look beyond the structure, if always through its frame of a window. The husband, a marshmallow salesman met at a school bazaar, will not let Sally talk on the phone or look out the window. The house is cheerfully appointed, though, and Sally can only gaze at the surface of its domestic stability. By the close of the book, the house itself has been superseded as an adequate dream by another structure. The house, Esperanza recognizes, must be owned by herself alone: "Not a flat. Not an apartment in back. Not a man's house. Not a daddy's. A house all my own. . . . Only a house quiet as snow, a space for myself to go, clean as paper before the poem" (108). Esperanza turns her longing for what we can call an adequate structure for her desire in the direction of writing itself. Her desire for the agency of self-representation becomes the focus of the last quarter of the book. The book itself as the structure of her desire is (re)cognizable through autobiographics. For the writing subject has not disappeared in the usual ways, voiceless and dismembered. The book replaces the house on Mango Street as a structure of self-representational identity.

As if playing with a suggestion of Roland Barthes's—"Does the text have human form, is it a figure, an anagram of the body? Yes, but of our erotic body"[19]—Cisneros somatizes her text by figuring the book as an autobiographical body. She seeks a landscape on which to place this body and house so that it may possess a historical and political address, a location from which to speak and in which to live. Esperanza's departure is represented as a critical precursor to this new narrative location: "One day I will go away. Friends and neighbors will say, What happened to that Esperanza? . . . They will not know I have gone away to come back. For the ones I left behind. For the ones who cannot out [sic]" (110).

A context for describing the autobiographics of *The House on Mango Street* can be fleshed out through reference to similar contemporary self-representational texts, such as Cherríe Moraga's *Loving in the War Years* and Gloria Anzaldúa's *Borderlands/La Frontera*, which share a similar relation to a marginalized community identified through ethnicity. All three texts share Steedman's commitment to representing the landscape of a particular life in relation to the landscape of the community, representing it in conjunction with political, historical, and aesthetic desire. Jamaica Kincaid's *Annie John* (1985) and *Lucy* (1990), as well as Jeanette Winterson's *Oranges Are Not the Only Fruit*, share an interest in the name as a site of experimentation, a figure that deflects the detective's tracking and stages the text's autobiographics. The communities of women, broadly defined through differing sexualities, form the major contours within which the autobiographical agents will build.

Jamaica Kincaid may well have initiated her experiments in naming when she renamed herself. Her parents named her Elaine Potter Richardson, but she baptized herself under a new name when she began writing; or put another way, she gave herself a new name for a newly explored identity. In an interview, Kincaid said she chose the name Jamaica to evoke the West Indies and her birthplace, Antigua, and the surname because it went well with the first.[20] The character Annie John is apparently modeled on Kincaid (Kincaid has continued the recycling of names by naming her daughter Annie, which is her mother's name). As the book concludes Annie is headed away from Antigua, and in Kincaid's subsequent book the same character seems to show up in New York, where she is now Lucy, with the same defining relationship with what appears to be the same mother. In

[19] Roland, Barthes, *The Pleasure of the Text*, trans. Richard Miller (New York: Noonday, 1975), 17.

[20] This information is drawn from Donna Perry's "Interview with Jamaica Kincaid," in *Reading Black, Reading Feminist*, ed. Henry Louis Gates (New York: Penguin, 1990), 492–510.

fact, Lucy's name is given in the final chapter in a discussion of her lack of investment in her name (149), and the island she is from in the West Indies goes unnamed. Kincaid has remarked in an interview that Lucy is short for Lucifer, and it is Annie John who identifies with a painting depicting Lucifer. Intertextual continuity is threaded throughout these texts and the signifier of change, of nonidentity, is the name. Kincaid's change of name, I would argue, is a way of deflecting the literal truth-telling demands of the autobiographical pact while inscribing a different discourse of truth telling, one that is more adequate to representing the "truth" and "identity" of a "post"-colonial subject.

Kincaid arrived in the United States in 1965, worked in New York as an au pair, and ultimately made connections at the *New Yorker*. She first appeared as a personage in "Talk of the Town" articles written by George W. S. Trow; then the editor, William Shawn, began publishing her works. Most of *Annie John* and *Lucy* appeared first in the *New Yorker*. Kincaid's long political essay, a postcolonial critique of tourism and other colonial legacies in Antigua titled *A Small Place* (1988), was rejected by the new editor at the magazine, Robert Gottlieb, because he thought it was too angry. It subsequently appeared as a book, and Kincaid's commitment to anger has flourished.

One subject of *Annie John* is rage, especially in its imbrication with love and identity, and the forms it takes.[21] The education of a colonial subject is detailed in scenes at Annie's schools where she is taught about the mother country and the dominions. The relationship is one of dominance. The relationship with her mother, fiercely compounded of rage and love, is also figured as a kind of colonial, revolutionary, and ultimately postcolonial narrative. The analogy is inexact, though, for the text preserves the historically specific landscape of postcolonial Antigua as well as the personal, or ahistorical in Steedman's sense, internal landscape of the mother-daughter relationship. Like the political and emotional chronology that organizes Cherríe Moraga's text, the chronology in *Annie John* is profoundly emotional and centers on the relationship with the mother. Two subjectivities are represented in relation to these coextensive, though distinct landscapes, and they coincide when Annie's class is assigned an "autobiographical essay." The essay is written during the period in which Annie's relationship with her mother is dying; indeed, images of the mother's death pervade the book, and the narrative of individuation is told as the story of life and death.

[21] See especially Kincaid's contribution to *Critical Fictions: The Politics of Imaginative Writing*, ed. Philomena Mariani (Seattle: Bay Press, 1991), 223–29.

Annie is infatuated with her mother's embodiment and experiences their separation as a death-dealing trauma. Until the rupture in their seamless domesticity, Annie is happily patterned in the form of her mother, who is represented as paradise. Of their mutual absorption, Kincaid writes:

> No small part of my life was so unimportant that she hadn't made a note of it, and now she would tell it to me over and over again. . . . As she told me the stories, I sometimes sat at her side, leaning against her, or I would crouch on my knees behind her back and lean over her shoulder. As I did this, I would occasionally sniff at her neck, or behind her ears, or at her hair. She smelled sometimes of lemons, sometimes of sage, sometimes of roses, sometimes of bay leaf. At times I would no longer hear what it was she was saying; I just liked to look at her mouth as it opened and closed over words, or as she laughed. How terrible it must be for all the people who had no one to love them so and no one whom they loved so, I thought. (22–23)

During the summer when Annie turns twelve, the break between mother and daughter is initiated by the mother who refuses their custom of mother-daughter dress: "Up to then, my mother and I had many dresses made out of the same cloth, though hers had a different, more grownup style" (25). Mother and daughter, too, are cut from the same cloth, and their shared fashion drapes a shared identity that deemphasizes the separateness of their bodies. When Annie chooses a piece of cloth for their new dresses, her mother unexpectedly intervenes: "'Oh, no. You are getting too old for that. It's time you had your own clothes. You just cannot go around the rest of your life looking like a little me.' To say that I felt the earth swept away from under me would not be going too far" (26). The difference in clothes signals a profound shift in identity, which Annie understands in terms of her growing body. Paradoxically, it is the body of girlhood that resembles the mother's and not the body of young womanhood. This metaphor of their difference describes their actual developing similarity as women. Annie, though, accedes to the logic of bodily metaphor and struggles for a way to stay different from, hence attached to and the same as, her mother: "I thought of begging my mother to ask my father if he could build for me a set of clamps into which I could screw myself at night before I went to sleep and which would surely cut back on my growing" (27).

Annie's "autobiographical essay," written at the end of the summer, offers a condensed version of Kincaid's view of truth telling in autobiography in which what is symbolically real must be represented through events that did not occur. In the act of interpreting her life as autobiography, Annie must offer a conclusion that did not happen in order to tell the story of her relationship to her mother. In the essay, she recounts a day trip to Rat Island with her mother. Although her mother is a strong swimmer, Annie fears the water and the sea creatures, so different from what she can see and know. Her timidity as a swimmer, however, creates the opportunity for her to be carried about on her mother's back, their bodies borne up together, suspended in the sensuality of skin on skin in the salt water:

> When we swam around in this way, I would think how much we were like the pictures of sea mammals I had seen, my mother and I, naked in the seawater, my mother sometimes singing to me a song in a French patois I did not yet understand, or sometimes not saying anything at all. I would place my ear against her neck, and it was as if I were listening to a giant shell, for all the sounds around me—the sea, the wind, the birds screeching—would seem as if they came from inside her, the way the sounds of the sea are in a seashell. (42–43)

The mother is represented in the essay as Annie knew her, the perfect mother who contained everything and from whom there was no separation. The essay must turn though, as the text it is in does, on the change in this relationship and the meaning it has for Annie. The meaning it has for her mother is suspended somewhere beyond reach. In the text of the essay, the mother returns Annie to the shore and continues her swim. On this particular day, Annie becomes distracted by passing ships filled with celebrating people and loses sight of her mother: "I stood up and started to call out her name, but no sound would come out of my throat" (43). The shock of separation comes not from their physical distance from each other, but from her mother's unawareness that Annie missed her, her inability to feel Annie's agitation, to sense the difference of this moment from all the similar trips to Rat Island. Annie's mother is enacting the ritual of swimming out to the rock while Annie waits safely on shore, but the emotional content of this ritual is utterly changed for Annie. This scene reverses the positions of mother and daughter when Annie chose the cloth for matching outfits; then, it was Annie who repeated the familiar ritual and her mother who saw everything differently and made that difference felt. In both scenes, however, it is Annie who is shattered. When Annie spots her mother, who is sunning herself on the rock, she cannot attract her attention. When her mother returns to shore, she discovers a tear-stained and exhausted daughter, whom she strives to console.

After the summer in which this episode happens, Annie has a recurring dream in which the mother often swims out to the rock and sometimes the father joins her. Annie is never noticed. The dream becomes so distressing that Annie tells her mother. The autobiographical essay concludes: "My mother became instantly distressed; tears came to her eyes, and, taking me in her arms, she told me all the same things she had told me on the day at the sea, and this time the memory of the dark time when I felt I would never see her again did not come back to haunt me" (44–45). In analyzing Annie's dream as a feature of her autobiographical essay, several elements emerge: the narrative of traumatic separation is drawn from a time in which Annie and her mother were still close; thus she can still be consoled by her mother after the dream. The autobiographical essay, however, is written in the midst of the mother-daughter alienation in which no consolation or reconciliation is possible. Telling the story in this way allows Annie to report a true incident, to represent the symbolic reality of the relationship with her mother, and to alter the ending to make those levels of truth into a coherent narrative. In fact, when Annie had told her mother about the dream, she was dismissed. Annie explains: "I placed the old days' version before my classmates because, I thought, I couldn't bear to show my mother in a bad light before people who hardly knew her. But the real truth was that I couldn't bear to have anyone see how deep in disfavor I was with my mother" (45). Annie fears that her mother's disapproval will seep into all her relationships as a judgment. As an autobiographer, she refuses to let her mother's version of truth and Annie's identity stand in Annie's place in the eyes of her teacher and classmates. Annie shifts the grounds on which she will be judged by manipulating truth as an interpretation and identity as its conclusion. She succeeds to this extent: "I looked at these girls surrounding me, my heart filled with just-sprung-up love, and I wished then and there to spend the rest of my life only with them" (45).

Kincaid represents Annie in the act of interested self-representation in a way that expands our view of autobiography. In representing herself to herself and to others, Annie alters the script in which she feels she is being read and authors her own. The mother-daughter narrative has become a site of dismemberment and trauma in which Annie's feelings are all saturated with death. In the autobiographical essay, she represents the possibility of truth telling in her own terms, terms that offer her a way to re-member her life. Kincaid illuminates the social authority of autobiography within a particular community by representing Annie as an autobiographer. At the same time, Kincaid explores how a colonial subject may challenge the authority of the discourses of truth and identity experienced as imperial law by refusing the autobiographical pact because it is less than truthful. The subject of that law and the subject of self-representation are not metaphorically joined; rather, the law produces that subject through practices, codes, and judgments that subject her. When Kincaid chooses a series of names for a series of identities, she refuses this patterning and becomes an agent of self-representation running at cross-purposes (x) to the figures of colonial identity.

The text concludes, as *The House on Mango Street* does, with the narrator summing up her life as a narrative in which her name stands as a figure for a changing identity. Like Esperanza, Annie describes her relationship to her house and takes a stand on marriage. On the morning she is to leave Antigua, she again assumes the form of the autobiographical essay: "If someone had asked me for a little summing up of my life at that moment as I lay in bed, I would have said, 'My name is Annie John'" (132). After giving her parents' names, she concludes, "I plan not only never to marry an old man but certainly never to marry at all" (132). Building from herself to her parents to her mother's choice to marry an "old man" and her own decision not to marry, Annie takes in the house and its furnishings as extensions of her parents' labor, of which she, too, is a product: "I suppose I should say that the two of them made me with their own hands" (133). Continuing to respond in this imagined interlocution, Annie concludes: "If I had been asked to put into words why I felt this way, if I had been given years to reflect and come up with the words of why I felt this way, I would not have been able to come up with so much as the letter 'A'" (134). In this sentence, with the book in our hands, the temporality has shifted in order to account for a symbolic meaning in the same way time was telescoped in the autobiographical essay. For the account has already been given and Kincaid offers her new audience the letter with which to re-member her name, her mother's name, Antigua, and autobiographics.

3

Policing Truth

Lying So Near the Truth

For the least glimmer of truth is conditioned by politics.
—Michel Foucault, *The History of Sexuality*

As Madonna, that Rorschach test of our time, has shown, the game of truth or dare operates less as an innocent model of personal revelation than through the intricate structural dynamics of the confession in which, according to prescribed rules, one is authorized to question and the other is bound to confess. When I used to play the game "truth or dare," from which Madonna takes the title for her 1991 concert film, "truth" was not only the expected choice (thus revealing the false binary of truth *or* dare) but the easier choice. Certainly, a "dare" had its appeal; it involved movement, gesture, bodily risk. Functionally, however, it was an evasion, for it drew attention away from the conspirito-confessional moment in which I could become the one who whispers intimacies. I could be dared to do almost anything, but I would be asked to tell the truth only about a single topic. In the absence of witnesses who could deny or corroborate my answer, "truth" was always the best place to lie. That self-representational moment, structured and experienced as an exercise in truth production, reveals something crucial about autobiography. In that discursive setting, where truth is known at least partially through its proximity to risk, identity emerges not as a thing in itself patiently awaiting the moment of revelation but as the space from which confession issues. In this confessional space, there is a preferred topic already structured through another self-representational nexus. Sexuality as what is confessed, or the *topos* of truth, is represented through the nexus of gender, identity, and authority.[1]

[1] I would like to thank audiences at the International Association of Philosophy and Literature, Emory University, 1989; the Autobiography Conference, University of

When a writer is seen in relation to the dominant discourses of power s/he was simultaneously inscribing and resisting, the "innocence" of autobiography as a naive attempt to tell a universal truth is radically particularized by a specific culture's notion of what truth is, who may tell it, and who is authorized to judge it. What we have come to call truth or what a culture determines to be truth in autobiography, among other discourses, is largely the effect of a long and complex process of authorization. Thus the canonizing question "What is truth?" cannot be separated from the process of verifying that truth. These are not discrete moments in any history where authority is established, including literary history, for the production and authorization of truth emerge jointly in the confession, as in other exercises in truth telling. Some are positioned in closer proximity to "truth" depending on their relation to other terms of value: gender, class, race, and sexuality, among others. When autobiography criticism preserves truth telling as a major symbolic, thematic, and referential dimension of the text, the autobiographer's ability to write her/himself into some proximate relation to the terms of value determines how the text will be interpreted.

Although the problems that constitute interest in autobiography have undergone major epistemic shifts since the "first" autobiography in English (Margery Kempe's *Book*), little contemporary attention has focused on a relationship that surely underwrites the autobiographical project: the relationship between truth telling and agency.[2] Authority in autobiography springs from its proximity to the truth claim of the confession, a discourse that insists upon the possibility of telling the whole truth while paradoxically frustrating that goal through the structural demands placed on how one confesses. Indeed, "telling the truth" so totalizes the confession that it denotes the imperative to confess, the structure of that performance, and the grounds for its judgment. Telling the truth may be a form of punishment, as well as an effort to stave it off. In order to stand as an authoritative producer of "truth," then, one must successfully position oneself as a confessing subject whose account adequately fulfills

---

Southern Maine, 1989; the University of Texas, Austin, 1990, who responded to earlier versions of this chapter; and Lucinda Cole for her helpful comments.

[2] I accept Mary G. Mason's designation of Margery Kempe as the first autobiographer in English. See her article "The Other Voice." Much feminist criticism of autobiography has depended on just such "against the grain" readings of literary history and has produced the excellent work in such recent anthologies as Brodzki and Schenck's *Life/Lines* and Benstock's *The Private Self*. For a discussion of Margery Kempe in the context of community, see David Aers, *Community, Gender, and Individual Identity* (London: Routledge, 1988), 73–116.

enough of the requirements of confession. Insofar as truth telling is a cultural production that offers varying rewards, is both embraced and resisted, upheld and revised through its practice, and forms a site in the Middle Ages where power was contested, an examination of the influence of the confession upon autobiography can reveal the possibilities and limits of human agency in the production of truth. Thus, the relation of the confession to subsequent forms of self-representation in which "truth" is taken to be at stake, from this point of view, does not entail a narrative of genre formation. Rather, the legacy of the confession for autobiography can be introduced as a history of valuing and devaluing, of determining and misrecognizing the profoundly political dimension of all discourses of identity.

The confession's persistence in self-representation and the meaning attributed to that persistence largely structure authority in autobiography. As a mode of truth production the confession in both its oral and written forms grants the autobiographer a kind of authority derived from the confessor's proximity to "truth." Inasmuch as the confession's cultural authority, then, necessarily exists in relation to other discursive and historical formations—religion, psychology, philosophy—the grounds of cultural and autobiographical authority are subject to change. These shifts enable the confession's authority to be recuperated by a variety of practices and discourses interested in controlling and structuring the confessing subject's speech. Psychoanalysis, for example, is available to twentieth-century autobiographers as one of these "self"-authorizing discourses. Yet, the access to self-authorization is regulated, as I have suggested, in a variety of ways, and this way of contextualizing autobiography reveals how intimately bound up in the cultural practices of policing and resistance is a kind of writing that is more frequently thought of as simply private. That is, the confession did not merely prohibit, restrict, and censor speech. Indeed, the evident "thematic of regulation" in spiritual confessions enables the one confessing to develop alternative and rewarded "competencies" in "telling the truth."[3] I do not want to overemphasize the liberating possibilities of the confession, however, but only to insist, as Foucault does, that power does not only flow from the top down. For example, the pressure placed on the church/state by women's visionary experience prompted a discursive crisis: the language of the (patriarchal) ecclesiastical authority clashed with the language of mysticism (defined largely by women mystics)

---

[3] The phrase "thematic of regulation" is D. A. Miller's from *The Novel and the Police* (Berkeley: University of California Press, 1988), 38.

and the function of the confession was to police these contradictions.[4] In order to regulate potentially threatening speech in the Middle Ages, the church/state developed an elaborate vocabulary that controlled, through both the setting and the language of confession, what one could and must say. To be sure, one could always bring a competing agenda to the confession, but one still had to convince the confessor in "his" language.

Foucault links the confession to the discourse of sexuality, but I am concerned with a different history from the one he charts, and with women as subjects in and of history. He sees the confession as profoundly involved with the discourse of sexuality and the sexualization of discourse. He examines the Greek and Roman, eighteenth-century, and Victorian periods, charting the "deployment" of sexuality by the eighteenth-century sciences and gesturing toward its relation to the Christian tradition of confession. By contrast, I focus on the "beginning" and "end" of the confession, on how it has become embedded in self-representation, and on its meaning to and for women. More specifically, rather than trace the history of mysticism and confession in a particular region or within a limited historical frame, I want to let the challenge visionary experience posed to the church/state apparatus stand as an example of power relations as Foucault describes them. That is, power relations have a "strictly relational character. . . . Their existence depends on a multiplicity of points of resistance" (*History of Sexuality*, 95). Within this context, I wish to examine how women, in particular, negotiated the discourses of truth, how their writing reveals the widespread and relatively long-lasting practice of mysticism as a resisting force, as well as the ability of the church/state to adapt to, if not always to contain, its presence.

Autobiography cannot in this context be seen to draw its social authority simply from a privileged relation to real life. Rather, authority is derived through autobiography's proximity to the rhetoric of truth telling: the confession. The legacy of the confession for women's self-representational writing persists in two ways. First, the confession imports not only the spiritual but also the legal constraints of truth telling and potential punishment for error into the genre. The story of the self is constructed as one that must be sworn to and will be subject to verification. Second, truth is marked as a cultural production entwined with our notions of gender so completely that even

[4] I refer mainly to mysticism as it was practiced/experienced in cloistered settings. Although there were women who dashed about to take communion or who went on pilgrimages, the cloistered settings in which mysticism was expressed offer the grounds for examining the institutional emergence of mystical writing.

the structural underpinnings of truth production are masculinist; that is, the maintenance of patriarchal authority and male privilege follow from the formation of rules in confession to the installation of a man as judge (authorized through that massive tautology of male power legitimating males to power). The confession is a discourse that both requires and shapes "truth" according to the notions of heresy and orthodoxy in the religious confession and according to criminalized definitions of human activity in the legal confession. One confesses in both situations in order to be judged by a standard of truth that, despite its evident solidity, is nonetheless part of a cultural process. When readers of autobiography become detectives or confessors, when they seek to verify the facts of an autobiography, when they are dubious of an eyewitness account, yet look to the eyewitness for truth, they indicate the extent of the confession's power.

Thus, it is not enough to examine the role of the confession in literary history. If the legacy of the confession for self-representation persists, it does so by virtue of the confession's still effective history, the "policing" it engenders, and the "disciplinary" power it maintains. But how is autobiography a "discipline"? The church/state code of "truth" is enmeshed within a complex and diffuse network of power relations, and it participates in producing the notion of personhood, which brokers otherworldly payoffs and punishment. A person's relation to God and her or his spiritual decorum and social conduct were all defined in order to implicate the social subject in both "this" world and the "next." For this reason, the confession formed a crucial site for maintaining and generating power and exerted influence far beyond the darkened space of the confessional, a space we may now associate with secrecy but which was considerably more "public" in the Middle Ages. It is precisely the situation of the confession at a boundary which contributes to its authority: that it may therefore function as a place where one speaks not only *to* priests but *for* the fate of one's soul helps us to understand its influence.

In confession, the penitent becomes not only a person who pleads for her/his life but a kind of advocate for her/his fate after death. Her/his relation to death, always a live issue in spiritual confession, constructs a "dead" subject in the body of the living. The discipline of confession compels the penitent to speak in her/his own "voice" an appropriate language in order to save her/his soul. "Immortality," represented as the ability to avoid eternal punishment, is offered through confession. Thus the notion of some self-determination within that structure prompted allegiance to the confessors and the authority they represented. The subject of confession spoke in the voice of the living and the dead, projected, in a sense, a person's own voice beyond the limited sphere of the living into the potentially boundless sphere of death, and mounted her/his own defense. The confession offers the penitent a chance to argue before God in a voice s/he will not have in death. There, according to the New Testament, because Christ acts as the advocate, you can not try your own case. The "presence" of death, the vivid sense of its proximity, maintained the power of the confession to compel its subjects to speak. I have been veering from the language of spiritual confession to the language of legal confession in order to indicate the defensive posture of both as well as the form of agency allowed a person who must always speak of transgression, who learns to confess in order to codify sinning and manage its presence. Other "positive" forms of speaking in a spiritual context would include prayer and mystical experience, and it is precisely this excess of mysticism which the church/state sought to control, to bring within the purview of the confession.

During the Middle Ages, a woman's intervention into the discourses of truth was massively scrutinized, her confession policed according to the elaborate codes that ultimately produced this judgment: "The Church has always tended to react negatively to 'revelations', and sensible men everywhere will applaud such hesitance."[5] Although I am not claiming that confession invariantly persists in all women's autobiography, or in autobiography generally, I would like to explore the ways in which the confession underwrites the autobiographical project in relation to the agency revealed in women's self-representational texts. I will discuss the intertextualization of the institutional production of truth, represented as the internalized presence of the confessor and the confessional code, in Julian of Norwich's *Revelations of Divine Love* and trace that dynamic through its expression in Mary McCarthy's *Memories of a Catholic Girlhood*. Although both Julian and McCarthy adopt the self-representational strategy that Bella Brodzki and Celeste Schenck identify as "singularity in alterity," which Mary Mason first theorized as a paradigm of women's autobiography—representing the self in relation to an "other" or "others"—they do so within a cultural context of truth telling which uses gender politics as an organizing agenda and gender logic as a mode of judgment.[6] I will conclude by analyzing how critical practices sustain that agenda in evaluating women's autobiography.

[5] Clifton Wolters, "Introduction" to Julian of Norwich, *Revelations of Divine Love* (1966; London: Penguin, 1988).

[6] Brodzki and Schenck develop the term "singularity in alterity" in their introduction to *Life/Lines*. For an excellent discussion of confession, see Jeremy Tambling, *Confession: Sexuality, Sin, the Subject* (New York: St. Martin's Press, 1990).

Autobiography is rooted in the confession, a form in which telling the truth or not telling the truth can meet with dramatic and occasionally fatal results. After Foucault, we can see how confessor and penitent are positioned in a differential power relationship, though they should not be thought of exclusively as producer/penitent and consumer/confessor of truth but also as enjoined in a mutually productive performance of truth telling. Their mutual performance locates a cultural and discursive site of truth production in relation to the disciplinary boundary of punishment. As Foucault explains,

> The confession is a ritual of discourse in which the speaking subject is also the subject of the statement; it is also a ritual that unfolds within a power relationship, for one does not confess without the presence (or virtual presence) of a partner who is not simply the interlocutor but the authority who requires the confession, prescribes and appreciates it, and intervenes in order to judge, punish, forgive, console and reconcile; a ritual in which the truth is corroborated by the obstacles and resistances it has to surmount in order to be formulated; and finally, a ritual in which the expression alone, independently of its external consequences, produces intrinsic modifications in the person who articulates it: exonerates, redeems, and purifies him; it unburdens him of his wrongs, liberates him, and promises salvation. (*History of Sexuality*, 61–62)

The confession must be regarded, then, as relational: neither penitent nor confessor is the "source" of truth production. Instead, their relationship forms the locus from which confession is generated. In this sense, confession can be thought of as "self"-policing. In the self-representational texts with which I am concerned, the proximity of truth and torture, of confession and skepticism, critically construct interest in women's visionary experience and mystical writing. That is, the desire to report one's mystical experience and one's transformed perspective on identity is not simply *informed* by the consequences of error; the confession is *structured* through the penalties and payoffs already in place. Mary Mason has noted the tremendous anxiety women autobiographers exhibit "to get it right" and, by specifying the gendered production of confessional truth, focuses on an aspect of the power relationship which Foucault neglects. The confession, I would argue, installs the production of gender as a truth effect; one tells the truth insofar as one also produces gendered identity appropriately. In this sense, the confession hypostatizes gender, condenses the differences among women into an institutional whole, and enforces that construction. For this reason, I would locate what Mason has identified as the pressure "to get it right" in the confession's simultaneous construction of truth and torture and of self-represen-tation and self-incrimination *in relation to gender*. For the purposes of this discussion, I will explore how this construction operates as the confession's constantly reformulated legacy.

Gender both defines and saturates the notions of truth and confes-sion which circulated and were formalized during the late medieval fourteenth and fifteenth centuries when women's mystical experi-ences abounded. The visionary who wished to confess her mystical experience was positioned differently from her male counterpart with respect to truth because of her place in the signifying chain of sin, error, deception, and femininity. One hears the dominoes that pro-duce this judgment as inevitable "truth" falling through a metonymic chain of associations in which sex becomes gender becomes hetero-sexual desire becomes identity and which leaves in place the meta-phorical equation of sin and femininity, sex and identity. Within this gender logic, women and visionary experience were both seen as forms susceptible to the devil's seductions; indeed, negative values attached to women spill into definitions of mysticism and are ad-dressed in the progressively formalized regulations concerning "truth" in mystical experience. Such definitional discourses marked the limits of the confession by establishing what truth could be told and installing a confessor, specifically a theologian, who would police those limits. Yet despite the exclusion of medieval women mystics from the priesthood (a location so near the truth as to be virtually a metonym for it), the authority devolving from their charismatic and visionary experience was largely unassailable, and the presence of such complex regulations evidences the church/state's desire to gain control over this power. If visions were verified, mystics could claim the authority to address popes and kings, to speak for God and for all. If visions were deemed demonic, the penalties varied. Special advi-sorial codes were developed to aid clergy in verifying women's vi-sionary experience: confessors were to be especially wary of speech and undue curiosity.

Writing at the end of the fourteenth century on a topic of public interest and debate, Jean Gerson, chancellor of the University of Paris, formally took up the issue of authorizing women's visionary experi-ence. The challenge to church/state authority by these "others"—women, lay people—prompted great concern, and Gerson elaborated a set of definitions, cautionary remarks, and prohibitions to advise clergy about what to do when mystical practice cropped up. Specifi-cally, these codes offered a way to intervene in mystical and, from the church/state's point of view, self-authorizing speech. The codes allow us to see how women's mysticism was "organized" in terms of truth production:

> (49) If the visionary is a woman, it is especially necessary to learn how she acts towards her confessors or instructors. Is she prone to continual conversations, either under the pretext of frequent confession or in relating lengthy accounts of her visions, or by any other kind of discussion? . . . There is scarcely any plague that is more harmful or incurable than this.
>
> (50) Also, you must realize that a woman . . . has an unhealthy curiosity which leads to gazing about and talking (not to mention touching) . . . .
>
> (51) Moreover the abiding peace of God is in quiet. Consequently no one will be surprised if such people, having embraced false teachings, turn aside from truth. All the more is it true if these women, itching with curiosity, are the kind whom the Apostle describes: *Silly women who are sin-laden and led away by various lusts: ever learning yet never attaining knowledge of the truth* (2 Tim. 3:7).[7]

Gerson's interest in speech refers to the notion that women are closer to oral than to learned traditions; thus their speaking practices, a realm in which their "potential" authority could evolve, should be most carefully policed. In order to succeed, Gerson's "law" needed to become entwined with how people thought and talked about mysticism. To what extent did these and other regulations linking gender and authority succeed in policing the production and maintenance of truth? That is, how pervasive were its effects? Could they, for instance, be registered outside the formal purview of the confession, outside conduct manuals and instructional discourses? Had they saturated the culture to the extent that persons could themselves participate in policing the truth at the very moment they attempted to represent it for themselves?

Take, for example, *The Revelations of Divine Love* written by fourteenth-century English mystic Julian of Norwich. Already convinced of her vocation, Julian prayed for a deepening of her calling in the form of illness. She became mortally ill and on May 8, 1373, received a vision of the crucifixion composed of fifteen revelations and lasting

---

[7] Jean Gerson wrote widely on topics ranging from ecclesiastical law to mysticism. The codes are found in G. H. M. Posthumus Meyjes, *Jean Gerson et l'assemblée de Vincennes (1329): Ses conceptions de la juridiction temporelle de l'église* (Leiden: Brill, 1978). See also Catherine D. Brown, *Pastor and Laity in the Theology of Jean Gerson* (New York: Cambridge University Press, 1987). I wish to thank Kathleen Ashley for bringing this document to my attention.

five hours; one night later she received the sixteenth and final "shew-
ing." When she recovered, Julian spent the next twenty years in an
anchorage adjoining Saint Julian's Church in Conesford, Norwich,
where she reflected on and revised her short text, written directly
after the revelations, into the longer text we know as *The Revelations of
Divine Love*. Julian was prepared literally to emulate the death of
Christ. She prayed for and received the wounding grace of illness and
near-death: "When I was half way through my thirty-first year God
sent me an illness which prostrated me for three days and nights. On
the fourth night I received the last rites of Holy Church as it was
thought I could not survive till day" (64). The content of the first
twelve revelations mostly concerns a graphic depiction of Christ's
passion in which his bleeding head looms at the foot of her bed.
Throughout the exposition of the vision, Julian reveals much of herself. In her interaction with God we see her habits of mind, even in
this biographically pared down depiction of selfhood: she prays for
and receives a vision; she asks God questions concerning its meaning;
she agitates to see more or less at different moments; and she dedi-
cates her life to interpreting the experience. The vigor with which she
seeks visionary experience considerably revises the conventional link
between passivity and grace.

We know only the barest facts of Julian's life. Because her surname
is unknown, no family history can be traced, no explanatory apparatus can be brought to bear on the life prior to one very full night of
visions, and no parish registries reveal information about her family.
Yet scholars have subjected Julian to intense scrutiny, from speculation about her relationship with her own mother and its influence on
Julian's theology of the motherhood of God, to debates about her
literacy. Questions concerning her authority have kept pace with her
success in passing various tests: after her mystical experience had
already been judged authentic and orthodox, despite the waffle on
original sin (Julian's claim that we are all in God and there is no sin in
him pushes church teaching on the point of original sin rather farther
than many have liked), her role in writing *The Revelations* was challenged. Some scholars are more willing to accept her as an unedu-
cated and therefore "natural" recipient of God's grace than to honor
the evidence that Julian's text was the product of twenty years of
interpretation and revision. The current consensus holds that Julian
was probably educated at the convent of Carrow by Benedictine nuns
from whom she would have learned some reading and writing. The
literacy debate turns on her claim to be "a simple and unlearned

creature" (63),[8] by which she may have meant simply that she was not formally educated or that she depended on an amanuensis. More-over, the rhetoric of spiritual confessions is filled with such deference; the humility *topos* is common to the point of being pro forma. More to the point here is the response of her critics. Many accept her claim as "truthful" and are, therefore, baffled by the literary and scholarly allusions that fill her text.

Mason ascribes Julian's disclaimer to the defensiveness she finds in most women autobiographers and argues that the critics' confusion is consistent with a pattern that fails to reconcile a woman's achieve-ments with the cultural position she occupies. Perhaps Julian herself offers the best gloss on this issue when she links authority with gen-der and, in that connection, reveals the gender logic that equates writing and femaleness with transgression: "But because I am a wom-an, ought I therefore to believe that I should not tell you of the goodness of God, when I saw at the same time that it is his will that it be known?" Thus the debate over whether or not she wrote *The Revelations* in her own hand ignores the point Julian was raising about the marginalization of her authority due to gender, as well as the political dimension of all self-representation, and demonstrates the historically mobile forms of policing that would maintain marginality. For whereas Julian's developed imagery of Christ as a birthing and lactating mother is not unique in mystical writing, her expansion of the motherhood of God into a complex theology of mothering is a remarkable step. It is grounded not in theological debate—the field of male ecclesiastics and scholars—but rather in the mystical experi-ence of being "oned" with God. That is, Julian's theology of mother-hood follows from the totalizing insight into her own identity de-picted in the revelations, and in this move she manages, at least in her text, to shift the grounds of authority on which she could be judged.

The visionary's burden, then, lies not only in finding a language to correspond to the divine language she hears during an ecstatic experi-ence, although it may be difficult indeed to bring into writing an experience that mystics frequently describe as indescribable. Tropes of ineffability and unrepresentability abound in documents that also detail, with tireless precision, the whole range of bodily and mental effects. The point is, mystics do describe the experiences. References

[8] For more on the literacy debate concerning Julian, see Mason, "The Other Voice"; and Jennifer P. Heimmel, *"God Is Our Mother": Julian of Norwich and the Medieval Image of Christian Feminine Divinity* (Salzburg, Austria: Salzburg Studies in English Literature, 1982).

to the unrepresentability of the rapture do not, I am arguing, derive from a mystic's inability to interpret an anomalous event. Rather, visionary experience, with its rhetoric of the ecstatic body, its enactment of a lover's discourse, its eroticization of the relationship with God, is difficult to represent in the terms the confession demands: it cannot be described as a sin or transgression; yet this is the formal demand made by the confession. Thus visionary experience must be coded as a potential sin and then defended. There are no commandments regarding visionary experience, although there is sufficient biblical attention to false prophecy and demonic possession to put any mystic on the defensive. We should not underestimate the threat posed by a phenomenon that was so widespread that it was unusual by the thirteenth century to hear of a convent without a mystic.[9] Potentially heretical claims about God's direct communication with individual women created a crisis in ecclesiastical authority. Thus, the mystic's self-representation was pressured from two sides: first, from the policing mechanism of the confession and her own internalization of its demands and, second, from the oft-repeated desire to represent God's intervention in her mundane world accurately.

Julian interprets and represents *The Revelations* within the context of the confession she would later make. Her representation of the experience documents this regulatory presence and the extent to which she has internalized the demands of such policing. This internalization is demonstrated throughout *The Revelations* as she forms a judgment about her experience. The more perfectly the illness fits Julian's desire for it, the more it appears visited upon her by a merciful and accommodating God rather than by indifferent nature or cunning Satan. The less it fits those requirements, the more she suspects herself of raving. To interpret this illness as a gift from God enables her to control its capacity to "hurt." In *The Body in Pain*, Elaine Scarry suggests that pain empties consciousness of purpose and progress; there is only the growing moment of agony released from all boundaries.[10] Pain forces the past and the future to recede to the edges of consciousness. As Scarry describes it, this breakdown is the method of torture: the body is assaulted through a variety of degrading practices, and the voice, or capacity to speak at all, let alone to speak in one's defense, is reduced to a preverbal howl of pain. The mystics are rarely out of control in precisely this way, though the visionary found to be a

---

[9] See Caroline Walker Bynum, *Holy Feast and Holy Fast: The Religious Significance of Food to Medieval Women* (Berkeley: University of California Press, 1987).

[10] Elaine Scarry, *The Body in Pain* (Oxford: Oxford University Press, 1987).

heretic could expect horrifying consequences. Significantly, it was possible for confessors to disagree about the source of visions.[11] Thus, it is important to distinguish an out-of-body experience and the mystic's rapturous language from the language of the confession with its potential punishment for heresy in order to understand the controlling power to interpret that confession exerted on rapturous language. Between these irreconcilable possibilities, between the ecstatic body and the tortured body, lies the discourse of confession: the very language of "truth" in which the mystic who would confess every experience of rapture was trained to the point of self-policing.

The interpretation of pain as blessing, of vision as gift, of mystic as chosen is held in check by the confession. The connections between women's experiences and Christ's life must be situated within the confessional frame because those are the grounds on which to verify the mystic as authentic or condemn her as a heretic or the victim of demonic possession. Yet, once the authenticity of the experience could be confirmed, God's invisible presence could be read in the visible alterations of the body. The saint's ravaged or levitating body confers a kind of facticity on the unrepresentable deity: the body becomes evidentiary text. The tension between physical abasement (the body in extreme need) and spiritual salvation (the "new" body redeemed by and absorbed into the body of Christ) marks passion as the nexus of pain and ecstasy. When she confesses, her discourse derives meaning through a dialectical relation to the confession. Thus it would be misleading to read mystical discourse as an ahistorical version of "writing the body." This body was written and read as a text within a particular discursive network of power relations. Through their remapping of the body, mystics represented it as a network of possibilities and not simply a biological fact, insisting simultaneously on its undeniable materiality and fantastical possibility, making it the major figure for the acts, images, and promise of embodied mystical rapture.

Mysticism provided an interesting test for the possibility of a counterdiscourse, as it revealed the limits of the church/state's tolerance in authorizing women's speech as "truth." Although mysticism was busily assimilated to an orthodox agenda, it was a counterhegemonic form of worship and, most important, began to generate its own discourse. Significantly, it was practiced largely by women.[12] Al-

---

[11] Joan of Arc, for example, was found by some official confessors involved in her trial to be telling the "truth."

[12] For more on male mysticism, an interesting phenomenon in terms of the construction of gender and the representation of sexuality, see Bynum, *Holy Feast*.

though men's mystical experience was also challenged, the codes of verification were devised mainly to contain women's mysticism, and the codes specifically addressed this "norm." Mysticism was not practiced at the altar or in other "authorized" sites of worship. Mystics would display their power publicly, would rush about to take communion; in short, they made spectacles of themselves. Their visibility was part of the significance of mysticism and describes an incipient alternative form of authorization. Paradoxically, the power and authority of priests devolved from unseen sources; the abstractness of their power compounded its authority. Conversely, the seeming "mystery" of ecstatic and visionary experience was widely demonstrated, registered through the acts of the mystic herself or employing the rhetoric of bodily display.

In this sense and others, gender polarity and spiritual authenticity are mutually embedded structures, both sources and symptoms of policing. As Peter Stallybrass and Allon White have demonstrated in *The Politics and Poetics of Transgression*, it is useful to grasp the conceptual binarisms that determine cultural value.[13] While the structuring aspect of the high/low concept shapes the interpretations negotiated within it, gender polarity in a culture still allows for subtle distinctions within the male/female, high/low binarisms. Further, the high/low binarisms structuring gender, class, and religious devotion are articulated simultaneously through a variety of discursive effects. Although the high/low poles designate the ends of meaning, cultural meaning itself consists in the circulation of the values represented and constantly recombined between those poles.

The "need" for policing becomes especially evident when there is apparent dissonance in the codes of gender, authority, and truth. For example, a woman mystic in fourteenth-century England could be seen simultaneously as a privileged communicant with God and an error-prone, sin-laden daughter of Eve. Significantly, this tension does not always render her unknowable. Such dissonance in fact reveals the power of the high/low distinction. The high, here, of mysticism includes the low of femaleness. Women were seen as more susceptible than men to Satan's deception: it happened once in the Garden; it could happen again. The high/low distinction between men and women enforces the church/state's greater skepticism about the veracity of women's visionary experience, even while it acknowledges its occurrence. The high includes the low symbolically through

---

[13] Peter Stallybrass and Allon White, *The Politics and Poetics of Transgression* (Ithaca: Cornell University Press, 1986).

the figure of Eve as an interpretive device for women's ability to tell the truth and to speak with God. Thus, women could be socially marginal and symbolically central in making the church/state case about God's grace: if he speaks to women, surely he could speak to us all.

The liberatory power of women's visions, then, is less likely to obliterate the edicts against women's speech and authority when both of those can be assimilated to an official position. To deny female visionary experience any authority at a time when the mystics themselves were widely believed and much sought after would not serve the interests of the church/state. Thus the church/state is able to regulate a force that is, potentially, socially transformative. And insofar as it succeeds, visionary experience remains mostly individually transformative. The church/state controlled how visions were verified in order to maintain order. Women's visionary experience was not, therefore, a priori a force for social change. Many who saw long-contemplated icons begin to ooze blood and glow or who found themselves physically levitated during prayers never managed to naturalize the phenomenon and lived in a state of watchful "otherworldly" attention. Others viewed mystical experience as so sufficiently interpretable as to be no less normal than any other moment of daily life. Mysticism came to transform, for a time, the church/state's notion of who receives God's word and how, but the church/state maintained its hegemony by giving the last word to the confessor, as the one who would interpret and judge, rather than to the mystic alone.

Autobiography and Its Authorities

As an enlargement of the confession, autobiography retains many of its characteristics, though its historical transformations are critical. A contemporary example of the intertextualization of confession and its rhetorical apparatus of truth telling indicates the persistence as well as the historical contingency of the relationship between autobiographical authority and the forms of policing that regulate it. Mary McCarthy once rather dramatically (on *The Dick Cavett Show*, no less) accused Lillian Hellman of lying, insisted, in fact, that "every word" Hellman wrote in her series of autobiographies was a lie. This is an interesting charge from McCarthy, who is something of an expert in fictionalizing the past in order to tell a better story. Her first autobiography, *Memories of a Catholic Girlhood*, is a compilation of eight sketches describing events in her life collected from twelve years' worth of published material. The sketches are arranged in chronological order, preceded by a lengthy preface ("To the Reader") that foregrounds the collusion between fiction and nonfiction in autobiography. Indeed, the distinction is destabilized as soon as it is invoked. Between the numbered chapters, the purportedly truthful accounts drawn from life, is a sequence of italicized interchapters in which McCarthy distinguishes what she *really* remembers from what she invented to satisfy her own artistic sensibility: gaps in memory disappear into narrative continuity, conversations that never took place economically convey information, and characters behave as they must in a story even when they frustrate her with their "real" and unassimilable actions. Yet, she insists always that any departure from what she absolutely remembers occurs in the service of telling the truth or of squaring refractory memory with what "must" have happened. Mary McCarthy thus continuously discovers, as Julian of Norwich did, that it is never as simple to confess as one might wish it to be. The very act of confessing seems almost to conspire against the one bound to tell the truth. That is, in telling the *truth*, autobiographers usually narrate, and thereby shift the emphasis to *telling* the truth.

Because the subject of autobiography is a self-representation and not the autobiographer her/himself, most contemporary critics describe this "self" as a fiction. When we locate the pressure to tell the truth in the context of the fictive self accountable for producing truth, the problematical alliance between fact and fiction in autobiography begins to emerge. For autobiography's roots in the confession— spiritual and juridical—continue to mark it as a form in which it is both possible and necessary to tell the truth. The vow, "So help me God," seals the courtroom and the confessional account in the presence of a witness authorized to return a verdict, to determine veracity or perjury, to judge innocence or guilt, to decide on absolution or damnation. Some higher authority or recourse to its function is a fixture in scenes where truth is at issue, for it is necessary in this construction of truth telling to speak to someone. An immediate audience stands in for abstract authority because neither God nor the Law can speak in its own voice. Insofar as they emanate from the page and share mythic sources, they cannot be recovered, only represented. In order to catalyze the dynamics of what we recognize as confession, the stage must be set with a penitent/teller, a listener, and a tale. Even when the reader or the autobiographer replaces God as the implied audience, the structure of confession remains available. Indeed, the structure of confession, as I have described it, may be embedded in a specific autobiography, as it is in Mary McCarthy's *Memories of a Catholic Girlhood*. I have described confession as an "effect" of power relations, a discourse of truth produced by confessor and penitent within the context of a particular authority. In McCarthy, confessor and penitent become reader and writer and the language of confession is powerfully inflected by the practice of psychoanalysis, with its language of memory and repression and its practice of the talking cure.

In her preface, McCarthy claims: "This record lays a claim to being historical—that is, much of it can be checked. If there is more fiction in it than I know, I should like to be set right."[14] She thereby draws the reader into the confessional scene as a witness and judge. Yet the troubling equivocation, "more fiction in it than I know," indicates the extent to which the witness will be constrained by what is always a problem in confession: the tension engendered by the triangulation of penitent/teller, listener, and tale can be read in at least two competing ways. The witness may attempt to discover "truth" in the reality described by the autobiographer; thus, the witness suppresses the "construction" of truth to a conviction that the process of detection will reveal (rather than produce) it. This premise guides the practice of law (critical legal studies challenges precisely this view).[15] If we act as "detectives" of autobiography, a role prescribed by Philippe Lejeune among others, then we believe in the extratextual reality to which McCarthy's account refers. The investment of belief in a long-passed ground from which truth emerged and to which the reader must be able to return reveals this apparently ultraempiricist project as an exercise in metaphysics. Or we can interpret autobiography as a re-presentation, that is, a structuring of events, motives, and so on in an effort to position one's story within a discourse of truth and identity—in short, as an attempt to authorize the autobiography.

McCarthy's autobiography capitalizes on both constructions; her "truth" circulates within both. On one hand, she claims her account is the truth because it really happened. On the other, the fictions she creates to cover the gaps in history and memory have come to fit so neatly into her narrative that they attain the status of remembered

[14] Mary McCarthy, *Memories of a Catholic Girlhood* (Berkeley Medallion Edition; New York: Harcourt, Brace and World, 1966), 10.

[15] For the connection between literary studies and law, see Susan Sage Heinzelman, "Women's Petty Treason: Feminism, Narrative, and the Law," *Journal of Narrative Technique*, 20 (Spring 1990): 89–106; Victoria Kahn, "Rhetoric and the Law," *Diacritics* 19.2 (1989): 21–34; and David Kairys, ed., *The Politics of Law: A Progressive Critique* (New York: Pantheon, 1982).

fact. That is, the ability to ascertain the precise line marked by "more
. . . than I know" has receded beyond her ability to distinguish between the fiction in the text she has come to know—that is, remember and believe—as fact and fact itself. She acknowledges how this
might happen when she observes: "This is an example of 'storytelling'; I arranged actual events so as to make 'a good story' out of
them. It is hard to overcome this temptation if you are in the habit of
writing fiction; one does it almost automatically" (153).

McCarthy claims she lacks an authority against which to test her
sense of the past, because she was orphaned at a young age. And it is
the loss of her beloved parents that in some way generates her need
to confess her childhood. This wounding loss, wrapped in nostalgia
and grief, suffuses the autobiography and makes it, in part, an act of
re-creation. That it mainly succeeds in recreating grief and loss reveals the extent to which those emotional and, indeed, narrative
structures spur her writing. Although the parents are dead, writing
about them inscribes their presence in something less private and
potentially more sharable than memory; writing, however, cannot
avoid also inscribing this paradoxically generative sense of loss. More
germane to this discussion is the sense in which McCarthy presents
the death of her parents as the lack of a delimiting authority. Truth,
she writes, may not be verified because her parents cannot offer the
factual information standing between speculation and certainty. The
finality of their knowledge, their authority, is nevertheless repeatedly
undercut by McCarthy's refusal to privilege any eyewitness accounts
that compete with her own (see the tin butterfly episode in "Yonder
Peasant," for example). The loss of parental authority is coded as
something to be defended, a kind of transgression or straying from
proximity to the truth which causes McCarthy to position herself in
autobiography as a penitent. She attempts to pull her own account
into line with the rhetoric of truth telling and the rewards it offers.

Bereft of a corroborating other, she creates one in the interchapters
by textualizing the confessional space. These are the only sections of
the book written contemporaneously; that is, written *as* her autobiography. In direct address to the reader, she challenges her own
account, finds it accurate, and thereby preserves the structure of confession with the self of the interchapters playing confessor to the self
of the sketches. The reader is compelled to witness the account,
which, as early as the title of the preface, is clearly addressed to her or
him. The rhythms of confession McCarthy creates make it possible for
her to perform multiple roles while requiring her reader to fill in for
ones she temporarily vacates in order to inhabit others. At one time

skeptical and challenging (as in the interchapters when she admits to fictionalizing), at another fully convinced of her authenticity (as when she insists upon her accuracy), the reader and the autobiographer gaze into the unfathomability of memory and concede that the telling of lies is inextricable from the writing of memories.

In terms of how autobiography builds in authority, an analogy can be drawn here between the church/state as an informing context of self-representation in the Middle Ages and psychoanalysis in the twentieth century. For self-representation that takes truth production as its mode, as *Memories of a Catholic Girlhood* does, and deploys the language of memory and repression as both impediment to and constituent of "truth" is informed by the pervasive influence of that other confessional space, the analyst's office, and the language disseminated through it. The effect of this language emerges through the kind of competency in truth telling McCarthy develops, the episodes she chooses to narrate, and how they function in the autobiography. Her interest in memory and repression, especially powerful in the final chapter on her grandmother, and the apocalyptic force attributed to forgetting reveal the persistence in twentieth-century autobiography of a confessional practice in which the dominant discourse of truth telling, at least for prominent white intellectuals such as McCarthy, is psychoanalysis.[16] The power of confession persists primarily through the psychoanalytic interest in the "self," the construction of that self through a specific discourse, and the power relationship between analyst and analysand which produces "truth." One sees this persistence by historicizing the project of confession and crediting its ability to structure discourses of "truth." Foucault's general historicizing approach yields this insight and also enables us to discern the crucial feature of "authorization" which configures confessor/penitent, analyst/analysand, writer/reader, and significantly, critic/autobiographer on the grounds of truth.

For both its writers and its critics, autobiography is driven by an authorization complex.[17] Its writers attempt to situate themselves in relation to discourses of "truth" and "identity" while recognizing, in various ways, the insufficiency of any single discourse to express the "subject" of their writing. In the absence of a single, unified model of

[16] Perhaps the connection to *Discipline and Punish* is too obvious to mention in this context, but Foucault's discussion of the emergence of psychiatry is significant here, as is the way in which this discussion generates his later interest in "the care of the self."

[17] See Shari Benstock, "Authorizing the Autobiographical," in *The Private Self*, 10–33; and Nancy K. Miller, "Changing the Subject: Authorship, Writing, and Readership," in *Subject to Change*, 102–21.

"autobiography," they weave testimonial texts from disparate discourses. The effect of this positioning defines autobiography's characteristic weirdness and accounts for its problematical status as a "genre." Somewhere between reporting and fiction writing, autobiography challenges the limits of generic definition through its bricolage-like bravado. Critics/scholars of autobiography attempt to authorize their texts with introductions that contextualize their arguments within a comprehensible and already-authorized field of study.[18] Indeed, critics even reveal traces of "canon envy" as they attempt to establish autobiography's legitimacy and authority through a series of familiar moves: claiming an origin, invoking formal continuity, stabilizing a canon, constructing alternative traditions, and so on. But we should consider these moves more closely. Under what circumstances could a kind of writing such as autobiography, a practice as diffuse as self-representation, be seen to take on thematic continuity? From what project must autobiography be distinguished such that it can be said to "begin"? That is, how did autobiography become recognizable as such, to the point it could require a history, a narrative of its development? These questions indicate an issue in the study of autobiography which has largely been obscured, namely, that critical practices have organized and continue to organize autobiography and are bound up with and indeed generate "authority" in autobiography. How, then, has authority been gendered and how is the maintenance of gender hierarchy policed?

Autobiography is a form in which the self is authorized, although autobiography is not itself simply a self-authorizing form. Those who seek to interpret autobiography as a self-authorizing form place its roots in the Romantic concept of the self.[19] Paradoxically, the influence of confessional practices has been minimized by tracing autobiography's literary history and formal characteristics from Augustine (a necessary origin for this argument) and subsuming him into a discussion of autobiography as an Enlightenment project. Autobiography can then be seen as a literary discourse that develops in line with the emergent political discourses of individualism.[20]

Contemporary critics committed to upholding autobiography as a

[18] For two tracings of this history with very different interests, see Sidonie Smith, *A Poetics of Women's Autobiography*; and Spengemann, *The Forms of Autobiography*.

[19] Much of the advanced work on Romanticism tends to show how the Romantics themselves deconstruct or complicate the very concept of the "self" with which they are credited/discredited. I am thinking here especially of Mary Jacobus, *Romanticism, Writing, and Sexual Difference*, and her chapter on autobiography.

[20] American autobiographers—for example, Benjamin Franklin, Henry Adams, and even Donald Trump—have been acutely aware of this.

post-Enlightenment project in which an individual produces truth bring their concerns to women's autobiography. Insofar as writers systematically and historically excluded from the rewards of a thoroughly patriarchal and class-bound individualism produce texts that resist this ideology—even, as is sometimes the case, in the very act of trying to reproduce it—they are deauthorized through this "failure." Although it may seem rather paranoid, if not grandiose, to describe the liberal literary criticism practiced in the late twentieth century as a form of "policing," I insist upon this description not only and most obviously to foreground its politics but also to underline its ironic position in relation to those politics. Liberal humanism values free speech and the subject who can utter it despite the fact that the consequence, and perhaps the aim, of certain forms of speech is necessarily a context in which some speech is marginalized and even criminalized.[21] The relationship that feminists have described between male speech and female silence is not a simple binary but rather a cultural context in which the enforced silence of women can be read as the norm even when women manage to write and publish, to speak and achieve influence. For example, women writers frequently describe writing an autobiography as an empowering process through which they reach an understanding, however provisional, of the relationships through which identity is produced. Yet, until very recently, they were excluded from virtually all studies of autobiography. I would like to suggest that their absence can be read as the critic's participation in policing the limits of female "truth" and enforcing the remnants of Gerson's powerful interdictions.

As a "policing" critic, Philippe Lejeune would be a rather obvious autobiography gendarme. But perhaps this is the wrong word. Lejeune's autobiography cops belong to a liberal state imaginary in which the police lack preventive and interdictive powers. Rather, Lejeune's policing of the autobiographical pact authorizes a mobile readership of detectives who concern themselves with verifying the facts. One imagines them running credit checks rather than knocking on doors and demanding documentation, gathering and generating more paper as they track the facts to the truth. What do these inquiring minds most want to know? What really happened. Although this caricature is intended to indicate the lingering and reduced effects of some of the confession's more brutal legacy—the Inquisition, most notably—it is also meant to sketch the critical context in which wom-

---

[21] The feminist critique of liberal humanism is undertaken by Alison Jaggar in *Feminist Politics and Human Nature* (Brighton: Harvester, 1983).

en autobiographers have been read. The question "What really happened?" has only infrequently been a plea for more information. Usually it contains a way of valuing the testimony in question. As I have noted, when Hannah Tillich wrote her autobiography, she was widely criticized for missing the point. According to many of her reviewers and much of her reading public, she *should* have written the biography of her husband. How could she cheat history of the opportunity to know more of "a great man"? Ironically, Tillich supplied her readers with a good deal more than many of them wished to know about Paul Tillich. Thus questions of how to read autobiography frequently support an agenda for how to value the autobiographer.

Further illustrations of this claim abound, but Karl Weintraub's *Value of the Individual: Self and Circumstance in Autobiography* (1974) is especially appropriate for this context. Weintraub construes the generic emergence of autobiography as a corollary to the cultural hegemony of individualism. Without an "individual" who can be defined through "his" developing self-consciousness, there can be no autobiography. Weintraub defines the "proper form" of autobiography as the self-conscious search for individuality guided by the questions: "'Who am I?' and 'how did I become what I am?'" (1). The similarity of responses in men's writing indicates the extent to which the questions themselves also participate in the production of "autobiography" as we know it. That is, the responses are embedded in the question—both in the form of the question and in the answer it recognizes. "Who am I" assumes that the *I* is contained within a set of boundaries that distinguish it from everything else around it, and "how did I become what I am" assumes that the history of this distinctive *I* is the process of constructing those delimiting boundaries. Further, these two questions imply a third, which is perhaps the most important, namely, "What is the significance of this *I* that has been thus distinguished?" When the self is construed as an autonomous and self-authorized figure, the agency of others is reduced to their participation in "how did I become what I am"; that is, they are extensions of the self rather than selves in their own right. If we pursue Weintraub's definition of autobiography, we see that the growth of nations, the temper of the times, the political and cultural zeitgeist, and the "exemplary man" form a mutually reinforcing network of identity. The man is the mirror of his times; history can be told as the story of this self. Indeed, it is frequently the autobiographer's task to place—in the sense of both find and put—"himself" at the center of history and interpret from this perspective.

Forming a canon of autobiography depends on agreeing with a

particular narrative of history and choosing autobiographers who reproduce it. Such a construction is always a political retrospective with the following limitation: what were once rather more clearly ideological and political criteria get recoded as aesthetic criteria. This process also confers upon the writer the frequently dehistoricizing status of "artist" and allows, even requires, one to view textual production in familiarly generic ways, even when this interpretation is at odds with the broader discursive practices within which the writer was working. Precisely these limitations would require that I reorient my argument here, for example, within a discussion of more traditional literary categories, that I sufficiently distinguish literary from oral confessions, and finally, that I delimit the office of the confession in its ecclesiastical setting rather than implicate it in a far wider set of discursive and historical formations that are everywhere bound up with the power one seizes, reproduces, or resists by writing "I." Instead, as I have argued, the wide and shifting influence of the confession participates in the production of the *I* who writes autobiography, as well as in the structures in which autobiography is evaluated.

This canonizing impulse determines Weintraub's evaluation of two autobiographies by women in a chapter on the lives of saints: Saint Teresa of Avila's *Life* and Mme Guyon's *Autobiography*. Weintraub does not emphasize Teresa's successful manipulation of the church/state's massive technologies of "policing." In fact, Teresa, who wrote at the instruction of her confessors from 1561, when she was forty-five, through revision and amplification in successive drafts to completion in 1565, was especially successful at enlisting sympathetic confessors who would edit sections of the autobiography which otherwise would have been judged heretical. Her establishment of this network was a necessary condition for authorizing and, finally, canonizing this *converso* (a Jew who became a Catholic) whose "truth" was already suspect. By omitting this information, Weintraub, in effect, decontextualizes Teresa's position and self-positioning within an elaborate network of power relations. Instead, he aestheticizes her text and judges her account appropriately devout, finding affecting grace in a simple and direct style. Teresa's subjectivism is always tempered by fidelity to one of the two models of self-representation he authorizes, *imitatio Christi* and *individuum ineffabile est:* "Her self-conception stayed within the tradition of the model life" (220).

A discussion of literary merit, however, always has ample room for gender politics. Whether female gender is coded as emotionalism, chattiness, or subjectivism is not as crucial here as the persistence of its coding as negativity, its presence authorizing the police to take notice. Mme Guyon, whose lengthy tome was written over the years 1686–1709, does not fare so well with Weintraub, for she strays egregiously from the models of selfhood which underlie autobiography's "proper form." Whereas Saint Teresa is easily incorporated into the tradition of mystical writing and her reputation therein is without challenge, Mme Guyon is a fugitive from the models Weintraub acknowledges. He is put off by her lack of taste and proper restraint, both in perception and in language; he disdains the "exuberance of her expressions" (223), her egotism, and finally, her maddening self-sufficiency. His major complaint focuses on Mme Guyon's erotic mysticism, which explicitly surfaces in her descriptions of dreams. In one such dream, she is taken to Mount Lebanon, where her divine spouse shows her a room with two beds. Mme Guyon wonders, "For whom are these? [Christ] answered: One for my mother, and the other for thee, my spouse." "Surely," Weintraub sniffs, "God deserves the right to a more tasteful reporting of his inspirations" (225). Although Mme Guyon is inspired by the same Holy Spirit whose most celebrated activity was to cause the Virgin Mary to conceive, Weintraub denies this form of modeling and, in that gesture, Mme Guyon's authenticity as an autobiographer.

Mme Guyon's great failure, for Weintraub, is that she is generally unimpressed by the model of humanism he so affectingly sketches throughout the critique. It is her effective resistance to either mode of self-conception and self-representation, either *imitatio* or *individuum ineffabile est*, which he finds dangerous. Thus, she falls outside the limits of what he defines as humanism and of the study of autobiography set by his scholarship: "Where mystic leanings overstepped the normative lines drawn to guard the existence of sinful mortals, a dangerous, uncontrolled and uncontrollable subjectivism opened up which should not be confused with the ideal of individuality" (227). "Mystic leanings" are seen as an unofficial, extrainstitutional, ex-static form of knowledge and, as such, threatening to the "normative lines" maintained by what Althusser described as the institutional state apparatus. For Weintraub, subjectivism describes all marginalized forms of self-conception and self-representation. His analysis does not discriminate between forms of subjectivism; that is not its intent. Yet the two-model grid, which was initially offered as heuristic, has, by the end of the book, taken the form of an interrogation. What does not conform is open to suspicion and censure. Weintraub stands in for Gerson's confessor and finds Mme Guyon, who has clearly not been as fortunate in her confessors as Saint Teresa, to be in error. Her version of truth strays from the powerful criteria concern-

4

Genders, Bodies, Identities

Representing Gender in Medieval Mysticism

When I write "the body," I see nothing in particular. To write "my body" plunges me into lived experience, particularity: I see scars, disfigurements, discolorations, damages, losses, as well as what pleases me. . . . To say "the body" lifts me away from what has given me a primary perspective. To say "my body" reduces the temptation to grandiose assertions.
—Adrienne Rich, "Notes toward the Politics of Location"

For the essentialist, the body occupies a pure, pre-social, pre-discursive space. . . . For the constructionist, the body is never simply there, rather it is composed of a network of effects continually subject to sociopolitical determination.
—Diana Fuss, *Essentially Speaking*

As a concept, the body is overdetermined, weighted by a variety of approaches—religious, philosophical, medical, moral, sexological—and set into motion as a politically and aesthetically meaningful figure in a range of texts.[1] How the body comes to be seen as "possessing"

[1] Much of feminist criticism has turned its attention toward the body. See, for example, Susan Rubin Suleiman, ed., *The Female Body in Western Culture* (Cambridge: Harvard University Press, 1986); Jane Gallop, *Thinking through the Body* (New York: Columbia University Press, 1988); and Sandra Lee Bartky, *Femininity and Domination: Studies in the Phenomenology of Oppression* (New York: Routledge, 1990). A body discourse of tremendous promise is being articulated by gay and lesbian studies and queer theory. See, for example, Teresa de Lauretis, guest ed., "Queer Theory: Lesbian and Gay Sexualities," *differences* 3 (Summer 1991); and Diana Fuss, ed., *Inside/Out: Lesbian Theories/Gay Theories* (New York: Routledge, 1991). Social anthropologists and historians, Pierre Bourdieu and Michel Foucault chief among them, have established the body as a major focus of study. See, for example, Bourdieu, *Outline of a Theory of Practice*; Foucault, *History of Sexuality*, vol. 1; and Foucault, *Discipline and Punish: The Birth of the Prison*, trans. Alan Sheridan (New York: Random House, 1977). Of the overdetermined body, Bourdieu argues: "In a class society, all the products of a given agent, by an essential

certain *inherent* and *natural* attributes such as "race" and "gender" is intricately related to the political and social representation of persons. As a figure of identity, the body seems abstract, transhistorical, both alien and sharable, at once no one's body and *the* body. So, too, it is the intimate ground of lived experience, the material body, a body with organs and skin. In current feminist debates about essentialism and constructionism, the meaning of the body is vigorously contested.[2] In both critical positions, the location of gender identity is at stake.

Thematic approaches to the body find it everywhere and draw conclusions about gender's evident solidity and reality from its recurrence in representation. What I want to do here is claim the body as evidence of certain preoccupations about gendered identity, not as evidence of gender. This shift in focus necessitates a reading beyond thematics and correspondences, beyond and perhaps against the logic of identity-in-similarity which supports a naturalized reading of bodies. I would not, then, seek to re-place the body in the natural world in an effort to locate texts and practices in and through which women were more fully embodied. Rather, I seek the body in the world it has made to appear natural, a world in which skin, genitals, and physiognomy, the surfaces of the body, are seen as a manifestation of an inner truth flowing in the blood, a world in which assumptions may be projected onto the body's exterior and then read as proof of an interior truth. Such is the case not only or even primarily with gender but also, and with far-reaching implications, with race and sexuality, with nationality and ethnicity. This is an inside/out view of the body in which "traits" are seen as expressions of deep characteristics that make their way to the surface, either in signs read easily on the body (as with "the mark of Cain," for example), or in acts. The body, in this construction, can't keep a secret: "Blood will tell." Although the fallacy of this reading of the body can be readily demonstrated, its persistence allows "sex" to cling to female bodies through the "fact" of sexual difference and "race" to cling

---

overdetermination, speak inseparably and simultaneously of his class—or, more precisely, his position in the social structure and his rising or falling trajectory—and of his (or her) body—or, more precisely, all the properties, always socially qualified, of which he or she is the bearer—sexual properties of course, but also physical properties, praised, like strength or beauty, or stigmatized" (*Outline of a Theory of Practice*, 87).

[2] Diana Fuss, *Essentially Speaking: Feminism, Nature, and Difference* (New York: Routledge, 1989), 5. The term "essentialism" has been so stigmatized in the late 1980s and early 1990s, its epithet-power is so effective, that to be accused of it can utterly dismiss an argument/critic.

to nonwhite bodies through the "fact" of racial difference. Upon the logic of taxonomy, identity hierarchies build. The ways in which such identity hierarchies are written in relation to bodies are deeply implicated in the discourses of identity and truth and in acts of self-representation.

The mystics show that the embeddedness or distance of what Rich names "my body" as distinct from "the body" is historically and discursively specific. For many of the women mystics, what distance there is from the body of Christ they seek to span, and what embeddedness there is in "my body" they seek to challenge. The perspective offered from "my body" reveals both the body's materiality and its fantastical possibilities. "The body," then, in mystical writing is a complex figure signifying closure as well as the capacity for interpenetration. Through representations of the body, the mystic figures her relation to Christ. Frequently in these texts, gender difference is another trope and female and male bodies are used to figure kinds of relationships. Here, though, male and female body tropes are more freely substitutable because of the frame within which representation occurs. The body of Christ as the ground of mystical experience provides the occasion for what can be called a counterdiscourse of gender. That is, according to the Bible, in Christ there is *no* male or female, and in the mystic's self-representation of the relationship between Christ's body and her own, there is *both* male and female. These are possibilities, and in this sense, the mystics offer a perspective on the contemporary debate between essentialism and constructionism. The mystics enjoin the terms of the debate as a dialectic. Their texts insist upon the interchangeability of male- and female-gendered body tropes within a single, reconceived body. In this way, mystical self-representation of the body resists the duality and finality of gender, and even the orthodox mystical texts that I discuss here narrativize gender less as an inevitable identity than as a focus for self-representational agency.

Both Julian of Norwich, on whom I will focus again here, and Saint Teresa of Avila, to whom I will turn later, carved out spaces, material and discursive, in which they could exchange their culture's constraints for boundaries of their own choosing. Julian and Teresa led increasingly cloistered lives and exchanged the pattern of marriage, childbearing and child rearing, and domestic labor for religious life. Julian chose contemplation and seclusion, whereas Teresa became a vigorous reformer of the Carmelite order in her effort to offer religious women even further enclosure. The especially complex *habitus* in which they dwelled was the body: their own bodies were enfolded by and enfolded the body of Christ.[3] Both Julian's and Teresa's life-changing spiritual experiences began as illnesses, that is, as disturbances in the body. Each produced a discourse evolving from the body in pain, through the body on the cross, to the ecstatic and risen body. Their autobiographics are inscribed within an orthodox religious discourse of identity and faith; yet, this discourse is interrupted in both Julian and Teresa through their resistance to the representation and interpretation of female-gendered bodies and identities as unfailingly secondary. Further, they re-eroticize the female body as the site of mystical experience and pleasure.

Mystical (self-) representation insists upon the simultaneous presence of Christ's body in the mystic's and the mystic's body in Christ's. The mystic's experience of her own body and visions is framed within the conceptual boundaries of Christ's body. For the body of Christ, which is symbolically and semiotically "feminized" as a vision of interpenetrative possibility, forms the ultimate frame within which emotional, somatic, and perceptual events occur. To unmake the human body by mortifying the flesh is to remake it in the image of Christ in his Passion. Bodily wounds (which both Julian and Teresa desired, received, and counted as the benefits of grace) replicate Christ's own fragile and broken flesh in an embodied sympathy. To share in the wounded body—pierced, penetrable, and made into flowing liquid (as in the blood and water that poured from Christ's side)—creates a matrix for re-membering.

Medieval women mystics were obsessed with the body as metaphor, as material, and as the intimate ground of ecstasy, healing, and suffering. The body becomes for them the *topos* where mysticism is situated. In her massively documented work *Holy Feast and Holy Fast*, Caroline Walker Bynum focuses on the significance of food in medieval religious women's lives in a way that foregrounds the connections between women's spirituality and women's bodies as operating along other lines than the Pauline, Augustine, or Platonic separation of spirit (soul) from body (matter). For religious women, the body is irreducibly plural in its capacity to signify different levels of experience. Thus, it is a cliché of interpretation to attribute to the mystics a

---

[3] I am using Bourdieu's sense of *habitus*: "The structures constitutive of a particular type of environment (e.g. the material conditions of existence characteristic of a class condition) produce *habitus*, systems of durable, transposable *dispositions*, structured structures predisposed to function as structuring structures, that is, as principles of the generation and structuring of practices and representations which can be objectively 'regulated' and 'regular' without in any way being the product of obedience to rules" (*Outline*, 72).

hatred of the body inferred from their mortification of the flesh, extreme food practices, and withdrawal from general society. Indeed, the mystics emphasize the body as a theater of tremendous potential for self-representation. If we reduce their desire to control the body to acquiescence or masochism, Bynum argues, we misread as passivity their passionate activity.

Bynum reinterprets asceticism as a focus *on* the body rather than abnegation of it: "Medieval efforts to discipline and manipulate the body should be interpreted more as elaborate changes rung upon the *possibilities* provided by fleshliness rather than as flights from physicality" (6). That is, Bynum suggests, the mortification of the flesh so central to women's piety which appears to be little other than a masochistic attack on the body, can be better understood as a way of grounding spiritual experience in the body. Indeed, some of this behavior borders on the exotic in its creative playing out of the basic motifs of fasting and self-flagellation. Extensive study of this topic provokes Bynum to comment that "reading the lives of fourteenth- and fifteenth-century women saints greatly expands one's knowledge of Latin synonyms for whip, thong, flail, chain, etc. Ascetic practices commonly reported in these *vitae* include wearing hair shirts, binding the flesh tightly with twisted ropes, rubbing lice into self-inflicted wounds, denying oneself sleep, adulterating food and water with ashes or salt, performing thousands of genuflections, thrusting nettles into one's breasts, and praying barefoot in the winter" (210). Historians and other commentators have evinced an aversion to studying the women who pray for debilitating illnesses. Their intensity obliterates the category of passivity and mimetically reproduces the Passion and, in so doing, challenges commentators to read them in relation to gender codes by which the women themselves are less than fully bound. Thus this critical aversion makes it ever clearer that the "impropriety" of religious medieval women's discursive and material practices is specifically a reading effect, a displacement of the revulsion they "inspire" in many chroniclers. Similarly, a post-Freudian interpretation of sexuality as genital and directed toward a heterosexual object misses the rich sensuality of women's spirituality. And it seems equally limited historically to conclude that this behavior results from sublimation. A brief look at specific writings should reveal how little sublimated are the desires they describe and how oriented toward producing the body as a proof text of devotion were their practices.

For example, we know little more of Hadewijch, a Flemish leader of a beguine group who wrote between 1220 and 1240, than what is suggested by brief autobiographical references in her visions, poetry, and letters. But we do know that the union with the desired other, Christ, for which she yearned passionately and which defined her sense of self was figured as the fusion of their bodies in hers. Her representation of union emphasizes the orality of hungering for, tasting, and eating God in a way that intertwines nourishment and eroticism: "They [her self and God] penetrate each other in such a way that neither of the two distinguishes himself from the other. But they abide in one another in fruition, mouth in mouth, heart in heart, body in body, soul in soul" (qtd. in Bynum, 156). So central is her sense of the body in this context that she proliferates activities in which the bodies may join as her mode of explanation. The images of "mouth in mouth, heart in heart, body in body" indicate and extend the difference between simple contact and the graphic indwelling for which she longs: not mouth *to* mouth, heart *to* heart, but mouth *in* mouth, an image of desire as well as speech. For if God's mouth is in Hadewijch's mouth, she may speak him. The authoritative act of speaking in God's voice through God's mouth is then also self-authorizing. Hadewijch's self-evidence is authorized by God through this doubling and incorporation of their "bodies." But what, then, does God's body represent? If her heart is in God's, she trades on a body symbolism of love, of course, but also presents an external and internal fusion of bodies. Not only are organs joined but surfaces and orifices. For Hadewijch, the physical image of God's body is utterly broached and broachable: she introjects her own body into this figure, complete encorpsulation. Whereas mystical experience is figured at the boundary between the human and the divine, the body does not persist as an unbreachable surface.

The trope of commingled bodies and of commingling identities within a single body, represented through Christ's divinity in humanity, is assumed by women mystics. Bynum clarifies this point in her commentary on Hadewijch, to whom, she says "biological images for the love offered and received by the self are images of the utmost intimacy. To love is to give one's bodily fluid as food, to carry a foetus within oneself, to chew or to be chewed; it is not merely to kiss but also to feel the other within one's own bowels or heart. To love is to engulf and be engulfed, to masticate and to assimilate, to flow out with nurture so that one's body becomes food for another" (157). Wanting this and not having it is agony. When this desire goes unfulfilled and the experience borders on torment, the implied hunger in the scene leaps forward. In her poem, "Love's Seven Names," Hadewijch invokes this tense simultaneity in poetic antithesis:

What is sweetest in Love is her tempestuousness,
Her deepest abyss is her most beautiful form:

. . . . .

To die of hunger for her is to feed and taste;
Her despair is assurance;
Her sorest wounding is all curing;
To waste away for her sake is to be in repose;

. . . . .

Her tender care enlarges our wounds;

. . . . .

Her table is hunger. (qtd. in Bynum: 158)

Denial and longing may be coupled in her vision of love, but in her visions of God, the differences between their bodies dissolve in an orgasmic melting away of physical boundaries. In this passage, which should make any reference to her "sublimation" seem, at the very least, inadequate, Hadewijch describes meeting God:

He came in the form and clothing of a Man, as he was on the day when he gave his body for the first time. . . . he gave himself to me in the shape of the Sacrament, in its outward form . . . and then he gave me to drink from the chalice. . . . After that he came himself to me, took me entirely in his arms, and pressed me to him; and all my members felt his in full felicity, in accordance with the desire of my heart and my humanity. . . . So I was outwardly satisfied and fully transported. Also then, for a short while, I had the strength to bear this; but soon, after a short time, I lost that manly beauty outwardly in the sight of his form. I saw him completely come to nought and so fade and all at once dissolve that I could no longer distinguish him within me. Then it was to me as if we were one without difference. (qtd. in Bynum, 156)

In this passage, God first performs the duties of a priest, but God's and Hadewijch's attention turns directly toward increasing intimacy. So far from sublimation, these equally erotic and ecstatic visions dominate women's (and many men's) mystical writing. Through a carefully elaborated movement of incorporation, Hadewijch assimilates Christ's body into her own and remakes his Passion into their passion. She connects Christ's Passion on the cross to its symbolic enactment in the Eucharist in a conventional way and then adds to that the dimension of her own longing. It becomes an embrace like no other. Following from this passion for the body of Christ, some women became so obsessed with the Eucharist, that the body of Christ was the only food they could ingest, and they would rush from church to church in order to take communion repeatedly. Many would vomit out an unconsecrated host, a feat of miraculous discernment. In their eucharistic frenzy, women were responding intensely to the notion that the single perfect sacrifice provided by Christ's life and death is open to infinite repetition in the Eucharist.

The Mass emphasizes the structure of interpenetration. When one eats the body of Christ and drinks his blood, the promise of resurrection is renewed. Because the Eucharist as a ritual focuses on eating, the body of Christ as food becomes a part of the person taking communion; it is intimately nutrition. In communion, the boundaries between one's own body and Christ's body become permeable: one is no longer separate from the other, no longer alone, no longer, that is, an isolated self. Taking communion represents a devotional act toward Christ; one is instructed to "do this in remembrance of Me." Christ's body is taken into one's own, is re-membered in a human being's own renewed flesh and then formed, through the community, into the renewed body of Christ.

The miraculous bodies the mystics envision and inhabit are virtual fantasies of open wounds, flowing liquid, and porous bodies. Blood, tears, and milk stream abundantly.[4] The blood of Christ is as resonant an image as his body. Recall here how Julian of Norwich's first revelation, which remained present to her throughout the duration of all the "shewings," focused on bleeding, the first issue of Christ's wounding: "And at once I saw the red blood trickling down from under the garland, hot, fresh, and plentiful, just as it did at the time of his passion when the crown of thorns was pressed on to the blessed head of God-and-Man, who suffered for me" (*Revelations*, 66). The garland itself has disappeared from her vision: Christ is simply seen in his wounding and bleeding. The menstrual blood, the blood of childbirth, the virgin's blood all signal women's sexuality, and by association, the metonymic links between his blood and her blood make the possibilities for *imitatio* seem even richer to some. If love can be a wounding act ("For God so loved the world"), wounding can be a loving act. Medieval women mystics demonstrate no squeamishness in the face of this flowing, liquefying, bloodied body, which is so suggestively engaged in the passion of giving birth to the new body that will rise from Christ's labor. Yet neither heterosexual experience nor reproduction are prerequisites for making these compelling con-

---

[4] When I began reading the autobiographies of Saint Teresa and Julian of Norwich, as well as the lives of other women mystics, after studying French feminist theory, I felt I had found the bodies I assumed were strictly metaphorical.

nections. Nor would they have been sought by the majority of religious women. Although the transformations of the female body in
pregnancy and labor are certainly common enough for many women
to observe or experience, childbearing would have been no more
likely a personal experience for most religious women than their own
crucifixion and resurrection. In fact, many religious women's daily
lives would have been more filled with images of the latter than the
former. Their experiences with bodily transformation, with the theat-
rical dimension of the body, were acted out through their skill and
flair with flails, thongs, hair shirts, and other accoutrements.

Correspondingly, because women's devotional practices and the
substance of their faith were so structured on the imitation of this
particular body, there was virtually no limit to what they would do to
heal and merge with the broken body of humanity: they not only
tended the diseased and quarantined and broke the social boundary
between well and ill bodies; they also embraced the diseased body
vigorously and intimately by, for example, drinking pus and licking
open sores. In other instances, their own bodies became the source of
food. Although they were frequently engaged in heroic fasts and
severely limited diets that prevented the natural processes of ex-
cretion and menstruation, women's bodies frequently produced
nourishment. For even as the ordinary processes of alimentation
ceased, extraordinary bodily effluvia were produced: they exuded
sweet odors, oils, and milk that fed and strengthened others. Hagio-
graphers, if not the mystics themselves, make this connection explicit
when they claim that by converting the limited resources of the body
into supernatural sustenance, the women saints and mystics associated with eating and feeding miracles reproduced Christ's miraculous multiplication of the loaves and fishes described in Matthew
15:32–38.

Bynum has argued that "since Christ's body was a body that
nursed the hungry, both men and women naturally assimilated the
ordinary female body to it" (272). Yet, this "natural" identification is
problematical here. Bynum infers it from the vast record of art and
iconography which records this connection and from men's and
women's (lay and clerical) writing. This may have been a "natural"
connection, but one, it must be emphasized, that emerges "naturally"
from ideological imperatives. When the physicality and humanity of
Christ is emphasized, Bynum argues, it will be linked with the sym-
bolization of woman as flesh, and woman's body as food. The connection is most explicit in the Eucharist: when Christ becomes food

on the altar, his body behaves as the nurturing female body does (268). These are cultural discourses that Bynum elides somewhat with the language of natural phenomena by taking gender to be located in the female body that is primarily engaged in the experiences of pregnancy, birthing, and lactation. Although this was certainly the normative experience for medieval women, it should be remembered that the vast majority of women living in convents and having visionary experiences would not have experienced this "normal" relation to their own bodies. Yet the persistence of this imagery indicates the extent to which the discourses of identity, gender, and the body are intertwined and together constitute the technologies of autobiography in which mystical self-representation occurred.

It is not that gender disappears in mystical self-representation focused on the body, but its ideological construction as "limitation" and "flaw" is escaped in a particular way. As an identity, mysticism scrambles gender logic's effective functioning concerning women and reproductivity. Mystical identity is not defined or understood as building from gender logic. As I have maintained, gender logic interprets the following discontinuous steps (or demands that they be interpreted) as a natural and inevitable sequence: first, sex is interpreted as being at the base of gender; sex can then be interpreted as a natural cause and gender as a cultural effect and, therefore, heterosexual desire, in a constitutive and catachrestical swerve, as a natural effect of a cultural cause. When gender is understood as an opposition derived from a power relation between men and women, mystical identity can be seen as standing outside gender and can be figured in relation to a body that neither resembles nor redeems sexual difference as a natural given. The body of Christ offers something other than the absence of "male or female." In its anatomical maleness and its semiotic femaleness, it enacts two positionalities, to use a semiotic term, of desire. That is, we see the desire of and for both the female and the male functioning within this figure in a way that effectively undercuts the phallic mode of desiring.

Christ's body, semiotically, is a feminized body, insofar as it conflates woman and wound. Teresa de Lauretis reminds us: "It is still, to be sure, the 'wound' which psychoanalysis correctly identifies as the mark of woman, the inscription of (sexual) difference in the female body" (*Alice Doesn't*, 101). But what a wound makes legible, in Christ's body as well as Adam's, is that something has happened on this site: the wound in Christ's side, the wound in Adam's side contrast to a natural opening in women's bodies—the vagina—which is construed as the fearsome site of castration.[5] The psychoanalytic linking of woman and wound, as de Lauretis observes, is meant to symbolize "the figure of an irreducible difference, of that which is elided, left out, not represented, or representable" (101). Religious women interpreted this similarity not as lack but as a symbol of their power. When women hunger for Christ and long for union with him, their desire is not reducible to desire for the phallus but persists as desire for the whole body of Christ and especially for a body capable of representing the experiences of women. A startling number of women's miracles involved bodily change, and their meditations on and visions of Christ most frequently focus on the fantastic changes he underwent in the Passion and Resurrection. The specific form of their miracles and piety seems intimately linked to their modeling of a body capable of miraculous transformation: from the Incarnation through the bodily demonstration preceding the Ascension.

To read Christ's body as a figure that resists the logic of gender and the inevitable translation of sex into gender (and then into heterosexual desire and identity) allows us to see how fundamentally his textualization—the process whereby he becomes a textual figure and is circulated meaningfully within discourse—maps a contradictory discourse of gender hierarchy into religious discourse. We can also reconstruct how learning to read this text informs the lives of Saint Teresa and Julian of Norwich, who exchange normative secular practices of femininity for a lifelong attention to an eroticized body discourse that has moved beyond gender. The mystic learns to position herself in relation to this body and thereby reread herself as a subject in the process of being "oned" with God. Thus, her choice is not between two positions of gender difference, in which she learns to take her place as the "unrepresentable" or the "repressed" in phallic discourse. Rather, by rejecting the either/or dilemma of gender, she gains revisionary leverage against the cultural role prescribed in marriage. To join a convent, to choose the society of religious women and to invest desire in the Scriptures and the body of Christ, enacted a

[5] Christ's miraculous birth repeats God's creation of human life in the garden and partially redeems female sin by having a human female give birth to the Lord. Yet this miracle, this incredible narrative, capitalizes on certain male anxieties concerning the impossibility of proving paternity. Historically, such anxiety has prompted male birth fables (for example, Athena being born from the head of Zeus), which appropriate the female role in birthing. It is interesting that Solomon's wisdom was tested on a point that is usually without controversy: deciding who is the true mother. A test for finding the true father would have been seen as mundanely impossible. No man is involved in creating Jesus: he is a product of divinity and femininity.

change in social reality, for the history of the mystical tradition, which is so significant to understanding the development of faith and theology in this period, is largely defined by the mystical experiences of women and the ways in which that culture came to understand the centrality of that definition.

Pain and ecstasy are connected throughout the crucial concept of Christian salvation. The health or wholeness to be granted by salvation (from the Latin *salve*) results from Christ's agony on the cross. This ambivalence is condensed in a scriptural passage frequently cited as testimony to God's love: "For God so loved the world that he gave his only begotten Son, that whoever believes in him should not perish but have eternal life" (John 3:16). God's love is figured in the act of handing over his child to unimaginable pain from which Christ emerges as the image of salvation. This gift is fraught with levels of sacrifice and suffering which are not lost on those for whom *imitatio Christi* offers a compelling model of identity. The relationship between pain and ecstasy occurs as the imagination fuses the suffering self with the image of Christ during the Passion. This identification releases pain into possibility. The imitation of Christ is fully enacted if the person praying for and then suffering from pain is healed, but the sufferer merges with Christ at every point along the continuum even if s/he succumbs to illness (and to die in the state of grace conferred by a holy illness is a frequent feature of hagiography). In this shared experience, the sufferer experiences pain within a context that offers healing and resurrection as its closing frame. The promise of closure demonstrates the compelling lure of *imitatio*, for the one healed has not only symbolically joined Christ in his ridicule and scourging at the hands of tormentors but has merged with the broken and suffering body in the Passion and thereby receives the "new body" of the Resurrection. Ultimately, to be washed in the blood of the lamb becomes an act all the more precious for its choice of gift: the blood and body of Christ. Scriptural examples mingling pain with salvation in the figure of Christ's body abound. Indeed, the promise at work in the crucifixion saves the scene from its purely grotesque aspect. Objects and states that are not available in the natural world (visions and miracles) or are meaningless as natural states (illness, misery, hunger, pain, near death) are invested with meaning and transformed into miracles. An economy of absence and scarcity can be read as one of presence and abundance, where the lack of food, health, and comfort form occasions for God to fill up a need. Without the end of the story—the Resurrection—Christ's Passion is reduced to torture or to experience without meaning.

Again, in this context, Julian of Norwich's preparation to emulate the death of Christ is significant. She reports: "When I was half way through my thirty-first year God sent me an illness which prostrated me for three days and nights. On the fourth night I received the last rites of Holy Church as it was thought I could not survive till day" (64). Julian carefully prefigures her vision of the crucifixion by recording her own bodily symptoms with clinical precision: "Thus I endured till day. By then my body was dead from the waist downward. . . . Then the rest of my body began to die, and I could hardly feel a thing. As my breathing became shorter and shorter I knew for certain that I was passing away" (65). Immediately thereafter, the pain ceases and she is sensibly aware that the change is "a special miracle of God, and not something natural" (65). Her first thought as soon as the pain eases is to assimilate her experience to Christ's Passion because she originally prayed to receive three wounds: "Then it came suddenly to my mind that I should ask for the second wound of our Lord's gracious gift, that I might in my own body fully experience and understand his blessed passion. I wanted his pain to be my pain" (66).

As in confession, mystical experience lies at the boundary between activity and passivity. The structure of reception seems passive because it depends on the mysterious action of grace. If one could earn a vision, God's freedom would be limited by the realm of human action and God's dispensation of gifts would be based on the human notion of merit, that is, of labor and reward. Also, the experience often occurs in conjunction with illness. One receives, suffers, is visited from outside by a vision. It is not an experience attributable to a source in the natural world; yet it is experienced as occurring within the self in such a way that the boundaries of identity expand to include the "supernatural" other. So passionately is the other desired that the experience becomes active. Julian shapes her visionary experience by praying for an illness, specifies what she wants to result from the experience, and guides the pace and depth of the revelations themselves. Thus, the experience occurs at a whole series of intersections emphasizing the proximity of passivity and activity and the differences within rather than between those paired terms. Voluntarity/abandon, pain/rapture, doubt/faith, grace/merit, denial/exultation, and concealment/revelation mark the boundaries that mystical experience destabilizes even as it represents them. For each pair is generally subsumed under the leading couple, self (mystic)/other (variously and simultaneously God, Christ, Holy Spirit), which at first divides their roles in relation to passivity and activity, only to fuse them in the mystical experience of interpenetration.

Julian's text emphasizes its autobiographics, those elements of self-representational practices and discourses, rather than its consolidated status as an autobiography, for in *The Revelations* Julian refines autobiography to an instant—the day of the "shewings," May 8, 1373—and reinvents time from that point. Her text is stripped of the external trappings of autobiography; she represents them in almost schematic and demonstrative form. Spiritual autobiography now seems to come with a whole set of rhetorical baggage that constitutes the form, but Julian travels light. She represents the aspects of life on which autobiographers minimally focus; yet, she represents them only as they further her relationship with the divine other she has now incorporated as her self. Julian revises the experience of being acted on by illness, of being a prisoner to a body that suffers; passivity turns to passion as her wounded body is conflated with Christ's. This assimilation of bodies and identities through self-representation forms the ground from which meaning will henceforth proceed. With the body in pain at the center of her mystical experience, Julian of Norwich reinvents her world. Her vision of God's love and Christ's Passion transfigures her own way of seeing so thoroughly that the "shewings" and the twenty years of reflection between her first and second manuscripts focus on self-representational autobiographics, if not on the narrative of a life.

In her most striking theological innovation, Julian attributes the female role of mothering to the trinity and to Mary, not only in the tasks of nurturing and in the interpenetration of self and other which can characterize the mother-child bond but primarily in the physicality of the mother who of her own flesh creates the child. During the twenty years of reflection, Julian evolves a symbology grounded in the embodiment of faith promised in the Incarnation and the Passion. God, Christ, and Mary are incorporated into the consuming matrix of mothering, and the multiplication of mothers directly sustains her abiding sense of the revelations that "Love was his meaning" (211). Clearly, the relationship in which love "means" most completely and resonantly for Julian is mothering. She considers it significant that God assumes our fleshiness through the Incarnation and thereby has a share in all the pain to which the body is heir. By taking on our physical humanity, he also becomes a creation of the female body: just as a woman gives of herself to the fetus she bears, Julian suggests, so God gives of himself to Christ and, hence, to all humanity. By bearing the Word in her body, Mary is the mother of us all. For Julian, the ultimate symbol of this maternity becomes Christ "in whom we are endlessly borne":

For when God united himself to our humanity in the Virgin's womb he took also our sensual soul. When he took it—having included us all in himself—he united it to our essential nature. In this uniting he was perfect man, for Christ who unites himself with everyone who is to be saved is perfect man. So our Lady is *our* Mother too and, in Christ, we are incorporated in her, and born of her. She who is the Mother of our Saviour is Mother of all who are to be saved in our Saviour. Indeed, our Saviour himself is our true Mother for we are ever being born of him, and shall never be delivered! (164)

For Julian, Christ's body remains the one in which the divine and human merge and thus becomes the matrix or the womb that begets redemption and rebirth. Christ's injunction that one must be born again does not displace the first birth from female flesh as a lowly source to be shrugged off for a new creation; rather, Christ shares in a most embodied human function: pregnancy and birthing. Only through Christ's full submission to the body can all be saved, and salvation throughout Julian's text is symbolized not by a disembodied "father" who is responsible for contributing the soul or spirit or reason (as Aristotelian physiology would have it, and which Julian would probably have known) but by a "mother" who gives the child its physicality by bearing it in her body. As Julian sees it, the mother is the one "in whom our parts are kept unseparated" (160). Thus the possibility of wholeness promised in her concept of "oneing" is fulfilled.

For Julian to equate Christ's humanity with the mother's body is consistent with her theology, which was never seen as heretical, and with the medieval conception of woman as body and as food. Her elaboration of the concept, however, distinguishes her. Julian's emphasis on this imagery collects both theme and structure in such a way that the thematic aspects of the "shewings" are tethered to the matrix of mothering and love she sees everywhere. Her explanation of the revelations resists linear exegesis mainly because its structure is assimilative, as the movement of the passage just quoted indicates.

The centrality of motherhood in Julian's writing has prompted speculation about her relationship with her own mother. Jennifer Heimmel believes that Julian's development of the idea of God's maternity surpasses that of her predecessors in "new length, innovation, and directness": "For Julian the statement of God's maternity is no simple invocation or comparison, but a repeated, insistent reality. It is clearly a form of relationship which finds a natural and essential place in her thoughts and expression. . . . For Julian, there is ultimately no human relationship able to give an idea more exact and complete of the love of God than feminine maternal love" ("God Is Our Mother," 49–50). Surely, Heimmel claims, Julian must have inferred the qualities of motherhood she attributes to God from her relationship with her mother. Similarly, David Knowles finds little in conventional theology or mystical writing to account for Julian's dominating focus on this theme. Compelled by the appearance of "autobiography" in a text that refines the autobiographical to a point that is embryonic in its potential, Knowles asserts that "the concept of motherhood touched a very deep chord in her own being. We may remember that her own mother was by her during her grave illness, and made ready to close her eyes when she supposed that her daughter was dead. It is possible, also, that it was she in whose well-being Julian took particular interest. In any case, many of the phrases that follow seem to reflect deep memories of acts of love received in the past."[6]

Knowles is on highly hypothetical ground here, as his language suggests. Such phrases as "it is possible . . . in any case . . . seem . . . deep memories" reflect the problems of reading an autobiography that resists biographical information and inscribes, instead, auto-biographics drawn from a range of discursive practices. Knowles's and Heimmel's speculations about biography are motivated by the autobiographical form (the confession) in which Julian works. Yet the passage from The Revelations which Knowles offers to substantiate his musing on Julian's mother only hollowly suggests a physical other: "This fine and lovely word Mother is so sweet and so much its own that it cannot properly be used of any but him, and of her who is his own true Mother—and ours. In essence motherhood means love and kindness, wisdom, knowledge, goodness. Though in comparison with our spiritual birth our physical birth is a small, unimportant, straightforward sort of thing, it still remains that it is only through his working that it can be done at all by his creatures" (170).

Julian's account of Jesus as mother here and throughout the text does more to obscure a specific human mother than to suggest one. The maternity of Jesus makes Julian his child and thus displaces an earthly mother. Gender is thereby denaturalized, for it no longer attaches persons to their acts according to gender expectations. By focusing on the textuality of "mother," on the word and its significa-tions, Julian removes it from the signifying chain of material refer-ence: she translates anatomy into lexicon and selects out the words from material life which she would reserve for her own ecstasy. Julian

[6] David Knowles, The English Mystical Tradition (London: Burns, 1961), 128.

continues to use words that refer to earthly intimacy for intimacy with God. Spiritual rapture and communion come to replace familial attachments: Christ is mother and father, sister and brother, trusted friend and passionate lover.

Indeed, her reclusive life replicates the way she removes words from the world and devotes them to her lifelong meditation on the revelations. Her figures of identity focus on images of enfolding and ever-deepening enclosure which mime the physical enclosure she chose when she became an anchoress. Images of clothing—of "knitting," "joining," and "uniting"—establish the dynamics of a relationship that fuses the immateriality of spirit with the fleshiness of creation: "For just as the body is clothed in its garments, and the flesh in its skin, and the bones in their flesh, and the heart in its body, so too are we, soul and body, clothed from head to foot in the goodness of God" (70). The revelations are interpretable as a womb of self-imagery, one in which Julian is born and from which she will never come out. Both the mystical experience and the years of recording and revising them demonstrate the passionate patience she devoted to this (self-) representation of bodies, ecstasy, and identity.

To write about rapture as a way of defining one's identity, as both Julian and Teresa do, is to make visible and permanent an invisible and ephemeral experience, but only in the most difficult of conditions. For Christianity is founded on a single exemplary life and continues to renew itself in the spectacle of the Passion. Christ's miraculous birth and ministry set the stage for the climactic acts of the Passion and the Resurrection. So full an example was he, so successful an experiment, that God need never again become so fully human, nor any human so fully God-like: and in this balancing act, Christ maintains that difference and holds the worlds in tension. Thus, the imitation of Christ is a difficult road, not an easy ride to salvation. The way to God is clearer after the Incarnation because one has an advocate, a mediator, and an exemplum. At the same time, however, any imitation of Christ is inherently doomed from the start; thus, it is difficult "to take up the cross and follow" insofar as it is necessarily a belated task.

As the focus of faith, the image of Christ forms the standard for judging the acceptability of natural objects. Objects in the world anchor the mystic to the dynamic of loss and absence simultaneously inscribed as presence: things of this world help at first to construct a bond with God because this world is seen as God's handiwork; yet, natural objects soon come to be inimical to the saint, for they are not, finally, her goal. They offer less and less satisfaction for spiritual desire. In fact, they may draw the mystic away from her appropriate object of desire: Christ. So little satisfaction does the material world offer that the mystic is driven further into the imagination for solace. And the images formed from objects in the world must be revised as metaphors, symbols, and signs of God rather than as things in themselves lest the world be experienced falsely as substituting for the presence of God instead of evoking, painfully and sensuously, God's absence. The act of imagining takes place in the realm of images, of course, with no act apart from its image. The imagination is detectable not only in its creation of images—that is, in its making up—but also as it invests available images (those furnished by the church) with meaning.

Memory can also be an imaginative act: for the apostles, the remembered Christ may have been a disappointment compared to the living person, but compared to an absent and dead Christ, the memory is vibrant, comforting, and more present than the absent Christ. Absence is graspable in the dimension of loss and is not perceptible by the senses. The one-dimensionality of memory recovers some of that loss as constitutive of the remembered Christ. He must be dead, absent, to be resurrected; thus, his renewal in history depends on his absence. Re-membering, like imagining, is an act of making him up and thus no longer passive. The activity of transforming absence into presence is a project always already heavy with loss. Thus prayer in this context can be seen as a technology of autobiography for the mystic as it allows for self-representation in relation to a discourse of truth and identity.

What we can see from the preceding discussion is how very rich and flexible an object of desire the body of Christ can be, for in contrast to what one might expect to follow in the way of religious practices from the narrowness of orthodox faith, the expansive body of Christ constructs a tremendously varied body of self-representational response.

A Lover's Discourse: Identity/Body Politics in Self-Representation

> The body of the text subsumes all the words of the female body
> . . . To recite one's own body, to recite the body of the other, is
> to recite the words of which the book is made up. The fascina-
> tion for writing the never previously written and the fascination
> for the unattained body proceed from the same desire.
> —Monique Wittig, *The Lesbian Body*

The passion to be inscribes her body.
Until we find each other, we are alone.
—Adrienne Rich, "Hunger," *The Dream of a Common Language*

God of thy goodness give me thy self.
—Julian of Norwich, *The Revelations of Divine Love*

The concept of the "body" has been a simultaneous focus of and stumbling block to feminism. The extent to which "gender" comes to be understood as an intransigent feature of the body, especially of the female body, localizes feminist discourse in a kind of "no place" because the female body is not so much a permanent location of feminist representation and action as a concept that in both its literality and figurality is caught up within historical and discursive formations. The medieval mystics were positioned differently in relation to the gendered body from either the figure of Eve or their nonaristocratic female contemporaries in twelfth- through fourteenth-century England (not all of the mystics were aristocrats, to be sure; still, one way a woman from a wealthy family could escape the marriage plot was by joining a convent); nor did they occupy the same place as many women who currently position themselves as "women" within religious discourses and practices. The body as the stable location of gender is vigorously resisted by the changing representations of gender, bodies, and identities in self-representational texts. There are two related approaches, then, to exploring the place of the body within the technologies of autobiography. The first approach locates the writer in relation to the technologies of gender in order to understand the extent to which the body is taken as the site of a single stable gender identity. The second approach considers the extent to which the writer locates her identity in the body and how that degree of embodiment shapes the focus of self-representation.

A persistent feature of texts that conjoin women's self-representation and writing the body is to link the desire for what Monique Wittig calls the "unattained body" with the desire for self-representation. For Wittig, eros and ego "proceed from the same desire." Wittig employs the metaphorical substitution of body for text, drawing, in part, on the conventional metaphorization of bodies of knowledge (the body of the text, the author's corpus, etc.).[7] Adrienne Rich, like Wittig, locates lesbian desire in the body as the site of a passionate quest.[8] While Julian of Norwich may seem out of place

[7] Monique Wittig, *The Lesbian Body*, trans. David Le Vay (Boston: Beacon, 1986), 6–7.
[8] Adrienne Rich, "Hunger," in *The Dream*, 14.

in this context, she too is driven by a desire for an unattained "body," the body of Christ, which she also figures as God's "self": "God of thy goodness give me thy self." All three women use figures of the body to represent the location of solace or satisfaction as an intimate joining with and even incorporation of the "other." As a mystic, Julian is positioned in relation to real and fantastic bodies: she represents the boundary between Christ's body and her own as fluid, their bodies substitutable, their desires mutually evocative. The possibility of such interchangeability and "indwelling" grounds mystical experience, but I want to emphasize how both Wittig's lesbian discourse and Julian of Norwich's mystical discourse invoke figures of the body to represent intersubjectivity. The female body is a significant trope of self-representation in both medieval mystical texts and contemporary feminist writing. The female body may represent a space of mutuality, an interpenetrated, knowing, and desiring habitation for the self and other, and it may thus come to represent, both metaphorically and metonymically, the "self." Passion and ecstasy characterize this representation of the body as a locus of self-in/and-other positioning, as well as the attendant desires of hunger and longing which drive it.

The autobiographics of medieval mystical self-representation and some contemporary lesbian writing are analogous in their challenge to the framing power of genre, to Roland Barthes's notion of a lover's discourse, a discourse that breaks from the prescribed modes of analysis and commentary in order to "simulate" its subject. Barthes describes his intention to "stage an utterance, not an analysis," by simulating a lover's discourse through his "restoration" of its "fundamental person, the *I*":

> Everything follows from this principle: that the lover is not to be reduced to a simple symptomal subject, but rather that we hear in his voice what is "unreal," i.e., intractable. . . . The description of the lover's discourse has been replaced by its simulation, and to that discourse has been restored its fundamental person, the *I*, in order to stage an utterance, not an analysis. What is proposed, then, is a portrait—but not a psychological portrait; instead, a structural one which offers the reader a discursive site: the site of someone speaking within himself, *amorously*, confronting the other (the loved object), who does not speak" (*A Lover's Discourse*, 3).

Barthes constructs the subject of a lover's discourse as "a discursive site" for the reader, "the site of someone speaking within [her]self, *amorously*, confronting the other (the loved object), who does not speak." He prepares a discursive site in the same way a lover might prepare the setting of erotic possibility. Surely, in this passage, some celebration is at hand despite the silence of the other, for a restoration is promised—not through a heroic return, however, but through the liberation of a lover into the discourse of restoration. The site of this restoration is discursive, and the discourse is one of simulation. Hence, the erotics of the scene, though unchastened, cannot deny loss and the impossibility of a return to an unproblematized "real." Here, simulation is preferable to analysis, though any closer proximity to "truth" is dismissed. And in this formulation, Barthes is very close to the notion of self-representation and its relation to a desiring and desired body "simulated" by the mystics and by Wittig and Rich. Barthes's representation of intersubjectivity constructs subjectivity as the textual presence of an absent other in the body of writing. The following discussion links the self-representation of divine and human bodies and identities to the notion of a lover's discourse and examines this link as a form of autobiographics.

The interchangeability of selves for which Julian petitions—"God of thy goodness give me thy self"—illustrates how notions of the "self" differ historically. Julian embraces the possibility that her very "self" may be inhabited, dispersed, and reimagined by another. Indeed, as a believer, she would gladly abandon a lonely and hungering self for the redoubling plenitude offered by God's "self"-infusion. Whereas Julian anticipated this experience as a tremendous boon, a contemporary perspective would no doubt regard the potential displacement of identity more ambivalently. Self-sufficient and autonomous "individuals" would probably not experience themselves as profoundly penetrable by the Holy Spirit, nor, conversely, would they conceive of the Holy Spirit as the medium in which they live, move, and have their being. The desire for such experience and the particular form it takes are shaped by cultural factors, and our ability to interpret their expression is similarly bounded by our own historicity.

The particular problem here lies in the lingering mythic legacy manifested in depictions of female spirituality and sexuality. For example, when a woman desires to be filled with the Holy Spirit, the conventional analogy between empty vessel and Woman is repeated when she is seen as a passive receptacle, without agency or volition, waiting to submit and to serve. This prior assumption has been mobilized to interpret the specific form of Julian's request for God's gift throughout her *Revelations*. But we could considerably displace this assumption by noting the extent to which Julian has focused all her will and longing on self-transformation so that she and God would be "oned"

in spirit and in her flesh. While the plea is phrased humbly to acknowledge that such a gift comes by grace alone ("of thy goodness"),
Julian agitates for it so intensely that her "self" becomes defined, and
not obliterated, through the process.

Her wish to enflesh the spirit and to bear the Word represents a
culturally feminized function: the acceptance of service, submission,
and suffering. This marks the linkage of identity politics (a politics
that stabilizes a prior, existing essence, such as "women," and locates
it as the origin and audience of feminism) with body politics (a politics
that defines this essence as a property of all female bodies). But we
can see that this way of being in the world is prescribed scripturally
for the company of all believers. The selflessness and marginality that
has been culturally constructed as "woman's place" signifies differently in a medieval Christian context. Whereas the abandonment of
the self in other contexts—the family, work, politics, and so forth—
defines the powerlessness of women, the ability to shift the grounds
of identity from self to God in religious life represents the most fully
empowered human condition. The chiasmatic reversal in power between the self in a secular context and selflessness in a spiritual (here,
Christian) context points to a difference *within* selfhood, for as Barbara Johnson reminds us, "what is often most fundamentally dis-
agreed upon is whether a disagreement arises out of the complexities
of fact or out of the impulses of power . . . the differences *between*
entities (prose and poetry, man and woman, literature and theory,
guilt and innocence) are shown to be based on a repression of differences *within* entities, ways in which an entity differs from itself"
(*Critical Difference*, x). Perhaps, then, "selflessness" should be more
accurately defined as "fullness," wherein self and other exceed and
restructure the boundary *between* them as a redefinition of a space
within. Julian sees the individual and the Holy Spirit as dwelling
within the same flesh, which is in turn encircled by Spirit. The layers
of enfolding which mark her experience represent an achievement
and not a position of little worth. Hence, when we speak of the
earliest stirrings of self-representation in women's autobiography, it is
important to reveal the stratification within identity and gender as
concepts and experience, as well as the complexity of the situations in
which they emerge.

In the effort to speak historically and to connect Julian's and Teresa's collocation of identities, bodies, and representation with the
work of Wittig and Rich, an appeal to the notion of a universal,
female self will be of little use. Instead, we may focus on diversity and

contradiction in the discourses of gender and identity rather than affirm how they consolidate "women" as a category through the identity politics of "the female body." The first step away from reproducing the fiction of universal and homogeneous selfhood would be to point again to the evidence autobiographics offers: medieval and contemporary, spiritual and secular, and male and female constructions of subjectivity are sufficiently contradictory to undermine the notion of universality on which autobiography studies has depended. The dissonance between and among epistemic shifts in a culture's beliefs about subjectivity, however, is frequently conceptualized as a problem in form, where difference, rupture, and resistance are construed as blips in the otherwise steady upward curve of evolution. Studies of self-representation which claim progress as their historical dynamic reveal an inability to read in the past either discontinuity or the enforcement of tradition.

In two contemporary commentaries on the representation of mystical experience, the relations among gender identity, the female body, and self-representation are subsumed within a masculinist discourse that focuses on the politics of representation and interpretation. In the first, *The Man Who Mistook His Wife for a Hat*, a book of neurological case studies, Oliver Sacks analyzes Hildegard of Bingen, a German nun who shared Julian's and Teresa's visionary experience, as a sufferer from migraine. Sacks's medical discourse takes Hildegard's mystical text as a case study in which she reports her symptoms. She draws a radically different conclusion about her experience from the one Sacks reaches. As Sacks somatizes female self-representation, the female body becomes a symptomatic text in which he reads illness. Hildegard's own version of writing the body is considerably obscured by a discourse that already construes her as incapable of self-interpretation. Sacks's description of mystical experience takes Hildegard as a "victim" of some gripping force. In the tradition of the holy vessel analogy, she is without agency, and her capacity to reinterpret pain cannot obscure the "truth" that Sacks can read. He directs his scrutiny toward a cause (here, a neurological source) of which the text is a mere effect. He aims for the experience preceding language. Hildegard's interpretive powers and the constitutive role of language in determining meaning are thereby subordinated to his diagnosis: Hildegard is the sufferer not of God's inspiration but of migraine: "A careful consideration of these accounts [Hildegard's *Scivias* and *Liber divinorum operum*] and figures leaves no room for doubt concerning their nature: they were indisputably migrainous, and they illustrate, indeed, many of the varieties of visual aura earlier discussed."[9] Although Sacks appreciates the pleasure that could follow from such an extravagant response to migraine, the phenomenon is always codified as an organic failure, as a proof of illness. Migraine is the source of her symptoms, however artfully presented. Illness produces inspiration, though Hildegard would probably have considered this construction a metaleptic error and interpreted it the other way around. According to Sacks, Hildegard reports literally a condition she simply experiences. Her text speaks to him; her words, her experience are transparent. Yet here it is important to note that Hildegard cannot give herself a migraine—a distinctly unpleasant event—in order to receive a vision—an event that gives her pleasure. Her allegorical interpretation of the "visual aura" does not coincide with the neurological event but succeeds it.

Sacks's case study of Hildegard, like Freud's case study of Dora, offers the patient's self-representation as an illness narrative and the doctor's interpretation as the therapeutic discourse. Neither woman is "cured," for in rather different ways, they are not listening. The doctors come to have an understanding of their "patients" which the women have no access to, for their own interpretations are presented as what the doctors move through and beyond to the truth. Sacks's certainty—"no doubt concerning their nature"—is consistent with what another doctor has said of female ecstasy. This doctor shares a similar belief in the female body's inability to stage anything other than its simple physiological response in visionary experience. But before I examine Jacques Lacan's comments on Bernini's sculpture *The Ecstasy of Saint Teresa*, here is Teresa's description of the ecstatic experience on which Bernini modeled it:

> Beside me, on my left hand, an angel in bodily form—a type of vision which I am not in the habit of seeing, except very rarely. Though I often see representations of angels, my visions of them are of the type which I first mentioned. . . . It pleased the Lord that I should see this angel in the following way. He was not tall, but short, and very beautiful; his face so aflame that he appeared to be one of the highest types of angel, who seem to be all afire. They must be those who are called cherubim: they do not tell me their names but I am well aware that there is a great difference between certain angels and others, and between these and others still, of a kind that I could not possibly explain. In his hands I saw a long golden spear and at the end of the iron tip I seemed to see a point of fire. With this he seemed to pierce my heart several

[9] Oliver Sacks, *The Man Who Mistook His Wife for a Hat* (New York: Summit, 1985), 160.

times so that it penetrated to my entrails. When he drew it out, I thought he was drawing them out with it and he left me completely afire with a great love for God. The pain was so sharp that it made me utter several moans; and so excessive was the sweetness caused me by this intense pain that one can never wish to lose it, nor will one's soul be content with anything less than God. It is not a bodily pain, but spiritual, though the body has a share in it—indeed, a great share. So sweet are the colloquies of love which pass between the soul and God that if anyone thinks I am lying I beseech God, in His goodness, to give him the same experience.[10]

Bernini's statue is located in a niche above the altar in the Cornaro Chapel in Santa Maria della Vittoria, a small church built by the Carmelites, Teresa's order. Bernini's sculpture depicts the moment after the angel has pierced Teresa with the spear. Through her mystical experience, Bernini addresses the particular problem of representing the rapture. It is both a physical and a spiritual experience: the source is experienced as outside the body; yet, the experience itself is profoundly embodied. Bodily functions and sensation are employed metaphorically: Teresa "sees" angels, though not with bodily sight. Feelings of abandon, of being caught up in a divine embrace, and the swooning desire that precedes and follows ecstasy are not passively meditated upon. Teresa's sensations are physical enough to make her cry out, and she is famous for the miraculous levitations that caused her considerable consternation. So rapturous were her transports that the nuns had to hold her down to prevent her body from rising.

In Bernini's depiction she is in one of those flights, hovering in the void on a cloud that flows into the draping folds of her garment. Her body seems to collapse inward toward the base of her spine, while her shoulders and head yearn upward. The angel lightly fingers her robe over the right breast, just at the point where her body seems gripped forward. His touch is so gentle, though, that it could not be the source of her straining. Her eyes are sightless behind closed lids, her head falls back as her face turns upward, lips part in reference to the moans she mentions, and the left hand dangles as do her feet. The cascading drapery of her clothing almost has a sculptural life of its own: it seems independent of the body, not quite concealing or revealing the figure within its folds. In contrast, the angel's clothing is so light it appears to be fluttering over the body it defines. The angel's body lacks gravity, while Teresa's is marked by a sort of collapse into

[10] Teresa of Avila, *The Life of Teresa of Jesus: The Autobiography of Teresa of Avila*, trans. E. Allison Peers (Garden City, N.Y.: Doubleday, 1960), 275.

the pit of her stomach, despite the obvious suggestion that both are floating on a cloud. The two figures offer a beautiful study in contrasts, but are still joined in that gentle, almost proprietary gesture of the angel's hand at Teresa's robe and the fiery arrow now withdrawn from her breast.

Lacan reads Bernini's *Ecstasy of Saint Teresa*, and female pleasure in general, in this way: "You only have to go and look at the Bernini statue in Rome to understand immediately she's coming, no doubt about it."[11] The statue qua woman is adequate to itself: perfectly legible to Lacan and unambiguous in meaning. Indeed, the passage is striking in its certainty, "no doubt about it," as was Sacks's confidence in the female body as a record of symptoms he could read, "no doubt concerning their nature." It is significant in this discussion of the visionary to examine the visual dimension on which Lacan relies for his conclusion. Lacan assumes the relationship between seeing and knowing as if the woman's body can only stage the obvious, as if it must both betray and offer up its pleasure to the male spectator/ interpreter. Lacan's abandonment of theory—"you only have to go and look"—in the face of the sexual abandon he reads in the statue indicates he is reproducing an ideology he has not fully inspected: he is gripped by the demands of (its) vision. Lacan asserts that in this moment seeing and understanding are simultaneous and identical; that is, simply seeing an image unproblematically reproduces its meaning when the privileged observer regards the female body and pleasure. In this he repeats the unlikely vision-driven scenario that catalyzes penis envy and "normal" female development for Freud: at some point, the little girl "sees" the penis, recognizes its superiority and her consequent inferiority, and assumes the path toward heterosexual development. In Lacan's reading of Bernini's *Teresa*, no interpretation is necessary; the sign is instantly legible. The primacy of vision and the male's privileged relation to the visible are based for Lacan on *the* thing worth seeing: the phallus, "the symbolic use of which is possible," Lacan revealingly comments, "because it can be seen, because it is erect; of what cannot be seen, of what is hidden, there is no possible symbolic use" (*Seminaire XX*, quoted by Heath, 54).

Compare Lacan's reduction of Teresa's experience to the limits of his own vision, to Teresa's visionary thoroughness and her contrasting lack of satisfaction with the proof of one sense. One could also

[11] Jacques Lacan, *Seminaire XX*, 14, quoted in Stephen Heath, "Difference," *Screen* (1971): 51.

distinguish the simplicity of the masculine power to know, represented by the doctors, from the young girl's labor to interpret herself as castrated. When she "succeeds" in making this conclusion make sense, according to Freud, she has done so by imitating the process whereby seeing is believing, but only if she represses the interpretive step that would compel her into belief. To return to Teresa, who emphasizes rather than obscures interpretation, she distinguishes ranks and classes of angels, specifies and then fuses the levels of spiritual and physical experience; her discourse combines holiness and eroticism, passion and theology. In Lacan's interpretation, the female body is silent. Specifically, female pleasure is another manifestation of female silence: in the economy of *jouissance*, female ecstasy cannot speak itself; it is the unrepresentable. Yet Teresa, like Julian and others, developed a rich and flexible discourse of ecstasy, of the body, and of identity which has been displaced as a historical and interpretive possibility by Lacan's gendered discourse. Most significant, the narrative dimension is neglected. In relation to Lacan's, Freud's, and Sacks's own narratives, Hildegard's and Teresa's writing disappears. Suddenly, we seem to be peering with the doctors through the murky pool of women's writing and discerning experience itself. Hildegard's and Teresa's texts as autobiography, as interpretation, are obstacles to the doctors' diagnoses in the first event and subsequently to their own writing projects. That women's writing can be seen as a secondary and "fictive" version of a primary and literal experience is a persistent problem. The narrative dimension of women's writing is frequently suppressed, and the texts themselves "disappeared" or subordinated to the allegedly franker task of just talking about women's experience in a way that can only recapitulate the reading error of Lacan and Sacks who are caught in the metaleptic grip of their own gendered body logic. And what, we should ask, must be left out if the accounts of doctors turned storytellers are to be more persuasive as "truth" than women's own self-representational texts?

To continue to foreground the issue of representation, we can look at the stories embedded in the story of the self and the figures of identity which constitute the technologies of autobiography. Autobiography dramatizes the scripted nature of life by revealing the stories within stories we tell and are told about who we are and who we might become. It offers the insider's account of the doubled narrative of the feminine, where the story a woman struggles to tell about herself is inscribed within the scripts she receives from her culture. Body tropes and figures available to the female mystic compose the

rhetoric of self-representation. The swoon or "dying faint," the ener-
vation of illness, stigmata, ecstatic trances, and physical levitation
offer a range of figures that continue to dramatize the transformation-
al capacity embedded in the dynamic exchange between passivity and
activity.

Teresa of Avila's *Life* is an unproblematical autobiography in many
ways: it contains biographical information and historically verifiable
dates, persons, places, and events. It was written at the well-
documented urging and under the supervision of spiritual directors.
It is an exemplary study in prayer, mysticism, and service; and as a
major document of women's mysticism, it contributes the figure of
the ecstatic body to the growing study of how women "write the
body" and what it means to do so. In contrast to Julian of Norwich's
twenty-year dedication to her *Revelations*, Teresa's approach to writing
is more casual. Yet, both share the mystic's consuming passion for an
intimate relationship with God.

Saint Teresa labored at her autobiography for years, revised minimally, and expressed occasional dissatisfaction with the whole venture. She felt that writing distracted her from the other work she
should perform. In part, her restiveness was due to her sense that
writing about herself was inconsequential compared to the work of
her order. She confesses (and complains) that her memory is poor,
that she is too weak for this work, and that as a woman she is generally unsuited to the task:

> I am almost stealing the time for writing, and that with great difficulty,
> for it hinders me from spinning and I am living in a poor house and have
> numerous things to do. If the Lord had given me more ability, and a
> better memory, I might have profited by what I have heard or read, but I
> have little ability or memory of my own. If, then, I say any good thing, it
> will be because the Lord has been pleased, for some good purpose, that I
> should say it, while whatever is bad is my own work and Your Re-
> verence will delete it. In neither case is there any advantage in giving my
> name. (123)

We recognize in this protest something of Julian's demurrals, for to
write as a woman about spiritual matters is to transgress ecclesiastical
discourse and Paul's prohibition against female speech. Under the
direction of her superiors, Teresa persisted. It is possible, however, to
see in her autobiographical discourse something in addition to the
habit of an obedient nun who wrote under orders and supervision.
Teresa's responses to her spiritual directors, her autobiographics as
agency, are evident in her strategic demurrals in the face of continued

self-representational writing. Teresa is alert to those who would police the truth and limits of her authority. She is, in fact, working in relation to their demand. Yet through autobiographics she produces an extended discourse of self-representation articulated in relation to orthodox teaching and visionary experience that includes gestures that would deflect the policing powers from judging her a heretic, yet would allow her to continue writing with an authority that expanded.

Teresa's autobiography is marked by the stress she lays on others who may authorize her words and acts (priests, confessors) and could also deauthorize them. It is not surprising that with so much at stake she approached her search for a compatible confessor with consuming diligence. Once she found one, she was loathe to tamper with the bond. It was especially important for Teresa to find sympathetic confessors because she was a converso, a Spanish Jew compelled to convert to Catholicism. She continued, under trusted guidance, to finish *The Life* and to produce her major texts on prayer: *The Way of Perfection*, *Foundations*, and *The Interior Castle*. Indeed, in a book of the length, scope, and rather impressionistic construction of Teresa's autobiography, the significance of others offers one form of coherence. Teresa focuses on how others may influence an individual—for good or ill—and makes this issue a tenet of subjectivity. From the importance of "good parents" through her insistence on associating with "people of virtue" and ultimately to her search for earthly and heavenly guides, Teresa represents identity as subject to influence. Even her emphasis on the observance of conventional rules of enclosure reveals her conviction that others can distract even the most devout persons.

Because others may pull the focus of spiritual persons back into the secular world, Teresa's reforms for the Carmelite order stress the importance of enclosure. Her desire for an earthly community always points toward and prefigures the heavenly community in which her identity ultimately finds its society. Teresa's comments on daily life in the convent formulates the perils of influence and demonstrates explicitly how demanding God is as the chosen "other":

> Their [the nuns'] life consists in learning how to advance in the service of God. They find their greatest happiness in solitude and it troubles them to think of seeing anyone—even a near relative—unless doing so will help to enkindle them in the love of their Spouse. So none come to this house save with that aim; were they to do so it would give pleasure neither to themselves nor to the sisters. They speak only of God, and they understand no one who speaks of anything else, nor does such a person understand them. (352)

Although Teresa has an executive mind when it comes to reform, her interest in ordering the text and the past on which it depends is nonchalant. For her, meaning inheres in the pattern of seeking God. Thus, her ambivalence toward resolving conflict in her past is based partly on her sense of amelioration. Teresa concurs with Julian's sense that the spirit will cover human lapses in the unfolding of eternity. As Julian writes, emphasizing the implicit future underlying the salvific ideal, "All will be well." Teresa's perspective on events in her youth (friends, parents, siblings, community) changes as she ages, and she uses her evolving insights to revise her sense of what is significant in her early life in terms of her progress in "the way of perfection." Because she sustains this instability as she writes, her text cannot be considered closed. Its design follows the process of reporting and reinterpretation. In spite of the chaos of the world and the particular chaos of the body in pain, heaven, or what one can glimpse of it in meditation, is filled with order and health.

Teresa's ecstasy is situated at the margins of representation. The mystic's burden lies in writing about a phenomenon that is explicable mainly as inexplicable, describable mostly in its ineffability, and legible in the rapturous trance or lingering illness traced in the ecstatic body. When Teresa is in the rapture, she hears a "Divine language" that is virtually untranslatable. When she reports the substance of the vision, she can only gloss this language: "And then my soul, in such a state that it could not endure so much joy, went out from itself, and lost itself for its own greater gain. It abandoned its meditations, and, as it heard that Divine language, which seems to have been that of the Holy Spirit, I fell into a deep rapture, which caused me almost to lose my senses, though it lasted but for a short time" (329). The difficulty in translating the rhetoric of rapture and of incorporating mystical discourses of the body and identity into existing discourses of gender hierarchy appears in Teresa's fracturing of language into asyntactic exclamation and neologism. Her translator, E. Allison Peers, speaks to the difficulty of translating Teresa. Peers regularized many of her anomalous, nearly incomprehensible formulations and, against her own practice, used the masculine generic, substituting "he" whenever Teresa does not seem to be speaking of a specific woman. Teresa's spiritual directors, who were also her editors, were frequently baffled by her syntax. As Peers notes appreciatively: "Vivid, disjointed, elliptical, paradoxical and gaily ungrammatical, the nun of Avila continually confounds the successors of those 'learned men' to whom in her life she turned so often for enlightenment" (The Life, 18). The complexity of her language attests to the intertextuality of autobiographical representation and to the contradictory codes of identity the autobiographer must work within and against. If the overdetermined female body persists in feminist discourse as both a necessary and a problematical focus, it does so at least in part through the contradictory discursive and historical formation of gender, truth, and identity, which compose the technologies of autobiography.

In ecstasy, Teresa reaches an altered state of consciousness in which time collapses: moments seem to linger for hours, or stretches of time are distilled into moments of rapt attention. Although her experiences are prompted by supernatural sources, they are profoundly, even disconcertingly, embodied. She writes: "One sees one's body being lifted up from the ground; and although the spirit draws it after itself, and if no resistance is offered does so very gently, one does not lose consciousness—at least, I myself have had sufficient to enable me to realize that I was being lifted up" (192). Her hair stands on end, she levitates, cries out with nearly sensible pain and joy, and experiences the aftermath as "a strange detachment" that increasingly prevents her from concentrating on the "things of earth" (192).

Indeed, the pictures of her ecstasy have so compelled readers that the writing is almost forgotten. Nevertheless, Teresa's figuration of the body and ecstatic identity is represented through the language inscribed in the book of visionary experience. It is the text of the angelic other she must learn to read and write in order to see this newly ecstatic body as her self. At the beginning of chapter 23, halfway through her autobiography, Teresa declares: "From this point onward, I am speaking of another and a new book—I mean, of another and a new life. Until now the life I was describing was my own; but the life I have been living since I began to expound these matters concerning prayer is the life which God has been living in me—or so it has seemed to me. . . . Praised be the Lord, Who has delivered me from myself!" (219–20). In this passage, book and life have been exchanged, if momentarily, as the structure of self-representation. Her representation of identity *is* the construction of a new identity, profoundly embodied and recognizable as a lover's discourse. As in Sandra Cisneros's *House on Mango Street*, writing itself and identity as a writer become increasingly central concerns in self-representation, joined in the capacious figure of the book of life. For Teresa, self-representation offers precisely what she searches for in devotion: by writing her autobiography, she is delivered from what she perceives as self-isolation into a relationship with God. By testifying to her mysticism, she leaves a written record of her interpretation of their union. Hadewijch, Julian, and Teresa found their authority for self-

operating here between word and materiality, figured as the body, reveals an understanding of identity which, in both its enactment and subversion, informs the tradition of autobiography, literary and critical. In order to examine how cultural fictions of the creation of gender influence (self-) representation, I begin with "beginnings," with two narratives that announce themselves as creation stories.

In the first, the Genesis account of creation, the body becomes "sexed" through a movement of narrative, and gender becomes fixed as a site of difference. In the second, Maxine Hong Kingston's *Woman Warrior*, representations of the female body provide leverage against masculinist notions of flawed and limited femininity. In both, the creation of gender is represented as a kind of violence enacted on the body in order to make something visible qua gender which did not previously appear. Only then may the body be interpreted as possessing a female mark of identification and identity. The body is seen as "gender female" once it has been injured; thus, the "creation" of gender is represented in both texts as a kind of violence. In *The Woman Warrior*, the violence that engenders women remains part of the self-representational project.

As a technology of autobiography, rhetorical violence, when it produces cultural knowledge of gender (its identification and value), not only constitutes a repertoire of themes and images for the writer but also recalls the ambivalent legacy of the confession. Insofar as the confessional subject is poised between absolution and punishment, truth telling is enmeshed in a rhetoric of violence. One knows the effects of truth and absolution, in no small part, through their difference from error, sin, and punishment. But the problem for many confessional subjects is profoundly narrative: How does one confess an experience and subjectivity that are not fully assimilated to the rhetoric of the confession? In the same way that confessional subjects stumble over the contested discursive notions of truth, many autobiographical subjects have to contend with gender, with telling "a woman's story." When the way in which a woman does that is to splice together disparate self-representational discourses, gender may be represented as a "core" of identity that is nonetheless violated at that "core." Differing narratives follow. Certainly, gender is a core element in many discourses of identity, and no less powerful and intransigent for being discursive, but it is an unevenly experienced and applied element of identity, and just as certainly its "truthfulness," its ability to describe or predict, is less than complete.

How women autobiographers handle the task of representing gender—as personal identity and as female collectivity—frequently depends on their sense of the rhetoric of gender and violence within which they are positioned. In some versions of what we could call "gender re-membering," or the act of reinterpreting gender as an imposed and falsified construction with material effects, there is an implied collectivity of women or an implied unity of female identity that needs to be reassembled. Despite the causes or historical circumstances of this dispersal, some women writers appeal to the notion of an original closeness among women or an interior coherence to being a woman which was violated and needs to be restored. For other women, a theory of identity as a discursive assemblage is itself the premise from which feminist re-membering builds. These are significant differences, but they would not, I think, simply sort themselves out, with all the "postmodernists" lining up on one side to claim a constitutively composite subject and the "liberals" and even the "radicals" rallying to restore truly and authentically whole women. Even if the contestants were willing to declare these allegiances, it is less than clear to me that anyone could convincingly do so for very long if what I have been arguing about the discourses of truth and identity is accurate. When gender coherence is represented as primary, and gender fragmentation as the result of a secondary violence done to women in their cultures, to their lives, and to themselves, then one cannot read "gender restoration" in the same way one would read a text that takes the project of re-membering as an act of resistance occurring in a culture in which gender and identity do not cohere. An identity theory that takes a constitutive discursive dis-unity as a description of women's lives does not seek to represent subjectivity or agency through a "return," however far off in the future it may be, to a time when gender and harm were not linked. To focus this discussion, we can read texts in which gender acquires meaning *as* rhetorical violence, and the task of self-representation is subsequently organized around the body. This inquiry into creation stories that concern gender, then, begins with a question: How does women's self-representation come to connect gender with violence and bodies?

The Genesis account of creation ("In the beginning God created the heavens and the earth") is a narrative about the creation of language as a precondition of identity, and about the gendering of the world. Acts of dividing and knowing through opposition describe the method of creation (as in the separation and naming of first light and then darkness) and create a discourse of gendered bodies focused on the figure of the woman as a belated and secondary "helpmeet." Recall the form creation takes: "And God said, 'Let there be light'" (Gen. 1:3). This creation story instantiates a logocentric theology of creation.

Christ is the word made flesh, as is creation because it was spoken into being. It would seem here that the identification of speaking with creating marks a patriarchal locus of authority. Yet Genesis is a difficult text on which to hang a structure as monolithic as patriarchy because it contains two creation stories and has been identified by biblical scholars as the edited version of at least three documents. Although some would insist that each word in each source was divinely inspired, as were the arrangers of the whole, the evidence suggests that where there is arrangement, there is choice; where there is choice, so also is there an agenda. In effect, we have two creation stories side by side which differently describe the gendering of words and bodies.

In the first story, human life is created in the same way as the rest of the world; people are placed on earth, though they differ critically from the rest of creation: "So God created man in his own image, in the image of God he created him; male and female he created them" (Gen. 1:27). Thus, within the first six days and one chapter, a hierarchy is established with human beings, God's semiotic simulacra, heading all created things. Such mimesis does not raise the question of gender equality or inequality because the top level of the hierarchy is shared by male and female. In the story that follows, however, hierarchies are posited that reveal the values and assumptions that will come to constitute female identity. The second story, which features "woman" being created from "man's" rib, is not an amplification or continuation of the first story; rather, it comes from a different source altogether and probably predates the version offered in 1:27. In effect, the second version claims priority over the first version and rewrites the creation of the woman. Thus the representational politics of gender identity can be charted, as a different and historically earlier narrative of "the creation of Eve" supplants the textually prior narrative of human creation. In the second narrative, the woman is removed from all other first-order acts of creation (those occurring within the first six days), specifically by being nonlinguistic.

In the second chapter of Genesis, we read about Eden. It is a gardener's dream with God as master gardener: here, when creation is watered, rivers flow and trees bloom from its fertile ground. In a "green thumb" episode of unprecedented proportion, God forms man from this same ground and tells him a thing or two about the vegetation: "You may freely eat of every tree of the garden; but of the tree of the knowledge of good and evil you shall not eat, for in the day that you eat of it you shall die" (Gen. 2:16–17). Careful readers will wonder where the woman went. Genesis 2:18 erases the woman's existence, uncreates her, in effect, a mere chapter later, in order to recreate her out of a found object, the man's rib: "Then the Lord God said, 'It is not good that the man should be alone; I will make him a helper fit for him'" (Gen. 2:18). Although the man is created from dust, he is divinely inspired (God breathes life into him), and his place in creation is primary and intentional. The man's lack, his insufficiency unto himself revealed by his need for a helpmeet, generates the necessity for woman. His insufficiency results in her belatedness which is introduced both in the manner in which, as well as the matter from which (the man himself), she is fashioned. She scandalously *supplements*, to use Derrida's sense of the word as implying both lack and bounty, what should be understood as an order perfectly full and complete unto itself (creation after the seventh day). The issue is not a divine failure to foresee the need for a person or function as crucial to the command to "be fruitful and multiply" as woman. Nor should it be assumed that the Scripture writers or the church founders would attribute any lack of vision to the Creator. Rather, the second story supplies an epistemological model that begins to cover over the arbitrary but symbolic correspondence between belated bodies and belated words emerging in the very language of the second story.

Because of the textual uncreation of the female body, female speech concomitantly lags behind male experiments with language. The first human work, appropriately, mimes God's work as God turns over the authority of naming to the man. Language in paradise, where God and man converse freely, is unmediated and fully present. If a name is lacking, so is the thing, and vice versa; thus, the man can name creation according to a natural correspondence between signifier and signified. Ontology at this point needs no epistemological supplement. But when the name/thing "helpmeet" is discovered to be lacking, God performs the first surgery and extracts a rib from the man to serve as the foundation for a rather peculiar birthing fable that links woman with wound. He opens man's body and from man's own flesh revises natural reproduction to make the man the "mother" of the woman. She is formed from matter already used primarily for another purpose, and the name of this last fruit of creation is similarly fashioned, by the man, from found lexical elements. The man's speech is quoted for the first time when he proclaims: "This at last is bone of my bones and flesh of my flesh; she shall be called Woman, because she was taken out of Man" (Gen. 2:23).

The extraction of the rib mimes the form of God's first-order acts of creation without benefit of the word that accompanies them: that right is reserved for the man. God differentiates whole elements that in their unity are chaotic and after their separation are bound in oppositional relation to each other and have mutually reinforcing functions. The word is given over to the man who remains the signifying subject in this scene, the arbiter of epistemological propriety. He recognizes the relationship the woman bears to him and names her: "This at last is bone of my bones and flesh of my flesh; she shall be called Woman, because she was taken out of Man" (Gen. 2:23). After humanity is gendered (that is, differentiated into male and female), heterosexuality offers a return to unity and becomes codified as marriage law: "Therefore a man leaves his father and his mother and cleaves to his wife, and they become one flesh" (Gen. 2:24). Unity in this formulation is possible only through the sundering of a primary relationship (here, the parent-child bond), which further enforces the nostalgia built into this cyclic search, even as it offers itself as a coherent narrative to ground the ontological primacy of "one flesh."

In a developing "world" in which priority is increasingly associated with hierarchy (first, light before darkness, then heaven before earth, and ultimately man before woman), the promotion of the man to "first person" status and the relegation of the woman to "late arrival" establishes gender hierarchy. As figures of human existence and identity, man and woman are both metaphor (created in God's image) and metonymy (they represent a part of God's total creation and a part of God) in the first story. In the second story, the woman is further displaced down the signifying chain and stands in metonymic relation to the man. She is fashioned from a part of him, and this part, the rib, comes to symbolize her new position in the emerging social order: beneath his arm.

One critic sums up the traditional interpretation of Genesis 2:4–3:7; it is, he says, "an etiological tale intended to account for the existence of woman, for her subordinate status, and for the attraction she perennially exerts over man."[1] It also justifies the institutional misogyny of the church and is seen to prefigure and support Paul's injunction against women's speech (1 Tim. 2:11–14). The mode of subordinating woman to man which becomes codified in the second story works through the differentiation of male and female words and bodies, specifically, through the construction of gender as the site of difference and hierarchy. The gendering of the female involves consolidating her identity as "different from" the man and "same as" sin: on the

---

[1] Robert Alter, "Sacred History and the Beginnings of Prose Fiction," *Poetics Today* 1.3 (Spring 1980): 143–61.

one hand, her body and soul are unified in their corrupt and corrupting sameness; on the other, she is distinguished from the man, made into an "other," and through this "othering" is brought about the identification of her words and body with the semiotization of woman-as-sexuality, -sin, and -suffering.[2]

By restructuring male and female access to language and its authority in this way, the second story elevates male physical primacy as it demotes female embodiment. The representation of the female body as a different kind of creation, and the equation of that body with the emergence of sin, provides a look at the mythification of femininity as flawed and transgressive, the narrative signification Paul assumed by reading the conflicting creation stories as a developmental narrative of female identity. Mieke Bal offers a narratological interpretation of Paul's readerly logic:

> From a narratological point of view, the development from one myth—the text as it stands—into the other—the sexist view formulated by "Paul" [placed in quotation marks in Bal's text because the historical identity of the letter writer is uncertain]—is the result of what I propose to call the *retrospective fallacy*. It consists of the projection of an accomplished, singular and named character-image on previous textual elements which *lead* to the construction of that character. It is this circularity which entails the realistic illusion. As such, it contributes to the production of myths.[3]

By projecting the second creation story as an extension of the first, Paul further distances the woman from man as a body and attributes to her soul the consequences of her words. The orality of female action which leads to the Fall (speaking with the serpent, eating the fruit, enticing the man to eat) underscores for Paul the danger of female speech. The beguilement by the serpent forms the site where the female word and body are given a one-to-one correspondence with deception and transgression, and it is in this conjunction of word and body that "woman" emerges as a narrative sign whose truth and identity Paul feels confident to read.

Thus any attempt to arrive at the truth by determining which of the two stories is primary can only repeat Paul's participation in the pro-

---

[2] The diverse and interesting body of feminist work on woman-as-sign includes de Lauretis, *Alice Doesn't*, and a contemporary proliferation of semiotics in cultural, feminist, and lesbian and gay studies.

[3] Mieke Bal, "Sexuality, Sin, and Sorrow: The Emergence of Female Character," in *The Female Body*, ed. Suleiman, 319.

duction of myth by displacing textuality into a search for a kind of narrative continuity the text cannot support. That is, the two stories, following in the order they do, have been read—certainly by Paul—as the intentional unfolding of female character in a narrative that sets in motion the semiotization of the feminine as follows: Her secondary, hence lesser, body is a morally weaker one and is thus prey to the forces of corruption, or by another move, she embodies the corruption that will eventually reveal itself in the transgressive act ending in banishment. We witness in this myth of origins how the creation of the world consists in and entails the creation of narrative as a representation of social order, the gendering of identity, and the placement in this textual world of woman/Woman/women. For the ways in which this narrative creates identity through opposition; through separation, unity, and nostalgia; and through the gendered association of labor and desire reveal the rhetorical violence in this creation story about sexuality and textuality. A social order structured through domination needs identity categories, such as gender, to explain power in naturalistic terms. Identities emerge in power relations in this creation narrative and are not simply "there."

Significantly in this discussion of identity and naming, the proper names Adam and Eve appear without flourish. They arise in connection with a specific act that marks their symbolic and literal place in creation. Adam is connected with naming (Gen. 2:19), and the woman, who remains nameless for the duration of her stay in Eden, becomes Eve in this procreative signifying chain: "Now Adam knew Eve as his wife, and she conceived and bore Cain, saying, 'I have gotten a man with the help of the Lord'" (Gen. 4:1). The first three chapters establish naming as the significant and signifying action and make clear Eve's place in this order. She names nothing, creates nothing. Perhaps in this narrative we could say that Eve was the first to experience the relationship between signifier and signified as arbitrary. Her transgression (which should primarily be understood as the desire for knowledge, the desire to know what God knows), which results in the exile from the garden, initiates only a more formal exile than the one she already lives. Her exclusion from language carries tremendous consequences, and this first revolution of the dispossessed (she does not own her name, hence, her self) concludes God's experiment in the garden. When God first speaks directly to the woman, it is as a judge, and the first trial is initiated: "'What is this that you have done?'" (Gen. 3: 13).

The third chapter of Genesis begins with another creation story, one centered in the female body, which has become the site of labor and pain. God's punishment of the woman centers on her body and his curse makes clear the implicit consequences of gender: "To the woman He said, 'I will greatly multiply your grief *and* your suffering in pregnancy *and* the pangs of childbearing; with spasms of distress you shall bring forth children; yet your desire *and* craving shall be for your husband, and he shall rule over you'" (Gen. 3:16).[4] The final blow revises the man's caretaker role into mastery and, it would seem, tyranny. Because there has been no human procreation in the garden, God also predicts the future of heterosexuality with the constituents of desire and childbearing and prescribes the female role in it. Such a logic links the body whose desire is not for its own (other women) or for itself to subsequent subordination.

In its collocation of women's words and bodies and in the construction of gender in text this creation story is held together less by the unity of truth it propounds than by the dynamics of narrative and interpretation.[5] It is also the story of how the proper name comes to be seen as identical with the person/character to whom it refers. The movement toward the first name, "woman," defines her identity as symbol and as human: she is profoundly and complexly belated and "other"; she becomes the object of desire by replacing the tree of knowledge as creation's most compelling symbol. What is most deeply unknowable shifts from the tree of knowledge to woman. The movement toward the second name, Eve, is represented as the narrative of her desire for knowledge, narrated as a scene of seduction, and her forbidden choice prompts God to punish her and Adam through expulsion. Their removal from the source of perfectly met needs results from her transgression, and the hunger that must inevitably follow from this loss of immediate fulfillment is displaced onto Eve. This movement is also a useful illustration of—or does it establish?—the place of "woman" in narrative: her desire is for another; that is, she can neither possess nor redirect desire; it is neither owned nor for her own. Desire without authority or agency circulates within an economy of debt and loss. The woman pays for her transgression through the loss of owning her desire. From this loss, devolves Eve's legacy for the women—"real" and "textual"—who follow her. Inscribed in narrative, female desire is a primal loss; it is that which is one's own, though forever out of reach, its absence mourned, its presence a punishment.

This discussion of the biblical sources of textuality and sexuality

---

[4] *The Amplified Bible* (Grand Rapids, Mich.: Zondervan, 1965).
[5] I take the word "collocation" from Bal, "Sexuality, Sin, and Sorrow," 318.

and the gendered relationship between word and body has significance for contemporary autobiographers who understand and must
revise the logic that, in making writing and speaking transgressive for
women, joins rhetorical violence and self-representation. In *The Woman Warrior*, Maxine Hong Kingston creates a myth of identity which
shares with Genesis and John's Gospel the notion that language is the
controlling metaphor for the emergence of identity and that identity
consists in relation to language—or, more precisely, languages. For
The Woman Warrior is populated with fantastical and real female characters drawn from Chinese legend, American mass culture, and the
synthetic force of imagination. The swordswoman Fa Mu Lan of an-
cient Chinese lore and the young Kingston, who wants to score well
on exams so she can go to college, are pulled from different rhetorical
situations and histories and bound together through talk-story, her
mother's name for storytelling. Kingston's mother's talk-story is one
of the technologies of autobiography in relation to which Kingston
must represent herself. Kingston describes the ambivalence in the
Chinese discourses of gender identity as profoundly unsettling:
"When we Chinese girls listened to the adults talk-story, we learned
that we failed if we grew up to be but wives or slaves. We could be
heroines, swordswomen. Even if she had to rage across all China, a
swordswoman got even with anybody who hurt her family. Perhaps
women were once so dangerous that they had to have their feet
bound."[6] The practices of female infanticide and female slavery, however, more accurately represent the daily life of women in the China
from which the talk-stories are drawn. Kingston offers a litany of
epithets suggesting the value of women in no uncertain terms. They
are "maggots in the rice," "pigs" or "stink pigs," unprofitable in the
extreme: "It is better to raise geese than girls." From her position in
relation to the contradictory discourse of gender identity, Kingston
crafts tales in which women take charge. As Sidonie Smith has noted:
"Considered by some a 'novel' and by others an 'autobiography,' the
five narratives conjoined under the title *The Woman Warrior* are de-
cidedly five confrontations with the fictions of self-representation and
with the autobiographical possibilities embedded in cultural fictions,
specifically as they interpenetrate one another in the autobiography a
woman would write" (*Poetics of Women's Autobiography*, 151).

Central to the concerns of this discussion, the cultural fictions of
gender in Genesis, the Book of John, and *The Woman Warrior* quickly
realize a rhetoric of violence in the female body. In Kingston's self-

[6] Maxine Hong Kingston, *The Woman Warrior* (New York: Vintage, 1975), 23.

representational project, the female body is a metaphor for gender rather than gender's true and single source. Kingston imagines fantastical, mythic, and material bodies for herself, for her female relatives and ancestors, and for the female characters drawn into her text from a range of discourses and fashioned into autobiographical figures of identity. The two figures who embody the complexity of Kingston's relation to discourses of gender, identity, and agency on which I will focus here are No Name Woman, the father's aunt, whose legacy links silence, storytelling, and revenge; and Fa Mu Lan, the woman warrior, a seeming contradiction in terms with which Kingston struggles. In *The Woman Warrior*'s myths of identity and gender involving No Name Woman and Fa Mu Lan, gender is represented as violence done to the female body. As in the biblical accounts, gender as the mark of female identity emerges as the body is wounded, suggesting that for women, violence is entwined with self-representation. Kingston's text reveals, however, the danger surrounding violence does not threaten only the writer. Self-representation and confession are also acts of revenge sometimes visited upon an oppressive, punitive, or coercive community and family. Once violence and gender are put in discourse *as* female identity in the context of self-representation, threat is no longer static and no longer a shroud of silence. *The Woman Warrior* explores how stories use the rhetoric of violence to represent gender and reveal the violence of rhetoric in the legacy of those narratives for real women.[7]

The nexus of autobiographical words and representations of bodies forms the ground of the autobiographical act for many women; for Kingston, it also emerges as a thematic concern. For her, the body becomes a figure through which oppressive representations of gender identity and femaleness may also be resisted. In this sense, Kingston's revision of the belated and flawed relation of women's words to women's bodies produces the kind of resistance to the dominant discourse of gender identity which de Lauretis describes in *Alice Doesn't*:

Strategies of writing *and* of reading are forms of cultural resistance. Not only can they work to turn dominant discourses inside out (and show that it can be done), to undercut their enunciation and address, to unearth the archaeological stratifications on which they are built; but in affirming the historical existence of irreducible contradictions for women in discourse, they also challenge theory in its own terms, the terms of a

[7] For a discussion of the violence of rhetoric and the rhetoric of violence, see de Lauretis, *Technologies of Gender*, 31–33.

semiotic space constructed in language, its power based on social valida-
tion and well-established modes of enunciation and address. So well-
established that; paradoxically, the only way to position oneself *outside* of
that discourse is to displace oneself *within* it—to refuse the question as
formulated, or to answer deviously (though in its words), even to quote
(but against the grain). (7)

The Woman Warrior treats separation and the impossibility of separating self-representation from the discursive networks that construct truth and identity.[8] The structures of ideological oppression in
Kingston's life and text are precisely these intimate grounds of reality
and identity: her immigrant Chinese family, the mixture of cultural
influences in contemporary California, and her relationship with her
mother and her mother's stories. The encompassing method through
which Kingston comes to understand this network is her mother's
discourse, talk-stories, which works primarily through the modes of
mythmaking and translation. Whether invoking the moralistic tone of
the cautionary tale or the illustrative space of the fable, Kingston's
mother weaves her stories into her daughter's imagination and life.
Kingston explains: "Whenever she had to warn us about life, my
mother told stories that ran like this one [the story of No Name
Woman], a story to grow up on. She tested our strength to establish
realities" (5). But the impossibility of sorting these stories into a
monocultural whole and into the language spoken by a monocultural
identity, all of them pertaining to the real as Kingston experiences it
and her mother tells it, is evident. The discursive engagements that
structure this book involve Kingston as the emergent storyteller and
her mother as the figure of narrative itself, a woman who offers a
mythic and mundane discourse replete with the possibilities of voice
and silence. This is a charged engagement, for the stakes are high and
involve the possibility of Kingston's speaking at all. In Kingston's
developing epistemology of identity, "I thought talking and not talking made the difference between sanity and insanity" (216).

Kingston's sense of her identity and the epistemology through
which that sense is produced are created and recreated through "acts
of cultural resistance." Given the impact of her mother's talk-stories,
writing an autobiography functions as a dramatic and visible act of
self-definition even as it pays homage to her mother. Kingston's revi-

---

[8] For a discussion of this ambivalence in the context of feminist psychoanalytic accounts of the mother-daughter relationship, see Leslie Rabine, "No Lost Paradise:
Social Gender and Symbolic Gender in the Writings of Maxine Hong Kingston," *Signs*
12 (Spring 1987): 471–92.

sionary logic depends upon first taking fiction as a shaping force in her life. Stories have the power to do more than merely illustrate or influence; they construct the rhythms of life along narrative lines. As Carolyn Steedman argues in *Landscape for a Good Woman*, the autobiographer's confrontations with her mother's stories involve a struggle for the meaning of life itself. When interpretation is directed toward questions of family identity and historical truth, connected as they are to ideology, then the distinctiveness of "real" meanings and symbolic meanings is difficult for the child to discern, as it is for the adult who must look back through the child's eyes. Similarly, Audre Lorde imbues the stories her mother tells her with a mythic dimension figured through the name Zami, the Carriacou name for women together. Like Lorde, Kingston is the daughter of immigrant parents; the experience and understanding of her own life is interpenetrated by the mythic perspective of her mother and by the pervasive disorientation of multicultural identity as it collides with an assimilationist fiction of immigrant citizenship. There is also, at perhaps a basic level for the daughter, a sense that she doesn't recognize where she is. The mother's interpretive maps are drawn from elsewhere; they do not necessarily correspond to what the daughter sees. The mother's massive storytelling apparatus, especially the fullness of that narrative, is disorienting to Kingston, who cannot tell where the tales come from or the ends toward which they reach. It is this confusion that Kingston turns to productive advantage.

In the first chapter, "No Name Woman," Kingston retells the story her mother first told her on the day she began menstruating. The chapter begins with the mother's words—"'You must not tell anyone,' my mother said, 'what I am about to tell you'" (3)—and continues the mother's story without interruption. This injunction is, obviously, honored and dishonored simultaneously. Kingston judges the story worth repeating and in repeating it breaks the injunction. I would argue that Kingston has not simply reversed the injunction, not simply inverted the implied binary of silence/voice. Rather, to use de Lauretis's phrase, Kingston quotes against the grain, and by telling the tale in her mother's voice and then interpreting it in her own, she reveals quotation as a strategy to locate herself in the story differently. No longer the recipient of traditional warnings, Kingston tests the limits of ideology when she identifies less with the official interpretation of her aunt than with her own interpretive process. She fails to reproduce the story as a text with a single meaning and instead subjects it to interpretation.

This moralistic and violent parable concerns Kingston's aunt, who is punished for an illegitimate pregnancy by the villagers' devastating raid on the family's home. Everything is destroyed with the purpose of punishing and atoning for the aunt's adulterous "extravagance." The tale is a warning. The villagers are watchful; their threats still powerful. The tale does not simply illustrate the punishment for interrupting a legitimate line of descent; it also, and perhaps most important, installs the ancestral villagers as a still-present force. They are concerned with women's adherence to the law. A woman, like Kingston when she was first told the story, who reaches reproductive maturity is both in danger and a source of potential danger. Her body now shelters a reproductive possibility that may destroy her and those around her. On the night of the villagers' raid, the aunt kills herself and the baby she bears alone in the pigsty. Her sexual body is represented as a violent threat to the community, as are all women's bodies, the tale suggests. Because of this interpretation of her body, the aunt now has no name, no voice, no honored relation to the ancestral line. The sexualized body, then, forms Kingston's first level of inquiry as she questions the silence surrounding the story and offers counterinterpretations in an attempt to find herself in relation to her aunt.

Even as Kingston retells the aunt's story, which is also the mother's story, she problematizes speaking the unspeakable. Once the silence is broken, the threat does not disappear, though it is displaced from Kingston's body to the fraught interpretation itself. She wonders if her aunt had found a lover: a romantic myth. Doubtful, she decides: "My aunt could not have been the lone romantic who gave up everything for sex. Women in the old China did not choose" (7). The subsequent interpretation of rape follows from this reasoning, and the story becomes a tale of violence: "Some man had commanded her to lie with him and be his secret evil. . . . [He] was not, after all, much different from her husband. They both gave orders: she followed. 'If you tell your family, I'll beat you. I'll kill you. Be here again next week'" (7–8). As Kingston oscillates between the interpretive options of agent/victim, consenting and desiring/coerced and violated, she reveals the pitfalls of identification: one woman's story has been presented to her by her mother as exemplary; must it also be Kingston's story? If so, then even as her aunt was raped and cast out, so too could Kingston be. As narrator, however, Kingston suspends the binary logic she has installed and looks at the aunt's suicide as an act of revenge rather than the fulfillment of female destiny.

After working through the implications of the sexualized female body, Kingston places the body in the context of the family. In the middle of her revisions of the aunt's life story, Kingston includes her mother's revelation of who benefits most from keeping the aunt's silence: "Don't let your father know that I told you. He denies her. Now that you have started to menstruate, what happened to her could happen to you" (5). There are two imperatives here: sexual maturity has risks, and protect your father. These are related, but the ways in which the father must be protected are not all obvious. Obvious enough is the interpretation that insofar as he represents legitimate descent, the father's authority and position would be demeaned by the dishonor of illegitimate birth. Were this the only interpretation, however, one could assume the father would want this story to be told to all his daughters. It would be a frightening tale striking close to home, easy to identify with personal consequences. The father, it seems, has been struck down in some other way by this sister and has erased her presence, even as a figure in a grim menarche tale. The profusion of interpretive possibilities Kingston unearths makes clear how the current narrative of the aunt has been honed to a single meaning, a meaning it fails to convey.

Her experimentation with perspective as she tells the story from her mother's point of view and then from her own offers an insight into the complicity in protecting the father and punishing the aunt. The father was not an eyewitness to the villager's raid; only the mother tells the story as a witness: "My mother spoke about the raid as if she had seen it, when she and my aunt, a daughter-in-law to a different household, should not have been living together at all. Daughters-in-law lived with their husbands' parents, not their own; a synonym for marriage in Chinese is 'taking a daughter-in-law.' Her husband's parents could have sold her, mortgaged her, stoned her. But they had sent her back to her own mother and father, a mysterious act hinting at disgraces not told me" (8). At the time of the raid, all the men in the family had sailed for California. Kingston's mother, a daughter-in-law, observed the pregnancy and the villager's punishment. Despite the fact that the aunt's pregnancy could not be attributed to her husband, who had left the village much earlier, she did not live with her in-laws, but with her parents. Kingston speculates, "She may have been unusually beloved, the precious only daughter. . . . When her husband left, they welcomed the chance to take her back from the in-laws" (12). Thus she hints at another reason for the silence that surrounds her story. After all, the mother has told the story, as has Kingston; the protectiveness of the silence is imbued with deep ambiguity. Perhaps, for there were many family silences, the father did not know the specifics of his sister's life. Perhaps he knew only of her suicide, but would that have been sufficient to cause her erasure from family history? Kingston's father is the only man in the family who does not return to China. The deeper animosity between brother and sister, then, may have come from another incident altogether in which their father, Kingston's grandfather, "brought home a baby girl, wrapped up inside his brown western-style greatcoat. He had traded one of his sons, probably my father, the youngest, for her. My grandmother made him trade back. When he finally got a daughter of his own, he doted on her. They must have all loved her, except perhaps my father, the only brother who never went back to China, having once been traded for a girl" (12).

The tale does not resolve in the identification of Kingston and No Name Woman, and in this sense the mother's purpose is not accomplished. But No Name Woman remains a threat of a different kind, and the person she threatens is Kingston. The concluding interpretation of the meaning No Name Woman's story will have for Kingston focuses on the aunt's body. The meaning of the villagers' collective participation in the raid is explained through a philosophy of wholeness based on patriarchal right, most notably centered in legitimate patrilineal descent and figured through images of "roundness": "In the village structure, spirits shimmered among the living creatures, balanced and held in equilibrium by time and land. But one human being flaring up into violence could open up a black hole, a maelstrom that pulled in the sky. The frightened villagers, who depended on one another to maintain the real, went to my aunt to show her a personal, physical representation of the break she had made in the 'roundness'" (14).

From the philosophical "roundness" of generational continuity Kingston continues a signifying chain of "round moon cakes and round doorways, the round tables of graduated size that fit one roundness inside another, round windows and rice bowls" which represents the wholeness of families who "faithfully [keep] the descent line by having sons to feed the old and the dead, who in turn look after the family" (15). In order to make this logic illustratively powerful, the villagers circle the home, curse the aunt's transgressive "roundness," now figured as the swollen belly of pregnancy, and as she flees the ring of destruction, she breaks again this circle of avengers.

When the aunt is given words, it is in connection to her body: "When she felt the birth coming, she thought that she had been hurt. Her body seized together. 'They've hurt me too much,' she thought. 'This is gall, and it will kill me'" (16). The narrative turns to the aunt's labor and ultimate suicide and focuses on her body as the location of agency, in the sense not of possessing sexual desire but of having a will of its own. "With forehead and knees against the earth, her body convulsed and then relaxed. She turned on her back, lay on the ground. The black well of sky and stars went out and out and out forever; her body and her complexity seemed to disappear" (16). This vision becomes terrifying as the body loses its boundaries; her absorption into the sky and stars is interpreted as her disappearance: "Flayed, unprotected against space, she felt pain return, focusing her body" (16). The physical pain of labor locates her in her body, hence in the world. The release from pain dissolves the integrity of the body and leaves her vulnerable to disintegration. Between labor pains, the aunt runs to the pigsty in an effort, Kingston speculates, to protect the child from the immensity of space and from the "jealous, pain-dealing gods." Once the baby is born, the aunt makes her decision, carries the baby to an ultimate enclosure, and drowns them both in the family well. They are truly cast out of the roundness: the aunt, according to Kingston, knew well what her own fate would have been. She would have been an outcast, buried in an unmarked grave, and her child would not have had a descent line. Both would become ghosts, trailing each other through eternity, unprotected and vengeful.

In this mythic tale of the dangers of transgressing the laws of the community, Kingston finds that the power of the aunt rests in her revenge, an insoluble legacy. For even as Kingston breaks the injunction of silence—"Don't tell anyone you had an aunt"—and refuses to continue to punish the aunt through silence, she too breaks the community's laws. The raid itself was not the sole punishment, only a visible act to initiate the eternal punishment that would follow. Their curse is, " 'Ghost! You've never been born' " (16), and all who keep this silence, who uncreate the aunt, participate in maintaining the roundness. As if the language that creates the world can also uncreate a person, they speak her into oblivion. Without a story, without a name or ancestors, she cannot be re-membered. It is this dismemberment that Kingston responds to, but the consequences for breaking silence are evident: look at the aunt. Kingston concludes: "My aunt haunts me—her ghost drawn to me because now, after fifty years of neglect, I alone devote pages of paper to her. . . . I do not think she always means me well. I am telling on her, and she was a spite suicide, drowning herself in the drinking water" (19).

The route toward reclaiming the aunt's story goes through identification, and its perils are clear at the end of the chapter. Although

Kingston has invented a history, a self, and a kind of a name, which is "No Name," for her father's sister and although she makes explicit her interest in alternative interpretations of family and cultural myths, these myths nonetheless form the matter from which she is to fashion an identity, as her mother makes clear to her. In this respect, her similarity to the aunt is terrifying because it implies substitutability: "The Chinese are always very frightened of the drowned one, whose weeping ghost, wet hair hanging and skin bloated, waits silently by the water to pull down a substitute" (19).

In the following chapter, "White Tigers," Kingston tells the coming-of-age story she might have preferred. In her own talk-story involving her identification with the swordswoman Fa Mu Lan, Kingston fantasizes being taken from her family and trained by a wise couple to become the woman warrior of legendary power. The point of the apprenticeship is for her to return to her village and to defeat the army that has terrorized it. Blood figures prominently in this chapter. She not only gets her period during the fantastical, adventurous training by the mystical and benevolent old couple but marks her return to her parents by shedding blood. During her lengthy training, she begins menstruating and broods on the meaning of blood: "I bled and thought about the people to be killed; I bled and thought about the people to be born" (39). Yet blood is revised here as a creative metaphor, for bleeding is not passive, not simply suffered as a wound. Instead, Kingston's revised menstruation parable prefigures her submission to scarification as an act of bravery, as it represents the body's transfigurative possibilities. Upon her return to the village, she is welcomed home as a son.

Kingston's revised myth of the woman warrior turns on a ritualistic moment of mutilation. After her apprenticeship and before she puts on the armor of a man to lead an army, Kingston returns to her family and village, where her parents ritualistically engrave their names and grievances on her back: "'We are going to carve revenge on your back,' my father said. 'We'll write out oaths and names'" (41). Mutilation is reclaimed aesthetically as she asserts: "If an enemy should flay me, the light would shine through my skin like lace" (41). The entry into language, where the body becomes a text, propels the myth forward and marks the transition between initiation and action as it redefines the mythic Kingston's relation to her family and her culture and emphasizes the female body as the space where wrongs are both committed and memorialized. Thus, memory becomes as inescapable as one's own body. Language here does not grant a previously inarticulate or silenced woman the capacity for self-expression; rather, it signals a new phase of gendered identity in which "being a woman" will not limit a woman's action. This bodily text, this corporeal site of language, retextualizes the self and redefines the new body's script as a poetics of vengeance. In this myth, Kingston as heroine becomes a living war monument, her body iconized through scarification as a revenge text. Especially in its ritualistic structure, the etching of the family's lineage in her flesh recalls God's cursing of Eve in which God inscribes in the woman's flesh the simultaneous meanings of reproduction, femaleness, and pain. Images of blood recur throughout the text and build in the complementary structures of atonement and revenge.

The body is layered again as Kingston takes on man's armor. During her long campaign, the woman warrior gives birth. Her armor protects her gendered identity to the point that armor seems less like a disguise than like another performance of embodiment. Through these repeated rewritings of the female body—as a revenge text and then represented as a man—gender is displaced as the ground of meaning. In its vital sexuality and in its vengeful textuality, the body is no longer inarticulate; it has become a figure for self-representation. As a signifying subject, Kingston chooses to represent her body as something other than the hysterical space of male desire. She reconceptualizes the connection between "our bodies, our selves" as a problem in representation and not, finally, as a hypostatized fact. Her body, with rows of characters marching in files down her back, is the author's text. Commenting on this conjunction, Susan Gubar suggests that "women have had to experience cultural scripts in their lives by suffering them in their bodies. This is why Maxine Hong Kingston writes so movingly about her resemblance to the mythic woman warrior who went into battle scarred by the thin blades which her parents literally used to write fine lines of script on her body. For the artist, this sense that she is herself the text means that there is little distance between her life and her art."[9]

Yet it also means that this "little distance" between life and art, the space of autobiographical discourse, is a perilously expansive passage. Narrowed by the cultural imposition of silence and the compelling dogma that a woman's place is to be the art object and not the artist, the passage widens as the autobiographer finds the craft that sustains her crossing. Kingston has internalized conditions she can now report. Still the possibility of having the female body read as if it

[9] Susan Gubar, "'The Blank Page' and the Issues of Female Creativity," in *Writing and Sexual Difference*, ed. Elizabeth Abel (Chicago: University of Chicago Press, 1982), 81.

could only stage the obvious, as if its meaning were only gendered identity, persists. In the woman warrior's ultimate confrontation with the baron who had drafted her brother, she leaves her troops and horse behind and stalks him alone. When she interrupts him as he is counting money, he asks: "'Who are you? What do you want?'" Kingston delivers the introduction to her revenge text: "'I want your life in payment for your crimes against the villagers'" (51). The baron then makes a series of what we could call reading errors. When he defends his profits as justly earned, Kingston challenges his rights by describing herself as an avenger. She is the one who knows what he wishes to hide, namely, his guilt. She, though, has also been hiding and discloses herself with this self-identification: "'I am a female avenger.'" Her combat "drag" determines the baron's response. He not only tries to appeal to her man-to-man by saying nobody would miss the girls and women he destroyed but also tries to charm her into masculine complicity: "'I haven't done anything other men— even you—wouldn't have done in my place.'" The baron is convinced by Kingston's performance of gender "drag"; he isn't thrown by the two gender identities supposedly combined in the "female avenger." His coolness under pressure comes from interpreting her bodily stance as the signifier of her male subjectivity. In this encounter, however, she is not wearing armor and could be fully legible as female. In order to push their confrontation beyond the baron's denials and equivocations, Kingston rips off her shirt to reveal the markings on her back. In that moment of dramatic "unmasking," the body as text of revenge becomes instead the female body that must be avenged. Kingston's body is, in a sense, a two-sided text that reads "female" on the front and "avenger" on the back. The baron reads only gender in this text: "When I saw his startled eyes at my breasts, I slashed him across the face and on the second stroke cut off his head" (52).[10]

The woman warrior of her mother's talk-stories has emerged through Kingston's own retelling of the tale with her self in the central role: she has become the woman writer whose revenge is to claim

---

[10] Kingston makes the connection between his startled leer at her breasts and his crimes against her. His execution, then, is equally compelling as a kind of intended, planned, "community-supported" vengeance and as a kind of *Thelma and Louise* moment that reveals the full meaning of the name "female avenger." She is not only the avenger who is female but also the one who seeks vengeance for all women, for the crimes committed against that community, as when Louise blows away the would-be rapist after rescuing Thelma.

selfhood by identifying the power she possesses as a writer: "The swordswoman and I are not so dissimilar. . . . What we have in common are the words at our backs. The ideographs for *revenge* are 'report a crime' and 'report to five families.' The reporting is the vengeance—not the beheading, not the gutting, but the words. And I have so many words—'chink' words and 'gook' words too—that they do not fit on my skin" (62–63). Implicitly an act of revenge, this resistance dares to act out the roles duplicitously offered to women in narrative and myth. But as revenge, Kingston's revision of the discourse of identity and the body acknowledges the tremendous appeal of myths and mythmaking. We would miss the compelling attractions of ideology which win our participation if we suggested otherwise. Her autobiography foregrounds this tension by focusing on the self's balancing act with stories, myths, indeed, with language as a system that engenders identity and epistemology. The mother's talk-story is rich with suggestions of reward and regret. On the one hand, Kingston finds herself tightly inscribed in the daughter/wife/slave role of submission, silence, and self-abnegation. On the other hand, her mother has contradicted and complicated this prescription by teaching the daughter talk-stories of swordswomen reveling in the glory, power, and triumph of the role. Kingston struggles for a lifetime to come to terms with the paradox created by the simultaneous offering of a fable as fantasy and as role model, and she finds a subject position within her mother's stories from which she can quote against the grain: "She said I would grow up a wife and a slave, but she taught me the song of the warrior woman, Fa Mu Lan. I would have to grow up a warrior woman" (24). In this autobiographical act of resistance, Kingston appropriates both received myths and mythmaking as technologies of autobiography and capitalizes on the contradictions within the codes of female identity: she recreates/represents herself as a woman warrior.

Although becoming a signifying subject means living through the double bind of oppression/expression, Kingston suggests that the discourses of truth and identity, while they certainly operate to reduce women, do not only operate in that way, nor do they operate on all women in the same way. From her parents' Chinese culture, Kingston received a contradictory discourse of female identity: tales of the swordswoman exist alongside fables that comment on female uselessness. "Better to raise geese than girls" and "girls are maggots in the rice" are the grandfather's remarks on the unproductivity of women. Female worth is located in a gendered body that consumes, yet produces little of worth other than children, and when it reproduces itself through female children, the unproductivity is doubled. Kingston's staged encounter between cultural fictions and self-representation shows how insoluble are inscriptions of ethnic/racial/cultural and gender identities. Against the homogenizing and inaccurate sense that identity is located at the crossroads of the universal and the particular, a reading of Kingston's autobiographics emphasizes how this location is less the name of a specific place than an autobiographical function.

The axis of identity indicated by the intersection of the universal and the particular is one conceptual framework among many, and it is a paradigm that has, primarily, obscured how gender identities are specified in cultural identities, how racial identities are sexualized, how ethnic identities are gendered, and how sexual identities are inflected by class. In short, that paradigm does not specify how the *I* shifts within those places and how power is distributed. Efforts to sustain an inspection into the complex particular frequently contain universalizing assumptions. The universal presents itself as a point, as "the" universal, while the particular struggles to represent simultaneity in unhelpfully linear schematics. For example, the signifying chain "race, class, gender" unfolds spatially in a linear, horizontal dimension that corresponds to a temporal unfolding. We read the words from left to right, hear them in "real time" as additions in which the cumulative identity, to borrow from Derrida, is constantly deferred, never fully present, always differing from itself in the language of identity. Kingston indicates how the simultaneity of this chain of signifiers operates ideologically. The differences are sustained and masked through rhetorical constructions with multiple interpretations but hegemonic meaning, as when Kingston writes: "There is a Chinese word for the female *I*—which is 'slave.' Break the women with their own tongues!" (56). The *I* is situated in multiple identity constructions at once and functions in a range of representational politics, resisting some while reproducing the effects of others. The heuristic value of feminist lists such as "race, class, gender" lies in how they make visible the particular against the universal, how they remind feminists of the differences among women and in what some of those differences are constituted, but the lists also reveal the inadequacy of piling "objective" categories of experience upon one another, whether that is done in the service of ranking oppressions or of stabilizing the complex cultural field of identity.[11]

[11] See Moraga's critique of ranking oppressions, *Loving in the War Years: Lo que nunca pasó por sus labios* (Boston: South End, 1983), 50–59.

Guerrilla Autobiographics

If Cherríe Moraga can be said to represent what Teresa de Lauretis describes as a "feminist subject," a woman who sees her position within ideology from a vantage point of political critique, through what representational practices has Moraga displaced herself into this position, and what does war (and love) have to do with it? In this section I explore how Moraga's self-representational project, *Loving in the War Years* (1983), resists rhetorical violence and its material and emotional effects through a strategic use of autobiographics. In this sense, Moraga rereads crucial cultural myths of gender from a lesbian, feminist perspective, a perspective that is constructed as the threatening margin of Chicano culture. From this position, Moraga conducts strategic raids on the discourse of gendered identity, for her metaphors of war concern how women are imprisoned by sexist and homophobic ideology, how the love of daughters for the violated mother breaks all the rules, and how the rhetoric of gender, class, color, and sexuality marks the language of identity as hostile terrain for a lesbian, feminist Chicana. Given this understanding of her project, Moraga's genre-busting book can be read as a manifesto for a guerrilla autobiographics that explores the many meanings of the title, *Loving in the War Years: Lo que nunca pasó por sus labios.*

To recall the formulation with which I began, I offered autobiographics to describe those elements of self-representation which are not bound by a philosophical definition of the self derived from Augustine or the literary history or concept of the book which defines autobiography as a genre; instead, autobiographics marks a location in a text where self-invention, self-discovery, and self-representation emerge within the technologies of autobiography, namely, those legalistic, literary, cultural, and ecclesiastical discourses of truth and identity through which the subject of autobiography is produced. While the subject of autobiography has come to designate a stable *I* anchored within a relatively stable genre, this definition has come at the cost of dramatically narrowing the field of self-representation. Autobiographics, as a description of self-representation and as a reading practice, is concerned with resistance, contradiction, and interruption as strategies of self-representation. A text's autobiographics consists in the following emphases in self-representational writing, or writing that emphasizes the autobiographical *I*: writing itself as constitutive of autobiographical identity, discursive contradictions (rather than unity) in the representation of identity, the name as a potential site of experimentation rather than a contractual sign of identity, and the effects of the gendered connection of word and body. This approach gives initial conceptual precedence to positioning the subject and to describing "identity" and the networks of identification. An exploration of a text's autobiographics allows us to recognize that the *I* is multiply coded in a range of discourses: it is the site of multiple solicitations, multiple markings of "identity," multiple figurations of agency. Thus, autobiographics avoids the terminal questions of genre and close delimitation and offers a way, instead, to ask: Where is the autobiographical? What constitutes its representation? The *I*, then, does not disappear into an identity-less textual universe; rather, the autobiographicality of the *I* in a variety of discourses is emphasized as a point of resistance in self-representation.

Through poems, journal entries, and short essays, Moraga explores how the autobiographical is embedded in the discourse of the *familia*. *Familia*, in its network of meanings, composes for Moraga the discourse of truth and identity within which she must struggle to make her lesbianism visible. She writes in "La Güera": "I am the very well-educated daughter of a woman who, by the standards in this country, would be considered largely illiterate. My mother was born in Santa Paula, Southern California, at a time when much of the central valley there was still farm land. Nearly thirty-five years later, in 1948, she was the only daughter of six to marry an anglo, my father" (50). The *familia* forms a nexus within which collide Catholicism, sexuality, and ethnicity, all of which have deeply layered, even formalized, meanings of their own. Moraga describes herself as the light-skinned daughter of a Chicana and an Anglo who knew from the time she was ten years old that she was queer. But within her home and religion, queerness attached to the powerful imagery of the chosen: "Queer to believe that God cared so much about me, he intended to see me burn in hell; that unlike the other children, I was not to get by with a clean slate. I was born into this world with complications. I had been chosen, marked to *prove* my salvation" (ii). The figure of *familia* represents a highly charged and shifting place of loving and combat. For Moraga, writing about home in *Loving* traces a path within and across Chicano and lesbian communities, through a sustained encounter with the meaning of her love for her mother which will clarify the pulls of lesbianism, Catholicism, and ethnicity—all struggles, in Moraga's bodily figures, of the identity network Minnie Bruce Pratt has named "skin blood heart."[12]

---

[12] Minnie Bruce Pratt, "Identity: Skin Blood Heart," in *Yours in Struggle*, ed. Elly Bulkin, Pratt, and Barbara Smith (Ithaca: Firebrand, 1984), 11–64.

In a section called, "Like Family: Loving on the Run," a title that reinforces the compulsory transience of some lesbian love, Moraga's companion poems "Loving on the Run" and "Loving in the War Years" search for the places of "loving" offered Chicanas. Here, Moraga renders the autobiographical in poetry. "Loving on the Run" describes an encounter between the speaker of the poem and "you on a street corner / hangin out with a bunch of boys" (25). The poem is dedicated to "women who travel in packs of one" and traces through a moment of recognition the difficulties of seeing, being seen, and seeing oneself as a lesbian:

> I found you on a street corner
> hangin out with a bunch of boys
> lean brown boys
> you too lean
> into them
> talkin your girl-head off
> with your glasses like some wizard
> sayin
> "I know what that feels like."

There is tension in this street corner scene of loving, hanging out, speculating, and communing. The community in which this lesbian feels "at home" in her desire for women is formed with heterosexual men. Her "disguise" offers the only opportunity, in this section of the poem, for a sense of belonging. But it has its costs:

> For all your talk about women
> likin them
> they don't catch the difference
> for all your talk about your common enemy
> you operatin on a street sense
> so keen that it can spot danger
> before he makes it around the corner
> before he scarcely notices you
> as a woman
> *they marvel at this.*

The disjunction between a threatening "he" and a group, "they," who can "marvel" at the lesbian's street smarts, maps the social and psychic geography of the neighborhood. The lesbian and her street-corner group are engaged in a war of territory, of place, and, consequently, of identity. They share a stake in that war, a sense of the enemy: "They believin you/ because you know/ you got/ no reason/ to lie to them" (26). What is made visible in this section of the poem is how invisible the lesbian's sexuality is despite her voicing of desire, as well as the neighborhood that represses her sexuality while offering an ambivalent "home."

In the second section, the intimacies of location open into sexual intimacy:

> While walkin thru the neighborhood
> there you were
> kicked back on some porch
> actin like family
> like you belonged
> callin to me
> hangin over the railing
> wavin
> coaxin me to your steps
> gettin me to sit there
> you strokin my head
> slow and soft, sayin
> "you are soooo sweet"
> drawin out the "so"
> like a long drink
> like a deep moan
> comin out from inside you
> like a deep sigh
> of lovin.

This stanza juxtaposes the intimacy of the familiar, "like family," to the unsustainability of lesbian love within the unreconstructed world of this family. After two sections, the lesbian connections remain fleeting, precarious, still "lovin on the run."

In the third and final section, Moraga collects the fragmented moments of intimacy and gathers together love for women with the identification with men as family:

> collecting me
> into your thin arms
> you are woman to me
> and brother to them
> in the same breath
> *you marvel at this.*

The "home" offered by men on the street corner is not simply replaced by a lesbian home; rather, the women's sexual intimacy allows a change of vision which shifts the possibilities for identification, for self-knowledge, in the poem:

> Seeing yourself
> for the first time
> in the body of this sister
> like family
> like you belong
> you moving up against this woman
> like you this streetfighter
> like you whom
> you've taken in
> under your bruised wing
> your shoulderblade bent
> on bearing alone
> seeing yourself
> for the *first* time
> in the body of her boyhood
> her passion to survive
> female and *un*compromising.

The poem signals the shifts in identity by breaking from the I-you mode of address to a point outside, where the *I* can now be "seeing yourself / for the *first* time / in the body of her boyhood / her passion to survive / female and *un*compromising." And it is finally this changed view of home and identity which welds epistemology to politics through female agency: "Taking all this under your wing / letting it wrestle there / into your skin / changing you." Moraga offers an image of flight and shelter ("your wing"), an image of struggle, and has shifted from "I" to "you" through a performance of lesbian poetics and erotics. Throughout the poem, the speaker recharts the neighborhood until it can be read as a lesbian space. The place of revision, of course, is the poem, and the changed mode of address between lovers, but it is situated in the language of the neighborhood in which the lovers live. In order to move into this discursive space, Moraga begins with what appears as the thoroughly heterosexualized street corner where men talk about women, and reveals both the lesbian in the center of the scene and the lesbian speaker of the poem who recognizes her. In what is clearly not a lesbian-defined space, until revision makes it so, Moraga reveals the moment of recognition between the lesbian lovers as an act capable of altering the heterosexist narrative of lesbian disidentification: "Seeing yourself / for the *first* time / in the body of her boyhood."

The title poem, "Loving in the War Years," follows "Loving on the

Run"; both poems lie in the middle of a section titled "Like Family," in which Moraga represents relationships and places that do and do not feel like home and are connected in her search for *familia*. The section, however, is not about the simulation of a prior family or home, nor is it an effort to approximate or reproduce an edenic home. "Like" signifies the space of desire and the standard of reckoning for a future configuration to be named "Family." In this section and throughout the book, Moraga presents the feelings that prevent the possibility of family as a complex network of attraction and repulsion within the matrix of home, defined crucially through love for women and for her mother. Mostly, there is movement through, toward, and away from "home," for Moraga insists that racial and sexual oppression mark the memory and experience of the first home and border every other social context in which a lesbian home is established.

"Loving in the War Years," like "Loving on the Run," performs a dialogue between "I" and "you." The poem opens with the speaker offering her lover an analogy: "Loving you is like living / in the war years" (29). The speaker seeks another analogy, a place in which she can situate the lesbian relationship, and as if there is no concrete place or image that comes immediately to mind, she offers a Hollywood comparison, aware of its limitations:

> I *do* think of Bogart & Bergman
> not clear who's who
> but still singin a long smoky
> mood into the piano bar
> drinks straight up
> while bombs split
> outside, a broken
> world.

The near analogy seems suited to the war-torn times and ways of surviving which are fleshed out in the poem. The speaker enunciates the code of survival in this war as dependent on clear vision and graphic speech and revises the reactions of survival into the agency of resistance:

> Loving in the war years
> calls for this kind of risking
> without a home to call our own
> I've got to take you as you come
> to me, each time like a stranger
> all over again.

> Not knowing
> what deaths you saw today
> I've got to take you
> as you come, battle bruised
> refusing our enemy, fear.

In an effort to refuse "our enemy/fear," Moraga takes on the cultural myths of gender which structure male prerogative in the family. Moraga represents her family as a replication of the mestiza mixing of Anglo and Mexican-Indian blood which began with Cortéz and Doña Maria, who goes by many names that mostly add up to metonymic signifiers of female treachery. She is Malinche, Malintzin, La Chingada (the "fucked one"), La Vendida (sellout), and she is woven through the dichotomous representations of Woman as whore or madonna (La Virgen de Guadalupe). As Moraga recounts the central meaning of the myth for Mexicanas/Chicanas, "The sexual legacy passed down to the Mexicana/Chicana is the legacy of betrayal, pivoting around the historical/mythical female figure of Malintzin Tenepal. As translator and strategic advisor and mistress to the Spanish conqueror of México, Hernán Cortéz, Malintzin is considered the mother of the mestizo people. But unlike La Virgen de Guadalupe, she is not revered as the Virgin Mother, but rather slandered as La Chingada, meaning the 'fucked one,' or La Vendida, sell-out to the white race" (99). By rereading the myth of Malinche *as* mother as a way to understand her relationship to desire—for women, for spirituality, for her mother—Moraga negotiates the discourses of truth and identity which construct her as both historical and mythical subject.

In *Labyrinth of Solitude*, Octavio Paz describes the meaning of the word *chingar*: "The verb is masculine, active, cruel: it stings, wounds, gashes, stains. And it provokes a bitter, resentful satisfaction. The person who suffers this action is passive, inert and open, in contrast to the active, aggressive and closed person who inflicts it. The *chingón* is the *macho*, the male; he rips open the *chingada*, the female, who is pure passivity, defenseless against the exterior world. The relationship between them is violent and it is determined by the cynical power of the first and the impotence of the second."[13] The violence signified through this verb has a crucial meaning in the cultural myths of gender for Chicanas; insofar as it refers to the historical allegory of Malinche, it carries her legacy of betrayal for the Mexican

---

[13] Octavio Paz, *Labyrinth of Solitude: Life and Thought in Mexico* (New York: Grove, 1961), 77.

mestizo population. Chicanos are "los hijos de la chingada" ("the sons of the violated mother") and Chicanas are always both a re- minder of her betrayal and potential betrayers themselves. Gender violence in Chicano/a culture is partly interpretable through the con- text of this powerful cultural fiction.[14] Moraga, like other Chicanas, has had to understand the place of this myth in her own self- representation, and how it reproduces other practices of violence, betrayal, and silencing.[15] In order to explore the complexity of this situation, Moraga rereads the mythic/historical figure of Malinche, the sellout, in her long essay, "From a Long Line of Vendidas."

The essay traces Moraga's acculturation as female and Chicana, as lesbian and light-skinned, as an aspiring writer of a mother who cannot write. The crisscrossing of hierarchies of value in this network produces some unpredictable scenes, as well as those that are grimly *familiar*. There is the home training in gender hierarchy within color hierarchy: as light-skinned daughter, Moraga is encouraged to "pass" in Anglo culture. As a Chicana, she must wait on all the men who come through the family home, including her older brother and his friends. Moraga recounts: "When my sister and I were fifteen and fourteen, respectively, and my brother a few years older, we were still waiting on him. I write 'were' as if now, nearly two decades later, it were over. But that would be a lie. To this day in my mother's home, my brother and father are waited on, including by me. . . . the only thing that earned my brother my servitude was his maleness" (90). The location of this servitude within the Chicano family leads Moraga to this early self-representation and identification: "If somebody would have asked me when I was a teenager what it means to be Chicana, I would probably have listed the grievances done me" (90). True to the internalization of privilege, her brother can claim years later: "*'I've* never felt "culturally deprived",' which I guess is the term

---

[14] See also the feminist Chicana rereadings of this myth by Norma Alarcón, "Chi- cana's Feminist Literature: A Re-Vision Through Malintzin/or Malintzin: Putting Flesh Back on the Object," in *This Bridge Called My Back: Writings by Radical Women of Color* (Watertown, Mass.: Persephone, 1981), 182–90; Ana Castillo, "Massacre of the Dream- ers: Reflections on Mexican-Indian Women in the U.S. 500 Years after the Conquest," in *Critical Fictions: The Politics of Imaginative Writing*, ed. Philomena Mariani (Seattle: Bay Press, 1991), 161–76. See also Tomás Almaguer's excellent discussion of the relation of this myth to Chicano homosexuality, "Chicano Men: A Cartography of Homosexual Identity and Behavior," *differences* 3 (Summer 1991): esp. 79–80.

[15] For other Chicana writers who are experimenting with multicultural (self-) repre- sentation and are developing multigeneric writing strategies, see especially Gloria Anzaldúa, *Borderlands/La Frontera: The New Mestiza* (San Francisco: Spinsters, 1987); and Ana Castillo, *The Mixquiahuala Letters* (New York: Doubleday, 1992).

'white' people use to describe Third World people being denied access to *their* culture. At the time, I wasn't exactly sure what he meant, but I remember in re-telling the story to my sister, she responded, 'Of course, he didn't. He grew up male in our house. He got the best of both worlds.' . . . *Male in a man's world. Light-skinned in a white world. Why change?"* (92).

Why change? This question underwrites Moraga's work on oppression. Moraga rejects a political and emotional model that would seek to understand oppression by ranking it, deciding which is the graver insult and who the most deeply aggrieved. To comprehend oppression through a hierarchical model of analysis is to replicate the method of oppression. Moraga instead offers a way of comprehending the simultaneity of oppression as a way to understand the dynamic contours of ideology within a culture. Through her experience of passing as Anglo and heterosexual, "un"-classed by higher education and language, an exile who experienced the mark of cultural displacement as her color, Moraga explores how each of these attributes she is said to "possess" functions primarily as a term of value. Through the experience of passing as "straight" and "white," Moraga confronts the mythic construction of "true" ethnic origins and "false" assimilated culture as an oversimplified dichotomy. In a sense, her birth culture reveals the complicity of assimilationist and preservationist impulses. Her mother's passion for her daughter's advancement does not fit the dichotomy, nor does Moraga's experience of homophobia in the Chicano community make it feel like a truer home than the community she found first with primarily non-Chicana lesbians. Her mother furthered her education at every point, "anglocized" her daughter, giving her a "passport" to the better life inevitably associated with white culture; indeed, Moraga had to take lessons to acquire her "mother" tongue: "In fact, everything about my upbringing (at least what occurred on a conscious level) attempted to bleach me of what color I did have. Although my mother was fluent in it, I was never taught much Spanish at home. I picked up what I did learn from school and from over-heard snatches of conversation among my relatives and mother" (51). In the family home, Moraga learned the sexual and gender politics of Chicano culture. Relentlessly patriarchal and homophobic, the home was represented through these oppressions as the last stand against assimilation. Identities are fashioned in Moraga, then, from conflicted sources, in hard times, through political and emotional passions, and are represented in multiple genres. Passing marks her as a double exile: exiled from Chicanos because she is light-skinned; exiled from Anglos because she is culturally her mother's daughter. When embraced by the predominantly Anglo lesbian culture, she feels the absence of Chicana connections; when embraced by her family, she feels the homophobia directed at her.

Moraga links Anglo imperialism and gender hierarchy as the forces that have colonized the minds and sexuality of Chicanas. Chicanas, Moraga argues, have developed defensive structures to contain their sexuality: it is always, as in Genesis, *for* the man. To own one's sexuality as a Chicana places one perilously close to the betrayal of Malinche. To choose, then, the love of women is to betray Chicanos by turning away from the bonds of family and to betray Chicanas by creating one more *vendida*. As Moraga explains, "What looks like betrayal between women on the basis of race originates, I believe, in sexism/heterosexism. Chicanas begin to turn our backs on each other either to gain male approval or to avoid being sexually stigmatized by them under the name of puta, vendida, jota" (98). In all these representations of femaleness, women are thoroughly sexualized, their identities variously saturated with the (always) potentially negative and inescapable taint of sex.

The extent to which the figure of Malinche represents an internalized specter for women of their proximity to sexuality and disaster complicates all relationships among women. It places a particular burden on the relationship between mother and daughter. When the mother of all traitors and one's own mother are represented in the same conceptual breath, then love for the mother becomes a revolutionary act of consciousness. The mother's participation in putting men first, in reproducing the myth of Malinche, forms another boundary for Moraga to cross as she attempts to negotiate her way to her mother through her lesbianism and not, as she had previously tried, in spite of it. Through all the tracings of home and family, through the two languages (Spanish and English) in which Moraga writes, and in all the kinds of writing that compose this "book," Moraga is putting into discourse the movement of desire for her mother. One converstion between Moraga and her mother develops into a scene of erotic self-identification. Her mother has asked her to have a man-to-man talk with her shy and sexually withdrawn father: "Grabbing my hand across the table, 'Honey, I know what it's like to be touched by a man who wants a woman. I don't feel this with your father,' squeezing me. . . . The room falls silent then as if the walls, themselves, begged for a moment to swallow back the secret that had just leaked out from them. And it takes every muscle in me, *not* to leave my chair, *not* to climb through the silence, *not* to clamber toward her, *not* to touch her the way I know she wants to be touched" (11).

At the heart of the myth of Malinche is the betrayal of a mother: she betrays her children, who in turn betray her with the reproduction of the myth. Moraga writes her way into the nexus of this rhetorical violence, as if she were making a guerrilla raid on the storehouse of cultural image-weaponry against the love among women, and declares the area a war zone in which: "I am my mother's lover" (32). When she asks herself rhetorically in the introduction to the themes of loving and war who she is writing for, she focuses again on the mother as a figure for possible relations among women: "But for whom have I tried so steadfastly to communicate? . . . It's the daughters who remain loyal to the mother. . . . It is not always reciprocated. . . . Free the daughter to love her own daughter. It is the daughters who are my audience" (vii).

Moraga's rereading of Malinche stages a process of consciousness, a strategy I am calling guerrilla autobiographics, for confronting the rhetorical violence in myths of gender identity. These myths construct sexuality as the degraded proof of gender and offer a "first woman" figure as the negative standard by which all women must continuously measure themselves and be measured, their identification with women barred by this dangerous similarity. By enacting this strategy as both an emotional and a political response, Moraga reveals how women are "fragmented" by culturally hegemonic models of female identity rather than by some sort of "internal" breakdown or splitting from an "external" originary whole. As a master narrative of female identity, the myth of Malinche constructs women's self-representation as a slave narrative, placing them in the lineage of the first slave to benefit from assimilation. Through this analysis, Moraga considerably complicates the critique of oppression. She goes beyond the terms "internalization" and "externalization" in order to express the simultaneity of influences, the partial saturation of gender ideology, the emergent resistance, and the embeddedness of the internal (women's personal senses of what it means to be a woman) within the external (myths, practices, and institutions of oppression which construct the "internal" as fragmented and partial).

The complexity of *familia* and home, through which the myth of Malinche runs, is written in the mutual articulation, the binding together, of mother's and daughter's sexuality. It is especially the graphic representations of the mother/daughter eroticism which challenge Moraga to rewrite the discourses of home in order to make visible not only lesbian sexuality but her identity as a writer. In the preface, she writes: "How can it be that I have always hungered for and feared falling in love as much as I do writing from my heart. Each changes you forever" (iv). In order to explore the places of change textually, to render the multiple identities separated in different rhetorical and formal traditions, Moraga blends Spanish and English, poetry and prose, critique and experience. Also, by combining poems written over several years with essays and journal entries, Moraga presents the book as a figure of process: "The selections are not arranged chronologically in terms of when each piece was written. Rather I have tried to create a kind of emotional/political chronology" (i). By the end of "From a Long Line of Vendidas," Moraga has revised the meaning of *familia* and expanded it to include the former prohibitions on female sexuality:

> Family is *not* by definition the man in a dominant position over women and children. Familia is cross-generational bonding, deep emotional ties between opposite sexes, and within our sex. It is sexuality, which involves, but is not limited to, intercourse or orgasm. It springs forth from touch, constant and daily. The ritual of kissing and the sign of the cross with every coming and going from home. . . . The strength of our families never came from domination. It has only endured in spite of it—like our women. (111)

These arguments replace negative constructions of women's sexuality in a general sense. Moraga addresses the specificity of lesbianism at the conclusion of the essay and also in her poetry. The love of women for the mother and other women is not synonymous with lesbianism, nor is it the logical or necessary conclusion of such love. Moraga does not find lesbianism as a preexisting element in all women or in the family itself; she does, however, find her own lesbianism there, tangled in and constituted by its power struggles and not existing in a transcendent place of pure discovery or nature. All women are not lesbians, nor does political feminist consciousness demand that "identity." Moraga resists the notion that because there is a political argument to justify that teleology, lesbianism carries an imperative for all women. Rather, for Moraga, lesbians are positioned within specific cultures that "influence" (129) sexuality and are influenced by it. Sexual identity is inseparable from this situation. Sexual identity, when that means lesbianism, is not a sufficient ground for identity politics. Thus her critique of her own culture and the threat of betrayal implied within it are precisely the knot of desire and identity through which Moraga must work. To displace herself into a separatist lesbian culture without a history and without her culture replicates the assimilation she has fought against.

Thus Moraga persistently analyzes the relationship between oppression and alienation and resists promoting a particular oppression as primary: "For, if race and class suffer the woman of color as much as her sexual identity, then the Radical Feminist must extend her own 'identity' politics to include her 'identity' as oppressor as well. (To say nothing of having to acknowledge that there are men who may suffer more than she)" (128). On the whole, then, feminist solutions that hold out lesbianism as the "logical personal response to a misogynist political system" (129), as a political response based in separation from specific cultures of oppression, are akin, in Moraga's view, to retaining race- and class-biased cultural superiority: "The lesbian separatist retreats from the specific cultural contexts that have shaped her and attempts to build a cultural-political movement based on an imagined oppression-free past. . . . The mistake lies in believing in this ideal past or imagined future so thoroughly and single-mindedly that finding solutions to present-day inequities loses priority, or we attempt to create too-easy solutions for the pain we feel today" (129). For Moraga, then, lesbianism is not about *the* mother but about her mother, the mother she was taught to distrust and betray within a specific culture.

Knowing this network of identifications, representing it in its discontinuities, in its rhetorical fragmentation of identities, is negotiated for Moraga in self-representational writing that seeks to make visible the complex experience and consciousness that conjoin being "in print" and being "out-to-the-world." In the effort to render her complexity of *situation*, Moraga crafts a self-representational rhetoric that will bring into expression the multiplicity of identity. To that end, she blends Spanish and English to create a hybrid rhetoric for a multicultural identity. Donna Haraway characterizes Moraga's response to the rhetorical violence that keeps these identities fractured: "Moraga's language is not 'whole'; it is self-consciously spliced, a chimera of English and Spanish, both conquerer's languages. But it is this chimeric monster, without claim to an original language before violation, that crafts the erotic, competent, potent identities of women of color."[16]

The Genesis myth of gender's origin legitimates violence against women, coded into the very language of law and human arrangements, for generations to come. *The Woman Warrior*'s gender myths legitimate the punishment of women and, through the complicitous silence of other women, the perpetuation of that punishment. King-

[16] Donna Haraway, "A Manifesto for Cyborgs: Science, Technology, and Socialist Feminism in the 1980s," *Socialist Review* 80 (April 1985): 94.

ston's revisionary myth of gender makes revenge on her Chinese immigrant culture possible, though at a cost, and ultimately also makes possible her reentry to that culture. Kingston ends *The Woman Warrior* with her own version of one of her mother's talk-stories, "Song for a Barbarian Reed Pipe"; as a tribute to her mother's legacy and to her own talent, it is double-voiced. The talk-story describes Ts'ai Yen, a kidnapped poet who lives among barbarians, has children, and ultimately writes songs that are drawn partly from her own culture, partly from the one she entered as a captive. Kingston offers Ts'ai Yen as a model of the transformative possibilities of cultural influences when she claims that Ts'ai Yen's song, like the talk-story Kingston presents here, "translates well." It is impossible to forget, however, the conditions under which Ts'ai Yen composed; thus, the ending is not a resolution of the cultural conflicts that structure Kingston's discourse but another instance of them. Moraga concurs that there is no way out but through specific cultural contradictions in identity.

Following "From a Long Line of Vendidas," Moraga concludes *Loving in the War Years* with three short poems and a fragment, all written in a mixture of Spanish and English, which reformulate key concepts in the network of themes the book has traveled. She begins with passion and connects the spiritual and sexual meanings in the geography of the body:

> I am a river cracking open. It's as if the parts of me were before just thin tributaries. Lines of water like veins running barely beneath the soil or skimming the bone surface of the earth—sometimes desert creek, sometimes city-wash, sometimes like sweat sliding down a woman's breastbone.
> Now I can see the point of juncture. Comunión. And I gather my forces to make the river run. (145)

Moraga's fusion of Catholicism and lesbian sexuality in passion prefigures the following poem's trope of hunger as a way of understanding the reconciliation among ethnicity, sexuality, and identity. The penultimate poem addresses mother and sister and establishes the return to a world of women within the family that Moraga can claim in the poem that concludes the volume, "Querida Compañera." The final poem offers the knowledge gained from the perspective of exile (within and outside of communities and homes) and finally names it as "lo que nunca / pasó / por sus labios" (what never passed through her lips) "but was / utterly / utterly / heard": the mother's gift, remembered in the body of the daughter, opened, and offered.

6

A Signature of Lesbian Autobiography

Coupling the Signature: Lesbian Representation and the Discourse of Autobiography

What a history is folded, folded inward and inward again, in the single word *I.*
—Walt Whitman, *An American Primer*

Identity always worries me and memory and eternity.
—Gertrude Stein, *Everybody's Autobiography*

In the summer of 1932, Gertrude Stein was writing two autobiographies. One, *Stanzas in Meditation*, records the standoff between Stein and Alice Toklas that developed after Toklas discovered the manuscript of *Q.E.D.*, a text in which Stein addressed her affair with May Bookstaver. Stein had not told Toklas about the affair, and when Toklas realized that one of the contexts of the wordplay was the sexual relationship with Bookstaver, she was furious.[1] The second, *The Autobiography of Alice B. Toklas*, takes the form of a long love letter to Alice, a compensatory gift Gertrude wrote to appease her partner. While it would be possible to read *The Autobiography* within the "context of production" suggested by these anecdotes, I offer them, instead, as a caution. Although biographical explanation informs our understanding of *The Autobiography* and *Stanzas* by, for instance, exposing the levels of parody and tension at play in seemingly simple statements in both, it may also naturalize Stein's discourse as an "expression" of identity and may miniaturize her as a member of a spatting couple. In this sense, autobiography may function as photography does: it naturalizes the subject, presents her as simply there, and in so doing represents a *time* (the biographical axis of representation) that no

[1] Ulla E. Dydo, "*Stanzas in Meditation*: The Other Autobiography," *Chicago Review* 35.2 (1985): 12.

longer exists as a *space* (the autobiographical axis of representation) that remains. As an object, an autobiography, like a photograph, simulates the action of the eye in a way that obscures how the apparatus of representation works on and within the scene it depicts. An analysis of Steinian autobiography may open onto biography rather than onto all that cannot readily be seen, but it does so by foreclosing an inspection of Stein's autobiographical experimentalism in *The Autobiography*. I focus here on how Stein writes an autobiography profoundly concerned with visibility, with what can and cannot be seen and why, as a way to explore the contradictory codes of lesbian and autobiographical (self-) representation she weaves together.

In contrast to the autobiographer bound by traditional laws of gender and genre, Stein reads the technologies of autobiography available at the beginning of the twentieth century for the gaps, discontinuities, and noncoincidences in gendered and sexual "identity" and reveals there a lesbian space of self-representation. Stein rewrites the illusory seamlessness of autobiography as a contradictory code of (self-) representation through three major displacements. First, she displaces the function of the autobiographical signature and the autobiographical *I*, which is to act as the referential anchor for the story of the self, onto the lesbian couple. Second, she relocates the meaning of gendered identity within a contradictory code of lesbian (self-) representation and mobilizes the recognizable constituents of autobiography—chief among them, chronological organization, a "truthful" narrator, and an individuated *I*—against autobiography itself. Third, she performs an autobiographical lesbian subject position as a major feature of this code located within a lesbian "economy" of exchange.

Given Stein's interest in verbal experimentation, we might well expect her work to have informed some of the current poststructuralist exploration of autobiography. This has not, however, generally been the case. In their introduction to *Life/Lines: Theorizing Women's Autobiography*, editors Bella Brodzki and Celeste Schenck offer *The Autobiography of Alice B. Toklas* as the "ultimate female autobiography —with a difference" for two reasons: to remark upon Stein's anticipation of and affiliation with poststructuralism and to question Stein's absence from contemporary studies of autobiography written by men (10–13). Brodzki and Schenck wonder how male critics, lured by the poststructuralist possibilities of autobiography, could have missed a star source such as Stein (11). Stein's fragmentary depiction of the self, her aggressively textual self-portraiture, and I would add, her enactment of Foucault's notion of writing as a game in which the author constantly disappears, make her an obvious candidate for such studies. Yet the omission of Stein reveals for Brodzki and Schenck the sexism of the recent boom in autobiography studies. "Is it only because [Gertrude Stein] is a woman," they ask, "that Michael Sprinker does not use her as a point of reference in 'The End of Autobiography'?" (11). Instead of seeking admission for Stein into critical works by male liberals in radicals' clothing, Brodzki and Schenck press their inquiry into this resistance by suggesting that Stein's decision to tell the story of the self as the story of the other enacts a specifically female autobiographical mode: "Being *between two covers* with somebody else ultimately replaces singularity with alterity in a way that is dramatically female, provides a mode of resisting reification and essentialism, and most important, allows for more radical experimentation in autobiographical form than recent critics . . . have been willing to attribute to women writers" (11).[2] In general, I agree with Brodzki and Schenck's insight, but instead of strictly pursuing the well-placed charge of sexism, I would like to confront sexism's ideological partner, heterosexism. To do so I must embolden Brodzki and Schenck's italicized flirtation, *"between two covers,"* in order to argue that the subject position Stein constructs in *The Autobiography* which enables this experimentation and revision is lesbian. I begin by exploring a signature and some lesbian signs as a context for discussion.

In the manuscript of "Lend a Hand," Wendy Steiner found a "doodle" that figured Gertrude Stein's lesbian relationship with Alice Toklas: "Gertrice/Altrude."[3] Through the combination of Stein's and Toklas's names, this marginal note represents a lesbian signature of "their" autobiography and underscores their coupling of the autobiographical signature in a way that the title and author identities represented as *"The Autobiography of Alice B. Toklas* by Gertrude Stein" do not. The commingled names "dragging at the margins" of Stein's manuscript, to use Jill Dolan's phrase, focus the complicated codes of lesbian semiotics, that is, the historically specific possibilities of making visible or invisible lesbian sexuality.[4] Given the contradictory

[2] As I have suggested, Brodzki and Schenck are significantly elaborating Mary Mason's groundbreaking essay on women's autobiography, "The Other Voice."

[3] Wendy Steiner, *Exact Resemblance to Exact Resemblance: The Literary Portraiture of Gertrude Stein* (New Haven: Yale University Press, 1978), 187. See also Catharine Stimpson, "Gertrice/Altrude: Stein, Toklas, and the Paradox of the Happy Marriage," in *Mothering the Mind*, eds. Ruth Perry and Martine Watson Brownley (New York: Holmes and Meier, 1984), 122–39.

[4] Jill Dolan, " 'Lesbian' Subjectivity in Realism: Dragging at the Margins of Structure and Ideology," in *Performing Feminisms: Feminist Critical Theory and Theatre*, ed. Sue-Ellen Case (Baltimore: Johns Hopkins University Press, 1990), 40.

codes available to Stein for representing lesbian sexuality, it is not surprising that she both inscribed and satirized them. From Richard von Krafft-Ebing's and Havelock Ellis's sexological discourse on inversion to the salon stylings of Natalie Clifford Barney and others, Stein and Toklas negotiated the space of sexual signification in Paris and beyond at least in part through their relation to autobiography.[5] My aim here is to examine how Stein used autobiography to inscribe the lesbian couple as the "subject" of *The Autobiography*, so that I may locate her extended autobiographical experimentation within two critical discourses—contemporary feminist and poststructuralist criticism of autobiography—neither of which has yet sufficiently incorporated an analysis of lesbian writing.

Until Stein was taken up by feminist critics, her early work was read as a densely textured kind of metapoetics, a discourse that referred almost entirely to itself. This reading enforced her canonization as a form-smashing modernist, undoubtedly significant but little read. Recently, feminist critics have "brought out" Gertrude Stein— beyond the conventional nod to her "longtime companion Alice Toklas"—by focusing on the "encoding" of a lesbian autobiography within Stein's asyntactic poetics. In one of the first essays in this phase of criticism, Elizabeth Fifer asserted: "Gertrude Stein's erotic works are demonstrations of disguised autobiography. Stein invented a witty code that played upon the details of her sexual and domestic self. In such a private autobiographical style she can tell everything— and she does."[6] In "Painted Lace" (1914), "Pink Melon Joy" (1915), and "Lifting Belly" (1917), according to Fifer, Stein creates a coded language and sign system that represents her lesbian relationship with Toklas. By describing this early work as a coherent and definable stage, Fifer offers new insight into Stein's refusal of classical realism and the lyric. Fifer's reading depends on recognizing the contradictory capacity of any sign system—here, specifically, a system that produces a lesbian subject that is not so much suppressed (and hence unavailable to the reader except as conjecture) as encoded and, therefore, not so much repressed (and hence unavailable to the writer except as confusion) as consistently recoded. Catharine Stimpson offers a similar explanation for Stein's complex name play and secret

[5] For an elaboration of this milieu, see Shari Benstock, *Women of the Left Bank: Paris, 1900–1940* (Austin: University of Texas Press, 1986), esp. 143–93.

[6] Elizabeth Fifer, "Is Flesh Advisable? The Interior Theater of Gertrude Stein," *Signs* 4 (1979): 472.

language.[7] Through her enactment of a lover's discourse, Stimpson's Stein can write a language of lesbian desire which plays with the names she and Toklas gave themselves and their sexual pleasures. Stimpson thereby links poetic invention with sexual subversiveness while remaining astute about Stein's reasons for reworking private matters into a private language. Following this stage of Stein criticism, Lisa Ruddick argues that Stein's linguistic experimentation is linked through its daring and depth to her personal evolution. Ruddick interprets the early experimental works as "serial acts of self-definition," suggesting that Stein's literary and lesbian "identities" emerge as a discourse that does not divide them as theory versus practice, public versus private.[8] The play of the signifier which characterizes Stein's writing, then, is situated in the context of lesbian self-representation. These feminist readings go a long way toward establishing a new spectator/reader for Stein's experimentation, a spectator capable of reading the lesbian *in* and *as* this complex encoding.

I would like to extend the insights into Stein's inscription of a lesbian subject position drawn from work on her "secret" autobiographies to a text she entitled "autobiography." The oscillation between the visible and the invisible in Stein's lesbian representation continues in *The Autobiography of Alice B. Toklas*, as well as in critical discourses that compound/elucidate invisibility/visibility. One of the ironies of Stein criticism is the extent to which its strategies sometimes obscure the lesbian as they explore Stein's verbal experimentation, and vice versa. For example, in situating Stein within the

[7] See Catharine Stimpson, "The Mind, the Body, and Gertrude Stein," *Critical Inquiry* 3 (1977): 491–96. See also Carolyn Burke, who, working along the same lines, claims: "For ten years, between 1903 and 1913, Gertrude Stein . . . converted the predicaments of her personal life into literary material, the better to solve and to exorcise them" ("The Cone Sisters," in *Writing and Sexual Difference*, ed. Elizabeth Abel [Chicago: University of Chicago Press, 1981], 221). Burke takes as her text the textualization of Stein's friendship with the Cone sisters, Etta and Claribel. She sees the dissolution of Stein's friendship with Etta Cone and Stein's growing dissatisfaction with the friendship's insufficient intimacy as prelude to her decision to live with Toklas. By combining biographical and literary evidence, Burke breaks the code that mutes the lesbian and the autobiographical in *Q.E.D.* (1903), *Fernhurst* (1904), *Three Lives* (1905–6), and *The Making of Americans* (1906–11). Taking the persona's declaration in *Q.E.D.*—"Why . . . it's like a piece of mathematics. Suddenly it does itself and you begin to see" (67)—as an autobiographical statement, Burke sees autobiography, encoded and transmuted though it may be, everywhere.

[8] Lisa Ruddick, *Reading Gertrude Stein: Body, Gnosis, Text* (Ithaca: Cornell University Press, 1990), 1.

discourse of autobiography, I depend upon the insights of decon-struction in the following ways: The doodle "Gertrice/Altrude" re-veals Stein's ambivalence about the self as a unified figure. This sug-gestive marginalia destabilizes the signature on which traditional interpretations of autobiography depend. Clearly, Stein is represent-ing autobiographical "identity" against the grain of identity politics and the politics of representation which they structure. For Stein, at least in this autobiography, the unified subject that stands before the law of gender and genre and represents itself through the signature is not the focus of this text. Both the concept of identity and the politics of representation that would offer up the autobiographer as an auton-omous and solitary self are undermined here by Stein's persistent play, as well as by the rhetorical resistance she enacts by refusing to follow the representational law.

Stein's representational politics, then, resists the notion that auto-biography is a discursive site for shoring up the self. Her experimen-tation is much more in line with the kind of lesbian representational politics that are less interested in an existing or preexisting identity (here, a sexual identity) that determines the "truth" of lesbian repre-sentation and more interested in representations that challenge the coding of sexuality, gender, and identity through models of coher-ence, stability, and causality. The insights of deconstruction have proved most effective in destabilizing what is already massively stabi-lized through institutions, laws, entrenched practices, and habits of mind, however. Lesbian identities are not surrounded and secured by the monumental cultural apparatuses that make deconstruction seem necessary. Stein's work requires a more flexibly articulated critical discourse that blends materialism with poststructuralism.

As a way to pursue a critical location that conjoins materialism and poststructuralism, we can turn to the French feminist materialist critic and experimental writer Monique Wittig for insight into lesbian and feminist concerns she shares with Stein. Stein's exploration of the autobiographical *I* and signature shares a general representational strategy with Wittig's rhetorical challenges to the language of identity. In "The Mark of Gender," Wittig discusses how personal pronoun use and gender are mutually reinforcing structures and offers *j/e* as an oppositional solution to the false unity of *je*.[9] Wittig is interested in the feminist politics of naming throughout her fiction and uses *j/e* in *The Lesbian Body* to signify a coupled rather than split female subject.

[9] Monique Wittig, "The Mark of Gender," in *Poetics of Gender*, ed. Nancy K. Miller (New York: Columbia University Press, 1986), 63–73.

In her Author's Note to *The Lesbian Body*, Wittig writes: "*J/e* is the symbol of the lived, rending experience which is *m/y* writing, of this cutting in two which throughout literature is the exercise of a language which does not constitute *m/e* as subject" (7). Just as these words create new possibilities for female definition and representation in Wittig's writing, they oppose the univocality of *je* and *ils* and erode their ability to signify unproblematically.[10] Gertrude Stein also subverts the conventions of naming in *The Autobiography* to call attention to the problem in it which draws her to the complexity of utterance, to the lesbian couple as an autobiographical subject position.

Wittig's severed *j/e* represents an identity cut at its center by a language of identity which reproduces this rhetorical violence in the material world every time a woman speaks or writes from the position of *I*. Stein's doodle, however, represents a position to the side of that language where "Gertrice/Altrude" signifies a lesbian identity that does not cut or deform, neither does it figure the Lacanian split subject. Rather, to borrow Sue-Ellen Case's bon mot, it "replac[es] a Lacanian slash with a lesbian bar."[11] The "identities" of lesbianism are figured in this autobiographical signature as the intermingling of syllables across a penetrable border. The subject position represented through this signature destabilizes the unified, solitary subject, whose ability to assure self-identity is the premise of the "autobiographical pact," and recasts the problem of (self-) representation in the context of a lesbian relationship.

"Gertrice/Altrude" flouts the kind of equivalency drawn between the solitary person and her or his recorded truth. In the terms of the "autobiographical pact" and the legal mythology of the signature it creates, the structure of autobiographical identity is a prolonged naming of the subject. The proper name collects experience, change and continuity, family relations, and social agency in a signifier of commanding proportions, for it signifies not only the person in the present whose birth certificate bears that name but the very possibility of the subject's temporal and spatial coherence. The name enforces the contractual oath of truth the autobiographer takes, and the reward of such fidelity is a "self" who survives. The guarantee of immortality, or at least remembrance, derives from the truthful solidity and the

---

[10] Although Wittig's experimentation usefully contextualizes Stein's interest in pronouns, it is still important to note that Wittig's work occurs at a different moment in a history of lesbian autobiographical representation. De Lauretis develops this history in "Sexual Indifference and Lesbian Representation," in *Performing Feminisms*, ed. Case, 17–39.

[11] Sue-Ellen Case, "Toward a Butch-Femme Aesthetic," *Discourse* 11.1 (1988–89): 57.

assertion that "I lived, I write, and I bear witness to my self." But Stein represents a lesbian autobiographical identity that history has not written. Thus she does not position herself in relation to confessional or testimonial rhetoric with its assertion of verifiable truth and its authority structure of authenticity. Rather, she plays upon the devices of fiction: Toklas is a character in her own "autobiography"; the "real" writer is a character in Toklas's autobiography. Stein is also a ghost writer, an invisible hand, who capitalizes on the role playing available within the subject of autobiography. By reading and writing linguistic and lesbian experimentation into the autobiographical *I*, Stein exploited its capacity to obscure and reveal particular kinds of difference and noncoincidence as well as the sameness of homosexuality (de Lauretis's term for same-sex sexuality). *The Autobiography of Alice B. Toklas*, Stein's auto- and homo-biography, constructs a lesbian subject position in autobiography.

Interpretation of lesbian representation is straightjacketed by the pervasiveness of what Wittig has called "the straight mind."[12] That is, the multiple networks in which structuralists and poststructuralists agree we exist assume heterosexuality as a premise from which all discourse derives. Wittig makes clear how an analysis such as semiotics derailed its political potential when it confronted the obligatory coding of heterosexuality. For Wittig, a political semiotics would confront the regularizing and enforcing tendencies of codes and view them as a method of control. Such an emphasis would focus on codes as instruments that train the subject in certain practices—including practices through which one is gendered and heterosexualized—and would expose the incoherence and contradiction within codes as the site of political opposition.[13] Given the critical context I have been elaborating here through Wittig's and Stein's emphasis on experimentalism, what more can be seen in Stein's own "encoded" works and the criticism that discovered them? While the insight that Stein's language is coded and that what is encoded is a lesbian language considerably advanced Stein criticism, the residual images of background/foreground, truth/simulation, identity/disguise haunt some of this criticism. What many critics, some of them Stein's most astute readers, assume is that a code is layered over an otherwise clear meaning; once the code is cracked, meaning spills out everywhere.

[12] Monique Wittig, "The Straight Mind," *Feminist Issues* 1.1 (1980): 107.

[13] I also take this idea to be very much in line with de Lauretis's analysis of narrative and desire; see especially chapter 5 of *Alice Doesn't* and the last four chapters in *Technologies of Gender*.

This conception assumes that what is being encoded is perfectly clear to the writer, who intends all her effects, and that representation is secondary, descriptive and not constructive. It also suggests that the impetus for formal experimentation lies in the urge/need to disguise lesbian content.[14]

I mean to argue, in contrast, that formal experimentation offers a way to make a lesbian subject position visible and not to disguise it. To suggest that Stein chose formal experimentation as one long end run around the problem of visibility rather than the most sustained, provocative, and imaginative encounter with it seems to obscure how her innovation works. Clearly, realist narrative was available to her and she rejected it, not because it fit her subject all too well and would therefore expose her as a lesbian, but because it did not. Citing other gay writers who created a textual space of sexual (self-) representation through experimental writing, Wittig also anticipates the ongoing political dimension of experimental forms of writing: "Since Proust we know that literary experimentation is a favored way to bring a subject to light. This experimentation is the ultimate subjective practice, a practice of the cognitive subject. Since Proust the subject has never been the same, for throughout *Remembrance of Things Past* he made 'homosexual' the axis of categorization from which to universalize."[15] The political valences of several paired terms, then, are not axiomatic or predictable: literary experimentation is no more automatically regressive and withdrawn from the field of visibility than realist narrative is automatically "open"; neither are experimental forms more radical or more conservative across the board than traditional ones. The point here is to keep from reproducing a critical narrative that suggests that lesbian and gay writers are more "out," more visible, when they write in traditional forms, that experimentation is a developmental phase that gives way to more "straightforward" writing practices. This historical terrain is certainly complicated, for while traditions often seem to move forward when viewed from an aesthet-

---

[14] Shari Benstock, for example, warning against "too literally 'decoding' the lesbian structures supporting Stein's writing, which risks reducing them to the formulaic and conventional," and calling attention to the constructive dimension of representation, later suggests that formal experimentation is a disguise rather than a construction: "The artistic risk takers (Djuna Barnes, Gertrude Stein, Virginia Woolf) disguised the lesbian content of their writing within experimental forms" ("Expatriate Sapphic Modernism: Entering Literary History," in *Lesbian Texts and Contexts*, ed. Karla Jay and Joanne Glasgow [New York: New York University Press, 1990], 195, 198).

[15] Monique Wittig, "Point of View: Universal or Particular?" *Feminist Issues* 3.2 (1983): 64–65.

ic context, the uses and forms of writing are not "progressive" in this developmental sense because they are always embedded in other social and discursive formations besides strictly literary ones.[16]

To pursue Stein's experimentalism within the specifics of autobiography, we can see how Stein challenges the question "Whose autobiography is it?" as well as the answers such a question seeks and the assumptions that produce it. Is "Whose autobiography is it?" reducible to or identical with "Whose life is it?" Must that question further be reducible to "Who is writing?" Stein's finely tuned sensitivity to verbal destabilizations found a provocative figure in the autobiographical *I*. Let us pose a question that will recontextualize Stein's autobiography: What is the discourse of the lesbian couple positioned within an identity-constructing form (autobiography) and what does this interpretive reorientation allow? Heterosexuality has been an unwritten context of the autobiographical subject, and it has bound women and men to each other through structural negativity. Questions of sexual difference deteriorate to sexual opposition when the program of self-definition becomes "a woman is a woman because she is not a man." By bracketing the negativity of heterosexual self-definition, Stein could explore other possibilities for self-representation.

At first glance, Stein and Toklas seem to have managed a superficially "straight"—or, more accurately, butch-femme—household. They organized their domestic economies according to divisions long entrenched in heterosexual arrangements: Stein was the reigning genius, whose writing was central; Toklas kept the household running. But here, perhaps, is a place to interrogate the interpretive habits of the "straight mind." Why does the butch-femme model of Stein's and Toklas's relationship appear to mimic heterosexuality? When we situate butch-femme within lesbian dynamics, the emergent subject position constructed by this practice has a performative force in *The Autobiography* which enables the signifiers of their life together to be read as roles encoded in butch-femme relations rather than as, for example, something derivative and grimly essentialist such as the natural expression of their different natures. That is, there is a certain playfulness, a self-construction, involved in adapting these roles.

In her essay "Toward a Butch-Femme Aesthetic," Sue-Ellen Case claims that butch-femme has always been a witty play on the domi-

---

[16] Marcia Aldrich and I address this issue in the context of Minnie Bruce Pratt's work. See our "Writing Home: 'Home' and Lesbian Representation in Minnie Bruce Pratt," *Genre* (Spring 1992).

nant culture's encoding of the couple; thus, it remains so whenever it appears. Butch-femme is a role lesbians inhabit together. Case quotes the old song: "You can't have one without the other" (70). Its performance layers an oppositional agency in behavior. Lesbians can act in certain stylized ways toward each other through a discourse of signs and gestures in which they become knowable as lesbians against tremendous cultural pressure toward invisibility and neutralization. Role playing underlies Stein's experimentation, especially as it destabilizes and shifts the possibilities for point of view in her portraiture. While the politics of a butch-femme arrangement and of a butch-femme interpretation remain troubling for some, I suggest we place such an approbative critique within a historical frame that makes Stein's and Toklas's choice visible primarily as a lesbian practice.[17]

Indeed, more complications emerge against the critique of butch-femme when we historicize its performance, and contextualize Stein's and Toklas's relationship within the Left Bank literary milieu of the 1920s. Take, for example, Alice's practice of "sitting with wives." In 1907 Alice visited Gertrude's home at 27, rue de Fleurus. She describes it as a bustling salon filled with chatty intimates and interesting strangers. Alice is moved by the strangeness and unfamiliarity of the paintings that Gertrude and her brother Leo collected and which lined the walls: "It is very difficult now that everybody is accustomed to everything to give some idea of the kind of uneasiness one felt when one looked at all these pictures on these walls" (*The Autobiography*, 10). Later in the evening, Gertrude places Alice with Picasso's "wife," Fernande: "Fernande was the first wife of a genius I sat with

[17] Case discusses Joan Nestle's *Lesbian Herstory Archives* and argues that "the butch-femme tradition went into the feminist closet" in the 1970s, following a two-pronged feminist attack ("Butch-Femme Aesthetic," 59). The heterosexual feminist movement sought to tame the butch's unfeminized self-presentation and thereby stigmatize the femme's desire for butch lovers. In other words, lesbians were to become more "regular," less threatening to a movement that was increasingly concerned with its mainstream image and decreasingly tolerant of lesbian sexuality. Pursuing the critique from a different angle, according to Case, lesbian feminists questioned the desirability of roles lifted from heterosexuality. The pressure from these convergent politics succeeded in forcing butch-femme role playing into the bars rather than out in the streets. Case considers the feminist critique of butch-femme thoroughly homophobic. She gives no credence to the argument that it is imitative and even reactionary for lesbians to play out the male-female, husband-wife roles of the dominant culture or to the argument that the roles carry heterosexist baggage, that they stultify, codify, and rigidify lesbianism, and participate in keeping lesbians bound to a heterosexual prison house of imagery and models. That is, butch-femme roles can offer neither a point of resistance nor a fully fledged lesbian code because they are always already written out of what Fredric Jameson has described as the political unconscious of the dominant culture.

and she was not the least amusing. We talked hats. Fernande had two subjects hats and perfumes. This first day we talked hats" (14). This tableau brings forward the stylization of Alice's relation to Gertrude more than it links Alice with heterosexual women or Gertrude with heterosexual men; it is a parody of heterosexual segregation. If we saw this scene on stage, and thus could read it as a sign, wouldn't we laugh at this "ironized and 'camped-up'" (Case, "Butch-Femme," 64) version of party behavior? For just such an emphasis on the semiotic send-ups that Stein presents in *The Autobiography*'s vignettes demonstrates how the gendered practice of "sitting with wives" cannot explain who Alice is, cannot fix her as "woman" in that scene. Gertrude has Alice warm to the topic with the ironic weariness of a connoisseur: "I have sat with wives who were not wives, of geniuses who were real geniuses. I have sat with real wives of geniuses who were not real geniuses. I have sat with wives of geniuses, of near geniuses, of would be geniuses, in short I have sat very often and very long with many wives and wives of many geniuses" (14).

Contextualizing Alice's and Fernande's chats about hats within Alice's lesbianism certainly underscores gender as performance, and allows us to imagine performances that construe gender and sexuality as anything but substitutable, structured through the following captions: If a woman sitting with wives equals a heterosexual, is Alice a "woman"? If a lesbian cooking dinner, tending garden, and doing needlepoint is a "wife," is her lover who shares the dinner, enjoys the garden, and proofreads in the afternoon with her feet propped up on a needlepointed cushion a "man"? Alice and Gertrude's "marriage" short-circuits the compulsory, four-square equivalences between man/woman, husband/wife as it asks, perhaps à la Gertrude herself, Is a woman a wife a wife a woman a husband a man a man a husband in a marriage?

In *Gender Trouble*, Judith Butler argues that gender is its own performance and asks: "To what extent do *regulatory practices* of gender formation and division constitute identity, the internal coherence of the subject, indeed, the self-identical status of the person?" (16). And this is precisely the kind of question raised by the problematic assignment of "wifely" attributes to the "femme" lesbian, a question turned back upon itself by a practice that seems to mime the "*regulatory practices* of gender formation and division"—here, for Alice, performing the practices through which one is trained to be a wife—without producing a woman who reads herself as a heterosexual. Butch-femme is an objectionable practice if one believes that role playing and roles themselves are grounded in the ontological categories "man" and "woman." These objections reveal an inquiry into origins. But if we pursue that inquiry and ask where butch-femme comes from and on what does it depend to make sense as a signifying system, the more likely answer locates butch-femme in "performances" of sexuality and gender, in the gestural and sartorial drapery of their significations, and not in the "essences" from which gender as the determinant of sexual desire can be said to derive.

Clearly, the performance of butch-femme "identities" is not mostly about clothes but about a representational nexus of identity, power, and sexuality, and thus it forms a lesbian technology of self-representation which lesbians negotiate in different ways, and it extends into all sorts of thinking about the gendered world. As de Lauretis points out in a discussion of *Nightwood* and *The Well of Loneliness*, "Gender reversal in the mannish lesbian . . . was not merely a claim to male social privilege or a sad pretense to male sexual behavior, but represented what may be called, in Foucault's phrase, a 'reverse discourse': an assertion of sexual agency and feelings, but autonomous from men, a reclaiming of erotic drives directed toward women, of a desire for women that is not to be confused with woman identification" ("Indifference," 24). Gendered sexuality informs our notions of lesbian (self-) representation; yet Stein camps up both gender and heterosexual roles in the wife/husband depiction of Alice and the Genius; she allegorizes their relationship through this depiction and in effect undercuts the referentiality on which this representation of domesticity depends. The reader must be willing to imagine how a lesbian relationship may indicate an alternatively gendered view of experience. Butch-femme roles do not flow naturally from sexuality, either from sexual difference (from men) or from sexual indifference to men. Neither sense of "difference" explains the lesbian subject of autobiography. If one reads for that kind of familiar definitional pressure—what is a woman as defined against what is a man—that reading will repeat the conventional heterosexist error of reading everything through its "normative" view. The narrative practice of inscribing and describing identity as engendered through hetero/sexual difference sustains the nonrepresentation of the lesbian subject. Viewing *The Autobiography* from within gender ideology, one sees the quaintness of Gertrude and Alice, all their witty guests, the fun they must have had. The view from Stein's lesbian subject, however, reveals how she compels the codes of heterosexual (self-) representation to detour wildly.

When Stein pursued the logic of autobiographical identity to the place within self-representation where the "self" and dominant culture collapse into the "representative man," she found some aspects of that subject position appealing, even apt. She, like Picasso, as *The Autobiography* reminds us, stood at the forefront of modernist experimentation; she and a small group of men, as *The Autobiography* also reminds us, composed an elite group of geniuses. Underscoring her own prescient insight into all this, Stein-as-Toklas writes: "I may say that only three times in my life have I met a genius and each time a bell within me rang and I was not mistaken, and I may say in each case it was before there was any general recognition of the quality of genius in them" (5). But at the same time as she found her similarity to that subject position, her difference from it was defined by being a woman and a lesbian. She found her own "otherness" within the subject position of autobiographer and not her "self." Her proximity to the subject position of "representative man" allowed her to remake that sameness into radical difference through literary experimentation and to remake her lesbian difference into a book-length, sustained autobiographical identity.

In this sense, Stein pursued a strategy to make lesbianism visible by exploring the possibilities within autobiography itself. She crafted a coherent subject position as her lover's *auto*biographer. Shari Benstock argues that Stein's representation of the seemingly "same" reveals her theoretical interest in the relationship between identity and representation: "Stein's writing interrogates the relation of sameness to itself and to a principle of difference within the field of representation. Stein took identity as her philosophic subject, rejecting out of hand identity as it has been constructed in the Western, European tradition and reconstructing (an)other id-entity" ("Expatriate," 194). Because the structural relationships between autobiography and identity have come to seem so close that it has been difficult to think them separately, to think them outside their shared narrativity, a fundamental criterion for judging the value of the autobiography has been the value of the autobiographer. Thus, the challenge to the notion of who is an appropriate autobiographer can incisively be staged as a challenge to what autobiography is. I want to focus next on how Stein enacted this challenge in *The Autobiography* by examining her use of portraits (in painting, photography, and autobiography), posing, and point of view.

Circulations: Posing, Portraits, and Gifts

Throughout *The Autobiography of Alice B. Toklas* a great many people are posed or caught posing. In this experiment in portraiture, what is seen is always linked to perspective: to what can be seen, by whom, and with what effects. Mostly, the subjects of these portraits are posed by Gertrude for Alice's pleasure and point of view. From their coupled subject position, one sees the hopeful and hapless, those in favor and those on the way out, the powerful and presumptuous as they come into the setting of 27, rue de Fleurus and are framed within its purview. This is the least complicated kind of portrait in *The Autobiography* and can be described as "semiotic send-ups," on the order of the portrait of Alice and Fernande which could be titled "sitting with wives." In many of these satirically "candid" portraits, Stein redefines the reputations of the modernists. She offers an ambivalent portrait of Picasso, her great friend and rival, in which he is posed in all his genius and more or less charming pettiness. Matisse, whose artistic highs and financial lows are chronicled with sympathy, is also caught exhibiting bad form when he responds to an invitation to dinner with a query about what will be served. Hélène, the valued cook, rebukes Matisse with a well-chosen insult: "She said a frenchman should not stay unexpectedly to a meal particularly if he asked the servant beforehand what there was for dinner. . . . So when Miss Stein said to her, Monsieur Matisse is staying for dinner this evening, she would say, in that case I will not make an omelette but fry the eggs. It takes the same number of eggs and the same amount of butter but it shows less respect, and he will understand" (7–8). Hemingway is deflated by being mocked as an imitator of his own self-image. In these "miniatures," Stein dodges dull guests and Alice punctures pretensions; character emerges in telling vignettes and personality is revealed through gestures.

The theme of many of these "studies" is the tension between the museum and the modern, the conservatory and the experimental. One of Stein's and Toklas's guests, Andrew Green, great-nephew of the Andrew Green who had been known as the father of New York, "had been born and reared in Chicago but he was a typical gaunt new englander, blond and gentle" (47). Andrew Green is a "type" in this hall of portraits; he is particular about his things and his point of view: "He adored as he said a simple centre and a continuous design. He loved pictures in museums and he hated everything modern" (47). His month-long stay at the rue de Fleurus wrecks these pleasures for him. Despite the care he takes not to be affected by the paintings in Stein's and Toklas's home—he covers them with cashmere shawls—somehow, they alter him, transforming his former pleasure into something alien: "He said that after the month was over that he had of course never come to like the new pictures but the worst of it was that not liking them he had lost his taste for the old and he never again in his life could go to any museum or look at any picture" (47). For Andrew Green, the paintings "reflected" something conservative, timid, and dull in himself. After discovering that he no longer likes the credentialed art that used to give him pleasure, he finds himself fascinated with Fernande.

In contrast, when Alice first encounters one of Picasso's paintings, which contributed to shattering conventional perspective, she is disturbed and compelled by this representation of women: "Against the wall was an enormous picture, a strange picture of light and dark colours, that is all I can say, of a group, an enormous group and next to it another in a sort of a red brown, of three women, square and posturing, all of it rather frightening. Picasso and Gertrude Stein stood together talking. I stood back and looked. I cannot say I realised anything but I felt that there was something painful and beautiful there and oppressive but imprisoned" (22). Andrew Green, in a sense, transfers his pleasure from one kind of conventional object to another, from formally predictable museum pieces to Fernande's formally predictable gendered presentation. Alice looks at women, and representations of women, from a different perspective. Her experience in Picasso's atelier suggests the deepening of portraiture's possibilities and implications.

Distinct from these illustrative portraits are the considerably more complicated treatments of subjects and poses which reveal *The Autobiography*'s persistent concern with seeing and being seen, with being captured by representational techniques. Not all are "done" by Gertrude or Alice, but all are of them. The "first" and absent one is a photograph of Stein and Toklas by Man Ray which Stein chose as the original frontispiece. In it, Stein sits at the desk, pen in hand. Something in her pose suggests Prospero's conjuring skills, for Alice seems summoned to the scene. Alice's hand is on the door handle, and she is emerging from a space unrepresented in the photograph which is flooded with light. Perhaps that part of the photograph is overexposed, but the effect is one of light spilling into a dark space, abundant, even excessive light from outside. The threshold figures the boundary where the differences in light blend in the place that contains Alice. A series of vertical lines punctuates the space between Gertrude and Alice: two tall candlesticks and an icon delineate or bar the space between them. A large cabinet runs the length of the same wall as the open door. On it are arranged more icons, a cross set in the middle of the mantelpiece, Victorian lady figurines arrayed about it— all somehow totemic. The scene is semiotically crowded. Paintings cover what can be seen of walls; objects cover what can be seen of furniture; all is *displayed*. And there is Alice's emerged form flashing at the door, her look blank, or guarded, or posed as if in the undifferentiated glow of a spotlight. Gertrude is the only photographic subject who has not taken the light. She is composing. On the original cover, only the title appears. We must wait until the last paragraph to understand how this photograph replaces the title page of autobiography: "About six weeks ago Gertrude Stein said, it does not look to me as if you were ever going to write that autobiography. You know what I am going to do. I am going to write it for you. I am going to write it as simply as Defoe did the autobiography of Robinson Crusoe. And she has and this is it" (252).

In a conventional understanding of autobiography, only the title is needed to indicate the "subject": title plus author plus photograph would pile repetition upon redundancy. In my Vintage paperback (1961), the reader's initiation into Stein's dislocation of the simple mirroring of identity in representation is foreshortened to the punch line. "Gertrude Stein," in large script, is placed above the title in the way a star's name dominates a movie title on a marquee. This cover photo, by Carl Van Vechten, shows Stein with her hair closely cropped, in profile, her gaze directed away from the viewer. The author and the photo are identical: there is no puzzling out of the perspective, no play on the subject of autobiography. In contrast, the Man Ray photograph rereads what can and cannot be seen, renders visible the otherwise invisible scene of lesbian domesticity, authorship, and autobiographical representation. The play between shadow and light, background and foreground, title and photograph redirects the focus from the *I* of autobiography to the couple in the frame. The Van Vechten portrait, used as an indexical sign of who/what lies within, forecloses this visibility. The photograph Stein chose and the photograph that replaced it are visual representations of the problem of reference Stein seized upon in autobiography.

It is not enough to notice all the portraits, poses, and their complications, for with Stein, the gallery, too, is significant. The house at 27, rue de Fleurus is a figure for a gallery that I would describe as a mode of exchange, even an "economy," in which portraits are shifted, including the most complex one, *The Autobiography* itself, and can function as gifts circulating within a lesbian "economy." I take this emphasis on exchange to underlie Stein's experimentation with the coupled subject described above, through which she deproprietarizes the autobiographical subject and thereby locates the meaning of this gift in the exchange of an *I*. The proprietary claims on identity and narrative (*the* story of *my* life), autobiography's deed and title, are troped here as what one gives rather than what one owns. *The Autobiography* as a gift derives meaning through the two economies in which it is valued and exchanged: the specific economy of a lesbian relationship and the market economy in which it became a best seller. Stein inscribes a code of lesbian gifts in antirealist and antiauthoritarian discursive practices and further distances herself from the indebtedness implicit in other theories and practices of gifting. The pressure of realist narrative techniques and nonfiction reporting (autobiography's traditional rhetoric) confront the subversions and oppositions of Stein's "autobiography," which are interested not so much in "truth" as a record of facts as in the lesbian subject of autobiography. Stein's lesbian subject position interrogates the ideology of autobiography and the textual apparatuses through which it is constructed and then refuses to authorize a single interpretive economy. She signals the grounds of her experimentation as early as the cover of the text with the Man Ray photograph.

The single portrait that compares most significantly to the autobiography and illuminates the problem of the subject's identity and self-possession is Picasso's famous portrait of Stein. In it, Stein is represented as a heavy figure sitting solidly, a mixture of browns, greys, and black. Her head, rendered in the masklike style of cubist faces, is set upon her body as if mounted there. This head is a solution to the problem that frustrated Picasso: "All of a sudden one day Picasso painted out the whole head. I can't see you any longer when I look, he said irritably. And so the picture was left like that" (53). The drapery that indicates the body and the background are in some sense the setting for this crowning feature of the portrait, its focus, and they are indistinguishable in color.

Picasso's portrait of Stein links the two as "composers" of art forms. Poised against Picasso's experience of painting is Stein's experience of posing. During the eighty or ninety sittings for Picasso's portrait, Stein began composing and perfecting the long sentences of *Three Lives*: "She had come to like posing, the long still hours followed by a long dark walk intensified the concentration with which she was creating her sentences" (50). Stein's dynamism during this period forms Picasso's "subject," and despite the chatty recounting of these early days in Paris, with a house full of charming guests and important art, a solitary Stein emerges. In relation to this increasingly self-defining Stein, Picasso's sense of his subject changed. Picasso confidently discusses the portrait, and implicitly Stein, in proprietary language: "Yes, he said, everybody says that she does not look like it but that does not make any difference, she will, he said" (12). Yet, he is defeated by the portrait; specifically, he cannot get the head right, at the same moment that Stein's head is alive with the invention of her own art form. It is Stein's head, as *The Autobiography* reminds us, that is the canvas and paint of her art—not the page, at first, so much as the rhythm caught and tested, the lines formed and revised, in the poser's head. When Picasso terminates the sittings, Stein leaves town and completes *Three Lives*, her own triptych of portraits. Picasso finishes the portrait in her absence. The simultaneous but unshared experiences of posing and composing are revealed when Picasso cannot go on and Stein can. When Stein returns to view her portrait, *The Making of Americans* is well begun.

The final anecdote about the portrait is offered as if to underscore that the depicted surface is not what cubism seeks primarily to represent; rather, its subject is the relationship between point of view and what can be made visible. Picasso painted Stein when she had long hair, which she usually wore coiled on her head. After she cuts it short in a caesar-do, Picasso wants to compare her new image to his portrait:

> Only a few years ago when Gertrude Stein had had her hair cut short, she had always up to that time worn it as a crown on top of her head as Picasso has painted it, when she had had her hair cut, a day or so later she happened to come into a room and Picasso was several rooms away. She had a hat on but he caught sight of her through two doorways and approaching her quickly called out, Gertrude, what is it, what is it. What is what, Pablo, she said. Let me see, he said. She let him see. And my portrait, said he sternly. Then his face softening he added, mais, quand même tout y est, all the same it is all there. (57)

Stein insisted that the principle to which all art must adhere is "objective realism." The objective dimension for Stein is not simply the object's surface but what constitutes it. Thus the problem in art is the relationship between representation and identity. That Picasso can now "see" Stein in the portrait, and the portrait in Stein, suggests successful posing. As Shari Benstock has pointed out, Stein was interested in the constructive dimension of representation, not the descriptive dimension: "Her work is a re-presentation that stages a dematerialization of the object of representation" ("Expatriate," 195). What happens, then, between the composer and the poser is considerably less about a power dynamic that would cast the two in a hierarchy of observer/observed, active/passive than about the problem of seeing and representation. As Charles Caramello argues, Stein does not reproduce a distant, unaffected point of view (neither does Picasso); rather, she rejects the position of the spectator on the sidelines in order "to express concretely not only the meaning of the thing being observed but also the meaning of the manner of observation and the meaning of the mode of its presentation."[18]

The most complicated and sustained posing in the autobiography is performed by Gertrude and Alice, as Alice poses for Stein's portrait of her, and Stein poses Alice and depicts herself. This arrangement and its "objective realism" raises the representational ante on the Picasso portrait. Put in painterly terms, this trompe l'oeil has occasioned considerable critical uneasiness. Stein capitalizes on the instability of the *I* when she inhabits it as an other, that is, inhabits the other's *I*. Critics have sensed danger in the usurpation of another's voice, of another's *I*, and their resistance has taken two forms. First, some critics perceive the text as an "appropriation" of Toklas's voice by Stein, rather than the ground of gifting and exchange. According to this view, Stein emerges as devouring and narcissistic, her egotism the theme of the text. In their study of modernism, Sandra Gilbert and Susan Gubar contend that Stein has appropriated Toklas's voice and the grounds for collaboration (or gifting) have degenerated into "collusion": "Usurping Alice's persona, appropriating Alice's voice, Stein presents herself as an unappreciated, isolated pioneer, and she thereby turns collaboration into collusion: living, listening, and talking do transform one into the other, but the result is a kind of cannibalism, as Stein makes Alice into a character of her own devising who, in turn, certifies Stein as the genius who will usher in the twentieth century."[19]

In this interpretation, the agency is all Stein's and all cannibalistic and can partly be explained as the persistent attachment of narcissism to lesbian and gay sexuality. Sue-Ellen Case has confronted the consistently negative Freudian reading of narcissism, its assumption of the regressive nature of same-sex attraction, and has questioned further:

What about the seduction of the same? . . . [W]hen I argued for the performance of the butch/femme roles, the masquerade of difference, I neglected to explore how the joke of that, the base that makes the camp masquerade operative is the base of the same. One part of this task

---

[18] Charles Caramello, "Gertrude Stein as Exemplary Theorist," in *Gertrude Stein and the Making of Literature,* ed. Shirley Neuman and Ira B. Nadel (Boston: Northeastern University Press, 1988), 4.

[19] Sandra Gilbert and Susan Gubar, *No Man's Land,* vol. 2: *Sexchanges* (New Haven: Yale University Press, 1989), 251.

would be to untie the notion of the seduction of the same from Freud's idea of narcissism which so dominates that figuration. At the same time, such a lesbian critique would reveal how Freud's notion of narcissism displays his heterosexual anxiety before the seduction of the same.[20]

Readers troubled by the appropriation of Alice's voice evidence a confused and confusing heterosexism. This heterosexism, I think, masquerades as feminist concern for female autonomy and glosses over the lesbian dynamic of the exchange. This homophobia involves a double movement in which heterosexualized readers project onto Stein the proprietary traits of the patriarch and attribute to her the act of stealing a woman's voice with the full sense of that theft intact. Even when an explanation of the motive force that would drive such an appropriation is evaded, the negative consequences are still attached to Stein's act. Readers define something in this impersonation as masculine and disturbing, and I would suggest that this "something" is the baggage of Freudian narcissism. Stein's impersonation of Toklas does not dissolve the other into a simple mirror of the self; rather, it displaces that conquering consequence in its affirmation of a doubled subject, a relation inscribed against the heterosexist logic of silence/voice.

The second line of resistance seeks answers to the referentiality Stein purposely obscures, tries to judge whose autobiography it "really" is. Again, this is exactly the kind of interpretation that cannot be sustained when we read the autobiography as a gift. The extent to which it is "their" autobiography is underscored by Stein's handling of temporality. She dispenses with the traditional narrative we expect, eschewing chronological order to place their relationship as the focal point of Toklas's life. Referentiality, or the founding reality upon which a gift's meaning traditionally depends, is re-presented in order to position the couple as the subject whose life is being told. Frequently, autobiographies begin with origins: with a place, a family, a birth. The Autobiography's opening sentence—"I was born in San Francisco, California"—is meaningful only as a comment on the weather, "I have in consequence always preferred living in a temperate climate" (3). Toklas's "origin" is a mise-en-scène, for it is to be found in a text by Stein. Toklas's life before Stein is displaced from a birthplace to a gloss on a text, Stein's gloss: "In the story Ada in Geography and Plays Gertrude Stein has given a very good description of me as I was

---

[20] Sue-Ellen Case, Introduction to *Performing Feminisms: Feminist Critical Theory and Theatre*, ed. Case (Baltimore: Johns Hopkins University Press, 1990), 13.

at that time" (4). Here is part of that "very good description": "Trembling was all living, living was all loving, some one was then the other one. Certainly this one was loving this Ada then. And certainly Ada all her living then was happier in living than any one else who ever could, who was, who is, who ever will be living."[21] This representation of Ada's immense and ongoing bliss totalizes the young Alice. Her coming into lesbian *jouissance* marks her origin. Because "Ada" is not quoted in the autobiography, we are pushed toward intertextuality. Toklas's "history" is dispersed across texts. In order to learn about her life, we need not turn to birth registries and newspaper clippings, for the emergence of the lesbian subject of autobiography is told through its appearance as a textual construction. The "real" dates and places of Alice's life reorganize around becoming Stein's lover.

Many critics have come to read the shape of Stein's career through her relationship with Toklas. Neil Schmitz, for example, has observed that Stein's work changed once her brother Leo had been moved out and Stein had begun her life with Toklas. He identifies *Tender Buttons* as the text that bridges Stein's transition from the philosophical to the poetic, from brooding to elation, from self-referential scrutiny to expansive gaiety and humor.[22] Stein alludes to the difficulties during this period of transition in *The Autobiography*. When she wrote *The Autobiography*, which has come to be thought of as a jeu d'esprit, her prospects for achieving a readership, let alone fame, were bleak. Although she was urged to write an autobiography—and indeed Alice pushed her to write what became a capital-generating best seller—the one she might well have produced would not have been to the public's liking. It might have been something more immersed in all her unpublished manuscripts, in which she more directly addressed her frustration and staked her claim for a serious reputation—an apologia for or vindication of her vocation—in short, a traditional autobiography. The gossipy tale of vibrant social life and companionable domesticity that we hear within Toklas's anecdotes still hints at Stein's great disappointment even as it displaces it: "After all, as she said, we do want to be printed. One writes for oneself and strangers but with no adventurous publishers how can one come in contact with those same strangers" (240).

Stein's isolation during the period that preceded her life with Toklas

---

[21] Gertrude Stein, "Ada," in *Geography and Plays* (1922; New York: Something Else Press, 1968), 16.

[22] Neil Schmitz, *Of Huck and Alice: Humorous Writing in American Literature* (Minneapolis: University of Minnesota Press, 1983), 12.

was profound. It is interesting that in the text that records this period even as it pronounces its end, Stein, like Defoe's Robinson Crusoe, writes an autobiography, with its opportunity for self-promotion, in order to disappear. At the end of Defoe's text, Robinson Crusoe's presence is figured as absence, as footprints in the sand. At the end of Stein's text, an invisible hand is left holding the pen: "You know what I am going to do. I am going to write it for you. I am going to write it as simply as Defoe did the autobiography of Robinson Crusoe. And she has and this is it" (252). The Crusoe/Friday parallel comments on the isolation Stein experiences, but her Defoe-like disappearance co-incides with her lesbian appearance. She, too, is only at home in an alien place after leaving the United States to settle in France. She, too, joins a companion who does not speak her language (her asyntactic poetics), but the language lesson here is quite complicated, for Stein learns to speak Toklas's language and Toklas learns to translate Stein's in a particular way: "As a matter of fact her handwriting has always been illegible and I am very often able to read it when she is not" (76). Such a dislocation, or translocation, of the ability to read the script of the other returns the gift in this lesbian "economy." Here Alice is authorized as the primary reader—if not writer—of her own life, and from this perspective, the autobiography appears more fully as a writer's/lover's gift. Authority is transferrable in this writerly text and functions as a form of gifting, as the reader becomes the writer implied in the autobiography's title.

Moreover, this device distances Stein from what she may not have wanted to write about: the lack of interest in her work. Alice's voice gestures toward "all her unpublished manuscripts" and thereby frames what Stein clearly considered traumatic within a deceptively simple style. Through this technique, Stein could write an autobiography the public would read. Yet this book must have been composed much in the way of all those others, in the late night and dawn hours of solitude. Therein lives Stein. In the scene that structures both her subjectivity and the writerly authority that scripts this text, Stein's present-tense identity is represented as "I am writing." Stein's experiments in literary point of view anticipate certain cinematic techniques. We can read Stein's self-representation as autobiography's version of the "space-off" shot, which Teresa de Lauretis explains as:

> The space not visible in the frame but inferable from what the frame makes visible. In classical and commercial cinema, the space-off is, in fact, erased, or, better, recontained and sealed into the image by the cinematic rules of narrativization (first among them, the shot/reverse-

shot system). But avant-garde cinema has shown the space-off to exist concurrently and alongside the represented space, has made it visible by remarking its absence in the frame or in the succession of frames, and has shown it to include not only the camera (the point of articulation and perspective from which the image is constructed) but also the spectator (the point where the image is received, reconstructed, and re-produced in/as subjectivity). (*Technologies*, 26)

Alice sleeps while Stein writes; thus she cannot narrate this activity in "her" autobiography. Correspondingly, Stein sleeps while Alice practices many of her domestic arts: cooking, sewing, corresponding. This is only one of the portraits (her portrait of Alice? her self-portrait?) whose authorial point of view is difficult to pin down. The coupled subject does not simply open the view to include both Stein and Toklas. It is a space from which to write, and it is also a space that controls perspective, a defining aspect of photography and portraiture. As in the Man Ray photograph, the representations Stein selects share a playful setting for the "subject," a setting that destabilizes point of view and dethrones the scopophilic gaze of the portraitist. By representing autobiographical subjectivity as a space-off shot, Stein can adjust the frame to focus on the lesbian couple where a solitary figure once posed. It is easy to speculate that had it not been for this solution at this point in her life, Stein might have reached the same conclusion Picasso did when he painted her portrait; that is, she could no longer "see" herself and was on the verge of painting out her head. And while the autobiography can be read as a series of portraits, it is through the portrait of a particular couple that Stein most fully explores portraiture, posing, and the possibilities of exchange.

As Gertrude Stein reinvented it, autobiography is no mere reflection of a life, no simple translation of lived daily experience into textual form. Rather, autobiography itself is a constructive dimension of shared lesbian identities. Within a text, within even the margins of a text, one can write "Gertrice/ Altrude" as a signature, as a sketch for a self-portrait, and as an autobiographical intertext in order to expose within the text of autobiography how "worrisome" identity depends on the possibility of writing the autobiography of (as) a lover. For Stein, lesbianism is not an identity with a predictable content and neither is autobiography. Rather, both become occasions for experimentation. The identity politics of autobiography as seen in the persistence of a belief in its historical reference, the realist manifesto written throughout criticism as versions of the autobiographical pact, are subverted in *The Autobiography of Alice B. Toklas*. Stein's lesbian identity politics, figured in the signature "Gertrice/Altrude," resists reinventing a unified lesbian subject. Rather, Stein persistently constructs a space where lesbian subjects can see and be seen. In order to "see" the lesbian in autobiography, however, we must widen our view within this framing device to see the other woman as the lesbian in this picture. Whether she is behind or before the camera or the text, she requires a place in feminist criticism beyond invocation and hasty retreat. Just such a figure, "the other woman," is having a renaissance in feminist criticism, but she is little known as the lesbian in (and out of) the text. More frequently she plays roles in the oedipal drama as mother, sister, daughter, or more problematically, the "racial" other, the postcolonial other, the subaltern woman. The latter positionalities are based still too much on the "self's" nonidentification with the "other" and require further work to displace a perspective that dangerously hypostatizes "otherness."

To read a lesbian signature requires a different view of otherness, and I invite the reader to sketch her own figure in the margins of this text, her own versions of "Gertrice/Altrude," to linger at the bar that marks her distance from and proximity to other women. Such marginalia may create a space "not visible in the frame but inferable from what the frame makes visible" and a perspective that re-views who poses for and who composes a (self-) portrait: a view of autobiography and, possibly, criticism which re-frames the feminist spectator/autobiographer/reader.

Conclusion

Confessional Subjects? Feminist Discourses
of Truth and Identity

I'm telling you stories. Trust me.
　　　　　　　　—Jeanette Winterson, *The Passion*

NOBODY KNOWS I'M A LESBIAN
　　　　　　　　—t-shirt logo

Feminist self-representation is central to the ongoing construction of a truth-telling apparatus for feminism, as are the critical narratives that establish contexts for interpretation and judgment. A range of self-representational and critical feminist writings can be understood in the context of the discourses of truth and identity, for they concern the possibilities and politics of women's self-representation, the shifting internal limits on feminist social and political engagements, and the relation between "identities"—sexuality, race, gender, class—and "institutions"—politics, law, science, and communities, among others.[1] How authoritative feminist subjects emerge, in what their au-

---

[1] The limits on a woman's ability to tell the truth about sex and power were recently dramatized, if not theatricalized, by the Anita Hill-Clarence Thomas hearings. Although the law professor Anita Hill told her story in a quasi-legal setting, she was unable to be heard as a truthful subject by the inquisitorial senators. Even though she passed a lie detector test, a truth-divining apparatus that is controversial at least in part because it takes the final call on truth telling out of the hands of human authority, Hill could not be "believed" by the small group of men in a position to judge. That she was widely believed by others who could not make their judgment ultimately count in that particular forum, however, may well prompt them to continue the hearing, in a sense, outside the setting in which it was judged a "lie," by championing Anita Hill's story elsewhere. As this incident showed, the multiple locations of truth within a culture often collide with a single location of the law, and it is frequently a hostile place without justice for those whose lives and experiences do not coincide with the preexisting standard for judging truth, eliciting justice, or provoking mercy.

thority consists, and how they are met by critical practice reveal some of the current stresses in the politics of identity and truth. I would like to sketch some current debates about feminist confessional and coming-out narratives. Following this discussion, I will turn to some contemporary feminist writing that posits "subjects" whose self-representation extends feminist identities into institutions otherwise considered hostile.

The mutual influence upon each other of feminist political rhetoric and feminist and women's "communities" has been explicated by several critics. The emergence of identity movements in relation to the name of "feminism" (variously embraced and resisted) has been charted across and through the proliferating subject positions of race, class, and sexuality, and in relation to a range of institutions, disciplines, and cultural traditions. Rita Felski, for example, has explored the effects of feminist rhetoric, specifically consciousness-raising rhetoric, on contemporary women's writing.[2] Felski argues that many writers within the feminist movement have appropriated confessional discourse in order to produce an authentic self. "Like consciousness-raising," she writes, "the confessional text makes public that which has been private, typically claiming to avoid filtering mechanisms of objectivity and detachment in its pursuit of the truth of subjective experience" (87–88). For Felski, these narratives lack the self-consciousness typically associated with modernist texts and thus strike critical readers as naive. When women use the confession, Felski claims, they avoid theory and ground subjectivity in the personal details of lived experience.[3]

Whereas Felski finds the confessional aspect of contemporary women's writing naive, I would say that women find in confessional discourse a subject position that grants them the authority from which to make truth claims. As I have maintained, the confession, as it persists in women's self-representation, may have little tolerance for irony, but the extent to which its subjects police themselves and strive to produce a "truthful" account defines them as highly "self"-conscious. Indeed, perhaps, they are as hyperconscious as the prisoners of the panopticon. As Foucault explains this by-now famous prison, the architectural design of the panopticon allowed the prison-

[2] Rita Felski, *Beyond Feminist Aesthetics: Feminist Literature and Social Change* (Cambridge: Harvard University Press, 1989).

[3] Among the texts Felski cites are Audre Lorde, *The Cancer Journals* (1980); Kate Millett, *Flying* (1974) and *Sita* (1977); Svende Merian, *Der Tod des Märchenprinzen* (The death of the fairy tale prince) (1980); Marie Cardinal, *The Words to Say It* (1975); Ann Oakley, *Taking It like a Woman* (1984).

er to be under constant surveillance by an unseen authority. The full success of this technique was achieved when the structure of surveillance had been sufficiently internalized to the point that the prisoner undertook self-surveillance.[4] Although many women are positioned within confessional discourse as liars, they engage a "reverse" discourse by speaking within the confession as truthful subjects. In order to do so effectively, they must be aware of what the dominant culture values and identifies as truth. Insofar as they become producers of truth, even co-conspirators, they are caught in its web. After all, one *confesses* in order to tell the *truth*. Other effects require other discourses; other discourses produce other effects. Thus I would put pressure on the suggestion that coming-out narratives, confessional narratives, and consciousness-raising narratives are regressive attempts to claim a representative and mimetic function for first-person writing. Instead, these narratives can be understood as a canny raid on the discourses of truth and identity. Further, they are effective as political rhetoric precisely to the extent that they claim to "speak the truth" at a particular time and in a particular place.

Such an invocation of the confession, however, which positions listeners as witnesses *and* judges, can always produce unintended, conflicted, or paradoxical results. They may even exploit the potential of these interpretive paradoxes. The confession is always a relational truth production; that is, "truth" issues from the confession and not from the speaker or listener alone. Jeanette Winterson's *The Passion* offers a version of the Cretan liar paradox in the mode of confession: "I'm telling you stories. Trust me."[5] The narrator locates "truthfulness" in the admission of storytelling and reveals this relation as a double bind. How else could a double bind catch up its object, the one who has been bound, and represent her as its subject? Without the enmeshment, the obligation, there could be no doubling and certainly no bind. The t-shirt logo that reads "NOBODY KNOWS I'M A LESBIAN" simultaneously conceals ("nobody knows") and discloses ("I'm a lesbian"). An ironic play on confession, this declaration asks how knowledge of sexual identity is constituted, even as it suggests the presence of that identity.

Truth telling has a formal logic that resembles confessional prac-

---

[4] See Foucault's discussion of the panopticon and the production of "docile bodies" in *Discipline and Punish*. See also Bartky's discussion of femininity as a technique of the panopticon of gender in "Foucault, Femininity, and the Modernization of Patriarchal Power," in *Femininity and Domination*, 63–82.

[5] Jeanette Winterson, *The Passion* (New York: Vintage, 1989), 13.

tices; questions hang in the air, challenges are presented, laws exist, and women's answers are partially defensive. But I want to question our certainty about the simplicity or transparency of these ironic answers: "I am telling you stories. Trust me" and "Nobody knows I'm a lesbian." For example, has the t-shirt wearer come out as a lesbian? Eve Sedgwick has noted how coming out is a sustained performance, a necessarily repeated act in the face of the massive cultural apparatus of the closet.[6] Does wearing the t-shirt do the work of coming out for that particular t-shirt wearer on that particular day, or does it more broadly insist to all who see it that they should not necessarily think they know who is and who is not a lesbian? The performance here is contoured with irony, with the possibility of similarity to or difference from the declaration on the t-shirt. What, after all, is the question to which the t-shirt responds? What I want to emphasize here is that such foundational claims to identity and truth, that is, the knowability of identity through a separable and single attribute that would make the whole picture make sense, are contingent upon repressing information that would make the picture not make the same kind of sense or information that may not be fully visible or even susceptible to revelation.[7] Trying to spend the whole day saying who you are with uncompromised clarity to all audiences would be an exhausting endeavor. Yet having to identify yourself—as a feminist, for example—in order not to be identified falsely by others is an ongoing pressure. The point is that members of the unmarked, dominant culture rarely face this pressure in the same way as those whose identities require authorization.

Also, in this context of whether or not feminist confessions or lesbian and gay coming-out stories are naively invested in the authentic, we could note that many claims to authenticity are on the verge of becoming passé. Current generational anxieties among feminists and the tensions adumbrated in lesbian and gay studies by the emergence of queer theory prove the contingency of persuasive claims to identity. Social movements change historically and culturally, as do forms of dominance, and styles of representation fall out of official favor

---

[6] Eve Kosofsky Sedgwick has charted the repetition of coming out as a performance without an end in, among other places, *Epistemology of the Closet* (Berkeley: University of California Press, 1990); and "Pedagogy in the Context of an Antihomophobic Project," *South Atlantic Quarterly* 89.1 (Winter 1990), 138–56.

[7] See Judith Butler, "Imitation and Gender Insubordination," in *Inside/Out*, 13–31; and Butler, "Contingent Foundations: Feminism and the Question of 'Postmodernism,'" in *Feminists Theorize the Political*, ed. Butler and Joan Scott (New York: Routledge, 1991), 3–21.

even while they are championed by marginalized persons. As with the movement of technologies between the so-called "first" and "third worlds," "obsolete" technologies of autobiography do not disappear; they travel to less privileged and less elite locations.[8] As the "progressive," whether it is industrially or textually high-tech, is preserved as a marker of currency, so too is the "regressive" preserved as a marker of obsolescence, as what we can do without. I would question the extent to which this dynamic informs contemporary criticism of "identity" politics and the self-representational narratives through which identities are expressed.[9] It is worth considering whether we are witnessing a similar movement in the technologies of truth and identity. Has the claim of representativeness, which characterized autobiography as practiced by an elite group, become passé and naive because the poststructuralist critique of such a grounding has been overwhelmingly persuasive? Or has representativeness been marginalized with the effect of forcing those who now claim it to the "margin" of representation? Why does the coincidence of poststructuralist skepticism and "truth telling" produce a judgment of naiveté when a representative identity is self-claimed by a non-"representative" person (in terms of dominant culture)? Although it is perfectly obvious that these judgments are produced on the historical move and never constitute a fixed standard or category of judgment, we can still see them moving. The effect here is the attachment of familiar and negative judgments to self-representational writing that seeks to claim, for persons who have been excluded from the subject position of the representative, the agency of truth telling.

Critical attention has also focused on the recent history of lesbian self-representation in order to acknowledge the complexity of lesbian "identities." The recent history may be said to begin in the mid-1970s, when, in the absence of a coherent political tradition of narratives about lesbian lives, some lesbian autobiographical writing began to create it. Autobiography was used strategically to put in place a discourse of lives that have been constructed as "marginal." The lesbian

[8] This analogy is inspired by Evan Watkins' discussion of obsolescence in *Throwaways* (forthcoming).

[9] I usually concur in the critique of identity politics, especially in its now familiar linkage with the critique of essentialism. Working on autobiography and autobiographics, however, has prompted me to think more about how the debates are represented, where the objectionable aspects of identity politics and essentialism are thought to lie. When they lie within self-representational texts, then I also consider the politics of the critique as an aspect of contemporary discourses of truth and identity. Given the considerable feminist attention that has focused on these debates, perhaps this slightly altered perspective will be useful.

coming-out story as a narrative with a specific act at its center initiated a narrative tradition informed by a desire for representation. Biddy Martin chronicles this historical development in the context of lesbianism's often-conflictual place within feminism.[10] Interpretation of lesbianism, she suggests, is bounded by the context of its representation. For example, Mab Segrest interprets lesbian storytelling as a route to affirmation in the context of positive self-definition.[11] By coming out, a lesbian sheds a formerly repressed identity and joins the lesbian community. This same narrative act and constitutive self-representation in a different context, however, signifies a detour or evasion rather than an identity. Katie King says that lesbianism functions as "feminism's magical sign of liberation" within a feminist critique of heterosexuality.[12] It is seen as "outside" heterosexuality and free from its corruption, just as lesbianism, in Segrest's formulation, is "inside" women and untamed by male domination and heterosexuality. The use of the inside/outside comparative seeks to make lesbianism visible as a different identity altogether, though knowable in contrast to heterosexuality.

Commenting further on the different contexts for lesbian interpretation, Martin emphasizes that politics does not necessarily derive from the categories of identity or experience, whether or not they are lesbian. According to Martin, then, these conflicting critical narratives of lesbian identity and autobiographical representation demonstrate "the effects of feminist rhetoric on definitions of lesbianism" ("Lesbian Identity," 88). As a dominant feminist rhetoric that was inattentive to nondominant identities emerged, it was compelled to take race, class, and sexual orientation into consideration, and when it did so, categories of identity first entered feminist rhetoric as "additives." This is no longer particularly the case, and earlier work has been surpassed by work done on the density and proliferation of subject positions within cultures. Considerable theoretical attention has focused on ways to read "color," "gender," "class," and "ethnicity" as more than attributes of the "person."[13] The translation of an identity

[10] Biddy Martin, "Lesbian Identity and Autobiographical Difference[s]," in Life/Lines, 77–103.

[11] Mab Segrest, My Mama's Dead Squirrel: Lesbian Essays on Southern Culture (Ithaca, N.Y.: Firebrand, 1985).

[12] Katie King, "The Situation of Lesbianism as Feminism's Magical Sign: Contests for Meaning and the U.S. Women's Movement, 1968–1972," Communication 9 (1986): 65–91.

[13] Homi K. Bhabha's notion of "hybridity" is significant here; see his "Interrogating Identity," in Identity: The Real Me, Institute of Contemporary Art Documents (London) 6 (1987): 5–11. See also Gayatri Spivak, "Can the Subaltern Speak?" in Marxism and the

understood primarily through its identification with an attribute (as in, "I am a ____") into a belief structure ("therefore, I believe____") has been a position from which to speak politically and theoretically.

Once this rhetoric puts into discourse a subject not previously represented, however, how is it possible to move beyond its repeated invocation? How and when does one capitalize on this significant intervention into representational politics in order to complicate further an "identity" that seems always on the verge of disappearing in political rhetoric in unmeaningful ways? The notion of the "person" and of "women" has been considerably altered and re-situated, but the consequences raise significant questions: What kind of politics is possible without a universal subject or identity representable through the statement "I am a ____, and I believe ____"? Indeed, the nearly defining and absorbing interest of many feminisms in identity seems driven by an entrenched performance anxiety where the questions "Who am I?" and "Who are we?" are raised simultaneously with "What shall we do?" How we understand the world of possibilities contained within identifications between who "we are" and what "we shall do" has defined feminist praxis across political and theoretical divisions.

By situating lesbian self-definition in the feminist rhetoric of the multiplicity of identification, Bonnie Zimmerman locates challenges to the narrative practices by which lesbianism, as well as other identities, is rendered authentic and natural, as evidence of a legitimate self.[14] Zimmerman finds these challenges specifically in lesbian autobiography committed to the representation of multiple identities, such as the work represented in Moraga and Anzaldúa's anthology *This Bridge Called My Back*, which emphasizes the politics of language in the practice of self-representation, the colonizing functions of institutions and their rhetoric, and the representational politics necessary to challenge ideological constructions of identity and experience. Moreover, writing against the notion that "identity" is a simpler content for lesbians, while acknowledging the strategic need to craft and deploy such identities, Martin contends that when "identity" is his-

---

Interpretation of Culture, ed. Nelson and Grossberg (Urbana: University of Illinois Press, 1988). Both share a concern with the crucial issue of visibility. Bhabha writes: "*To see* a missing person, or *to look* at Invisibleness, is to emphasize the subject's *transitive* demand for a *direct* object of self-reflection; a point of presence which would maintain its privileged enunciatory position *qua subject*" (5).

[14] Bonnie Zimmerman, "The Politics of Transliteration: Lesbian Personal Narratives," in *The Lesbian Issue: Essays from Signs*, ed. Estelle B. Freedman et al. (Chicago: University of Chicago Press, 1985), 251–70.

toricized and culturally specified and "experience" is denaturalized and analyzed in relation to ideology, then "lesbianism ceases to be an identity with predictable contents, to constitute a total political and self-identification, and yet it figures no less centrally for that shift. It remains a position from which to speak, to organize, to act politically, but it ceases to be the exclusive and continuous ground of identity or politics" ("Lesbian Identity," 103). In this sense, Martin applauds the more complex situation of current lesbian self-representation and tends to see the coming-out narratives as constituting, in their single focus on sexuality, the "past."

The arguments advanced by Zimmerman, King, and Martin all point up the complexity of lesbian self-representation with the political aim of articulating, rather than streamlining or masking, that complexity. As a political rhetoric, these narratives of lesbian identities do not focus on the metaphorical function of heroic autobiography ("I" for "we," exemplar for group) or the metonymic function of some women's autobiography (a lateral identification, a side-by-side relationship of differences among "us"). Rather, as Martin points out, lesbian autobiography characterized by an effort to render multiple identities provokes the reader "to examine the coimplication of 'my' history in 'yours,' to analyze the relations between" (103). This strikes me as a different claim of identification, one not based on differences acknowledged in the midst of sameness (*as* women, *as* lesbians, etc.), but of sameness explored in the midst of difference ("I" from "you").

Whereas all the critics I have cited have helped to articulate cultures of women's self-representation and to historicize the dense conceptual space of the contemporary, some critical narratives regard self-representation that had, and continues to have, significant strategical use for political representation as "the past," as obsolete. Yes, the coming-out or consciousness-raising narrative is simple, honed to a single meaning, but at some times and in some places, it is as simple as an **X** that marks the spot of identity and functions as a way to say *I* am here. Put another way, it is a way of saying an *I* is here in the discourse of political representation and is here specifically as an "identity" that is resisted by dominant culture. The person writing *I*, then, represents an identity and not necessarily the other way around. The person stands in for a marginalized or criminalized "identity" that nonetheless does not totalize her. Given the important function of representativeness in identity discourses, the distinction between person (as total entity) and identity (as an aspect of the person) reveals the subtleties that make possible coalition politics on the strategic grounds of "identity." The extent to which coming-out, confessional, and consciousness-raising narratives construct a political community in relation to which an identity may emerge is temporally complicated. Communities can be constructed through these acts and can even be made available textually when they are otherwise remote or inaccessible; moreover, through the construction of a community, subject positions and "identities" become possible for persons who previously were, in the context of political representation and representational politics, without them.[15]

One of the crucial insights of feminist theory is that politics is conceivable without a foundational subject (i.e., "women"); in fact, the condition of political agency lies in this conceptual refusal. The claim that "women" is a constructed category with varying histories and embodiments has not heralded the end of feminism or of the subject's agency; rather, it has adumbrated the end of "women" as the previously totalizing name of our identities. When "women" is only a record of wrongs, only the grounds of either immersed oppression or transcendent "womanhood," then being able *not* to identify with the category as the grid of self-knowing and self-representation makes agency possible. To "be" a woman, as some feminists have argued, already entails a kind of material violence. Monique Wittig has declared that women are knowable through the category of "sex," a category she considers thoroughly political, without ontology, and constituted through a violent assault on the grounds of ontology.[16] "Sex," as it prefigures "gender" and the autobiographical body for women, as I have claimed, is not primarily, then, a lived construction so much as a nonlived obstruction. For some contemporary feminist writers, the autobiographical text as the narrative account of a woman's subjection is refused for an autobiographical embodiment not currently recognizable without feminist technologies of self-representation.

Even as feminist theory has unsettled and inspired self-representation, self-representation has challenged theory in a reciprocal reworking of subjectivity, identity, and politics. Three texts exemplify the reworking of disciplinary and discursive boundaries and the ener-

---

[15] In particular, I am thinking of the historical significance to feminism of the Combahee River Collective's manifesto. The essay, which appears in *This Bridge Called My Back*, was produced by black feminists who opposed the racism and narrowness of a predominantly white and middle-class feminism. By signing the text as a collective, they constructed a community and identities within a single act, a signature of autobiographical community.

[16] See Monique Wittig, "Category of Sex," *The Straight Mind and Other Essays* (Boston: Beacon, 1992), 1–8.

gizing relations among politics, theory, and self-representation in feminist discourse. Through three figures or sites of feminist self-representation, I would like to read for the autobiographical as that which resists static identity categories. Donna Haraway's "Manifesto for Cyborgs" (1985), Patricia Williams's *Alchemy of Race and Rights: Diary of a Law Professor* (1991), and Minnie Bruce Pratt's "Identity: Skin Blood Heart" (1984) represent identity in specific networks rather than in entities or essences traditionally associated with women and feminists. All construe consciousness, identity, agency, and experience as key terms in the discourse of self-representation.

In "A Manifesto for Cyborgs: Science, Technology, and Socialist Feminism in the 1980s," Donna Haraway goes adventuring as a feminist subject in a discourse of truth that has seemed nearly implacable to feminism: science. In her essay, Haraway offers "an ironic political myth faithful to feminism" (65) which uses the figure of the cyborg to explicate the complexity of feminists' positions within discourses of truth and identity. Haraway offers the cyborg as the subject of feminist political self-representation; it "is our ontology; it gives us our politics" (66). It is a hybrid of machine and organism, recognizable as a fiction, a science fiction, and as a creature of social reality. Here, Haraway uses "social reality" in a specific and expansive sense; for her, social reality is "our most important political construction, a world-changing fiction" (65). The potential of this myth lies in its relation to history, its past tenses and possible futures revealed through a present-tense identity. The specter of faithfulness is raised in proximity to blasphemy. Irony and the potent effects of blasphemy, which Haraway is careful to distinguish from apostasy, offer feminism both "a rhetorical strategy and a political method" (65). It is important to focus on the irony in this "ironic political myth faithful to feminism" (66), especially in the confessional context I have discussed, for some may accuse Haraway of capitulating the contested ground of female identity and opting for an unrecognizable, unrealistic hybrid like the cyborg. The end result of Haraway's manifesto should not be capitulation, nor do I think this result is implicit in it. Saying "I am a cyborg" is different from saying "I am a woman" in some ways but not logically, in a politics of identity, for it makes visible what was not previously recognizable.

What is the cyborg's experience, agency, and identity? How can it be a self-representational fiction for feminists? We are all cyborgs, according to Haraway, poised in this identity on the cusp of the twenty-first century: "We are all chimeras, theorized and fabricated hybrids of machine and organism; in short, we are cyborgs" (66). And

Haraway likes it here, blurring the boundaries between natural and fabricated, human and machine, material and fantasy. The cyborg breaks with all previous mythologies of identity, all critical narratives, their ontology and epistemology. Most important, the cyborg confounds the possibility and desirability of a myth of origin founded on an originary whole or an identifying split. Cyborg identity becomes possible at the end of the twentieth century through breakdowns along three boundaries that previously structured identity and made it knowable: the human/animal boundary, the human-animal/machine boundary, and the physical/nonphysical boundary. This is our experiential past with respect to the concept of identity.

In this context, what are the possibilities for agency? The cyborg's agency lies in social relations and the identities it can access through heteroglossic naming. It is not surprising that cyborg affinity is based not in blood relations but in choice, but what Haraway uses the image of the cyborg to explore and to name is the extent to which its world already exists. She asks, "And who counts as 'us' in my own rhetoric? Which identities are available to ground such a powerful political myth called 'us,' and what could motivate enlistment in this collectivity?" (72–73). Affirming this already multiple collectivity, Haraway eschews any reconsolidation of the categories the cyborg—itself a powerful fiction—reveals as fictitious. Agency is made possible for Haraway when women are linked through affinity, not identity, for political purposes. The cyborg, then, is ultimately a political identity that emerges in relation to a collectivity that mirrors its own hybrid identity; here, coalitions represent the body politics of the cyborg. Identity is thereby conserved as a political category. Irony enables the cyborg's political agency within confessional technologies. The cyborg's faithfulness to feminism and faithlessness to gender distinguish its confessional project: the cyborg's confessors are positioned as scientists, as feminists, as consumers and producers of hybrid identities, that is, as already implicated in discourses that take identity seriously (a precondition for irony).

In *The Alchemy of Race and Rights: Diary of a Law Professor*, Patricia Williams locates identity at the boundary of historical possibility, legal representation, and political rhetoric. Like Haraway's cyborg, Williams's alchemist lives in a world whose past is distinctly undeserving of nostalgia. In her first chapter, "The Brass Ring and the Deep Blue Sea: (some parables about learning to think like a lawyer)," Williams presents her aims for her book through a dialogue with her sister. As Williams ticks off her theoretical goals, her sister agitates, "But what's the book *about*?"[17] As Williams explains, the book is not so much *about* something as it is itself a way of *doing*, and Williams puts the emphasis on writing as action: "I would like to write in a way that reveals the intersubjectivity of legal constructions, that forces the reader both to participate in the construction of meaning and to be conscious of that process" (7–8). Her writing is an attempt "to create a genre of legal writing to fill the gaps of traditional scholarship" (7).

The current genre of legal writing, as well as the practice and, as Williams suggests, the teaching of law, makes her identity "oxymoronic." This category is the negative version of the hybridity Haraway celebrates in the cyborg, and it lives by the law of genre. Williams describes it: "I am a commercial lawyer as well as a teacher of contract and property law. I am also black and female, a status that one of my former employers described as being 'at oxymoronic odds' with that of commercial lawyer" (6). Identity categories are at stake here because, in rhetorical terms, they are property, they are the properties of the person, and they define persons as property. Most significant, they are discursive constructions in discourses with normative predispositions. How else could one be "at oxymoronic odds" with oneself? The presumed objectivity of legal language flattens out the meaning of people's lives, and as it does so it fails to render them knowable to themselves and others. Williams, I think, sees this flattening out as a distortion that undermines the possibilities of justice, for it disallows the self-representation of the one whose evidence is always, in part, identity. Clearly, it will take an alchemist to produce this new writing, one who does not fear prosecution under the law of genre ("genres are not to be mixed").

Williams's use of confessional technologies can be seen through her invocation of a community that constructs meaning along with the writer. I think there is productive tension between her goals to force "the reader both to participate . . . and to be conscious of that process" and "to create a genre of legal writing." I see that tension as autobiographical; that is, the genre of legal writing is profoundly concerned with property rights, by which African Americans have been construed through slavery as property. Williams seeks to create a genre concerned with putting the disenfranchised "voice" and "self" into a legal discourse that has itself been one of the major instruments through which disenfranchisement was codified and rendered en-

---

[17] Patricia J. Williams, *The Alchemy of Race and Rights: Diary of a Law Professor* (Cambridge: Harvard University Press, 1990), 6.

forceable. What is at stake in the essays that follow is the development of the anecdotal as a far-reaching representational style concerned with the self and the extent to which it can be thought to be its own possession. The connection between identity and ownership affects legal discourse, for it focuses on the implication of being "a subject before the law" for self-representation.

The historical and cultural specificity of racial identity informs Williams's writing. By contextualizing African-American identities with legal notions of property, she explains that for Africans brought to the emerging United States as slaves, the conditions for preserving and reconstructing "identity" were violently constrained: the only possible legal identity was as property. The legacy of racism for African Americans, as Williams points out, is evident in the language of identity. She specifies her own use of this language: "A final note about some of my own decisions on categories: I wish to recognize that terms like 'black' and 'white' do not begin to capture the rich ethnic and political diversity of my subject. But I do believe that the simple matter of the color of one's skin so profoundly affects the way one is treated, so radically shapes what one is allowed to think and feel about this society, that the decision to generalize from such a division is valid" (256). As an identity category, "blackness" is not all, but all that it signifies is crucial to convey: "While being black has been the most powerful social attribution in my life, it is only one of a number of governing narratives or presiding fictions by which I am constantly reconfiguring myself in the world" (256).

In an essay titled "On Being the Object of Property," Williams frames an inquiry into property law with a historical and personal anecdote about the self and ownership. Just before her first day of law school, Williams's mother reminds her of her family history. Williams's knowledge of her mother's side of the family begins with her great-great-grandmother Sophie, who was purchased when she was eleven years old by a lawyer named Austin Miller. Williams has the document that is probably the contract of sale for her great-great-grandmother: "It is a very simple but lawyerly document, describing her as 'one female' and revealing her age as eleven; no price is specified, merely 'value exchanged'" (17). Miller impregnates Sophie, whose daughter Mary, Williams's grandmother, is taken from her to be brought up as a house servant. "While I don't remember what I was told about Austin Miller before I decided to go to law school, I do remember that just before my first day of class my mother said, in a voice full of secretive reassurance, 'The Millers were lawyers, so you have it in your blood'" (216). Identity, then, figured through the powerful symbol of blood, is bound up in a network of coerced histories, violently colonized persons, and rapes but also, as Williams emphasizes, in the ambivalent legacy of her own successes and demonstrated talents, of disenfranchisement and reclamations.

For Williams, the discourse of self-representation enacted in *The Alchemy of Race and Rights* remains centrally concerned with the significance of "truth" to identity. A series of experiential anecdotes emphasizes that to be seen as black and female by various institutions is already to have been placed in a position of defense, a position in which one is the transgressor, the liar, the criminal. Other subject positions are available, however, within the kind of writing Williams produces as an intervention in the connection of race-gender-identity-violence. For her, identity is forged in a crucible and the process is alchemical, mysterious; the third term between race and rights which produces an autobiographical identity is neither simply nor eternally given.[18] Autobiographical identity is expressed as Williams confounds boundaries, her political and imaginative goal in this book, and wages battles over their meanings and who will decide them.

Minnie Bruce Pratt's long essay, "Identity: Skin Blood Heart," is a critique of the feminist nostalgia for an identity discourse and its place within contemporary technologies of autobiography. Given the title, one might expect an essentialist view of female identity located in the body; however, Pratt considerably revises the conjunction of "skin blood heart" through a critical anatomization of anti-Semitism, racism, and homophobia. Like Williams, Pratt has received a racist and sexist indoctrination in which blood figured as a powerful symbol. She casts a critical eye on how her identity as a white, Christian, southern woman was constructed; she examines what she now understands as the networks in which identity is enmeshed, where the lures of racist and heterosexist identification lie, and offers the history of her resistance to the privileges of her former home. Pratt describes herself as being propelled into political consciousness when she came out as a lesbian and lost her two sons to her husband in a custody battle in which her mother threatened to testify against her.

Pratt's understanding of "experience," "consciousness," and "iden-

---

[18] In *Sexing the Cherry* (New York: Vintage, 1991), Jeanette Winterson explains alchemy through an analogy to imaginative processes: "The alchemists have a saying, '*Tertium non data*': the third is not given. That is, the transformation from one element to another, from waste matter into best gold, is a process that cannot be documented. It is fully mysterious. No one really knows what effects the change. And so it is with the mind that moves from its prison to a vast plain without any movement at all. We can only guess at what happened" (150).

tity" as aspects of political self-representation offers a dynamic model of feminist agency. Pratt suggests that the subject of self-representation is *experience*, understood as "an exhausting process, this moving from the experience of the 'unknowing majority' (as Maya Angelou called it) into consciousness" ("Identity," 12). When experience is further specified as "an ongoing process by which subjectivity is constructed semiotically and historically" (*Alice Doesn't*, 182), then it cannot be thought to simply accumulate, its dynamism defined through sheer bulk. It doesn't just add up. Rather, experience connotes a profoundly political, emotional, intellectual, and imaginative response, a series of alterations, differences, and repositionings in relation to sameness. The temporality of experience understood in this way is not exclusively or primarily linear, not additive or iterative but potentially transformative of the meaning of time. It does, however, engage this potential in specific cultural, historical, and narrative terms. Constitutive of feminist change are narratives of change, and Pratt offers a narrative of "consciousness" changing which foregrounds the relationship between "truth" and "lies" through the figure, place, and experience of home.

Marcia Aldrich and I have elsewhere discussed the centrality of "home" to Pratt's revisionary politics, but I would repeat here that Pratt constructs the home as a duplicitous site of acculturation which violently binds differences together under the sign of the same (as in the white, Christian family, and the construction of "our" people and "our" women who must be protected by "our" men from a malevolent black "them").[19] She explains how the stability of home is rendered through this violence and so wields its power through its continuous reproduction and the suppression of its reality. The identity enforced and experienced within this "home" is in large part refused, though it is precisely what Pratt must labor to understand in order not to be compelled by either the pull of nostalgia or the unknowing that comes from trying to raise one's own consciousness by analogy to someone else's oppression. To say "I am not what I was" and "I was not what I am," as Pratt does, locates identity on the move. Identity acts. It acts in relation to skin, to blood, and to heart, and the process of finding this relationship is itself an act of identity. But it is not final. The identity network, figured through the body as "skin blood heart" offers a dynamic model of self-representation: How do I know myself and how am I known by others? by skin? by blood? do I know myself by heart?

[19] See Leigh Gilmore and Marcia Aldrich, "Writing Home: 'Home' and Lesbian Representation in Minnie Bruce Pratt," *Genre* 25 (Spring 1992): 25–46.

As a feminist with home truths to tell, Pratt reworks confessional technologies through critical revision: she is seeing experience from an altered perspective and repositions herself to tell the truth rather than to have it told to her by father, mother, community, or husband. Her goal is to use the mode of truth telling to "get a little closer to the longed-for but unrealized world, where we are each able to live, but not by trying to make someone less than us, not by someone else's blood or pain: yes, that's what I'm trying to do with my living now" (13). Pratt's "living now" is represented in "Identity" as moments of "speaking-to" in which a truth is communicated not only in the content but in the quality of the exchange. These stand as confessional moments in which listener and speaker are joined in the production of truths that will reconstruct the world as an altogether different "home," one in which it will be possible to "tell the truth" from a subject position not based on exclusion, violent differentiation, or the compulsory masking of identities in the face of punitive institutions and identity authorities. It is necessary to speak what Pratt calls the "stark truth" (14) in order to create a context in which it can be heard: "This listening is one way of finding out how to get to the new place where we all can live and speak-to each other for more than a fragile moment" (14). Pratt recognizes the provisional nature of her confessional project, her refusal of nostalgia compels such an understanding, and she records the false starts and missteps in an effort to "expand my constricted eye" (17). She explains her perspective and enunciatory position: "I am speaking my small piece of truth, as best I can. . . . I'm putting it down for you to see if our fragments match anywhere, if our pieces, together, make another larger piece of the truth that can be part of the map we are making together to show us the way to get to the longed-for world" (16).

Pratt's description of her method exemplifies what I have been trying to convey through my exploration of autobiographics. The extent to which confessional technologies continue to operate in the discourses of truth and identity has put women writers on notice, but these technologies have also been negotiated in a variety of ways by writers who find other positions from which to tell the "truth." I have looked to women who intervene in the linkage of "lying" and "women," who refuse the violence of gender identity compelled by dominant discourses of self-representation in order to put themselves into their texts through the agency of re-membering. If autobiography provokes fantasies of the real, then autobiographics explores the constrained "real" for the reworking of identity in the discourses of women's self-representation.

Bibliography

Aers, David. *Community, Gender, and Individual Identity*. London: Routledge, 1988.

Almaguer, Tomás. "Chicano Men: A Cartography of Homosexual Identity and Behavior." *differences* 3 (Summer 1991): 75–100.

Alter, Robert. "Sacred History and the Beginnings of Prose Fiction." *Poetics Today* 1.3 (Spring 1980): 143–61.

Althusser, Louis. "Ideology and Ideological State Apparatuses." Trans. Ben Brewster. In *Critical Theory since 1965*. Ed. Hazard Adams and Leroy Searle. Tallahassee: University Press of Florida, 1986: 239–50.

Andrews, William. *To Tell a Free Story: The First Century of Afro-American Autobiography, 1760–1865*. Urbana: University of Illinois Press, 1986.

Anzaldúa, Gloria. *Borderlands/La Frontera: The New Mestiza*. San Francisco: Spinsters, 1987.

Bakhtin, Mikhail. *Marxism and the Philosophy of Language*. Trans. Ladislav Matejka and I. R. Titunik. Cambridge: Harvard University Press, 1986.

Bal, Mieke. "Sexuality, Sin, and Sorrow: The Emergence of Female Character." In *The Female Body in Western Culture*. Ed. Susan Rubin Suleiman. Cambridge: Harvard University Press, 1986: 317–38.

Barrett, Michèle. "Some Different Meanings of the Concept of 'Difference': Feminist Theory and the Concept of Ideology." In *The Difference Within*. Ed. Elizabeth Meese and Alice Parker. Amsterdam: John Benjamins, 1989: 37–48.

Barthes, Roland. *A Lover's Discourse: Fragments*. Trans. Richard Howard. New York: Hill and Wang, 1985.

——. *The Pleasure of the Text*. Trans. Richard Miller. New York: Noonday, 1975.

——. *Roland Barthes by Roland Barthes*. Trans. Richard Howard. New York: Hill and Wang, 1977.

Bartky, Sandra Lee. *Femininity and Domination: Studies in the Phenomenology of Oppression*. New York: Routledge, 1990.

Baudrillard, Jean. *Fatal Strategies*. Trans. Philip Beitchman and W. G. H. Niesluchowski. Ed. Jim Fleming. New York: Semiotext(e). 1990.

Benstock, Shari. "Authorizing the Autobiographical." In *The Private Self*. Ed. Benstock. Chapel Hill: University of North Carolina Press, 1988: 10–33.

——. "Expatriate Sapphic Modernism: Entering Literary History." In *Lesbian Texts and Contexts*. Ed. Karla Jay and Joanne Glasgow. New York: New York University Press, 1990: 183–203.

——. *Women of the Left Bank: Paris, 1900–1940*. Austin: University of Texas Press, 1986.

——, ed. *The Private Self*. Chapel Hill: University of North Carolina Press, 1988.

Benveniste, Emile. *Problems in General Linguistics*. Trans. Mary Elizabeth Meek. Coral Gables: University of Miami Press, 1971.

Bernheimer, Charles, and Claire Kahane, eds. *In Dora's Case: Freud—Hysteria—Feminism*. 1985; New York: Columbia University Press, 1990.

Bhabha, Homi K. "Interrogating Identity." In *Identity: The Real Me*. Institute of Contemporary Art Documents (London) 6 (1987): 5–11.

Bolton, Sarah Knowles. *Autobiography for My Son*. Boston: Published privately, 1915.

Bourdieu, Pierre. *Distinction: A Social Critique of the Judgement of Taste*. Trans. Richard Nice. Cambridge: Harvard University Press, 1984.

——. *Outline of a Theory of Practice*. Trans. Richard Nice. 1977; Cambridge: Cambridge University Press, 1985.

Braxton, Joanne M., and Andrée Nicola, eds. *Wild Women in the Whirlwind: Afra-American Culture and the Contemporary Literary Renaissance*. New Brunswick, N.J.: Rutgers University Press, 1990.

Brodzki, Bella. "Mothers, Displacement, and Language in the Autobiographies of Nathalie Sarraute and Christa Wolf." In *Life/Lines: Theorizing Women's Autobiography*. Ed. Brodzki and Celeste Schenck. Ithaca: Cornell University Press, 1988: 243–59.

Brodzki, Bella, and Celeste Schenck, eds. *Life/Lines: Theorizing Women's Autobiography*. Ithaca: Cornell University Press, 1988.

Brown, Catherine D. *Pastor and Laity in the Theology of Jean Gerson*. New York: Cambridge University Press, 1987.

Bruss, Elizabeth W. *Autobiographical Acts: The Changing Situation of a Literary Genre*. Baltimore: Johns Hopkins University Press, 1976.

Burke, Carolyn. "Gertrude Stein, the Cone Sisters, and the Puzzle of Female Friendship." In *Writing and Sexual Difference*. Ed. Elizabeth Abel. Chicago: University of Chicago Press, 1981: 221–42.

Butler, Judith. "Contingent Foundations: Feminism and the Question of 'Postmodernism.'" In *Feminists Theorize the Political*. Ed. Butler and Joan Scott. New York: Routledge, 1992: 3–21.

——. *Gender Trouble: Feminism and the Subversion of Identity*. New York: Routledge, 1990.

——. "Imitation and Gender Insubordination." In *Inside/Out*. Ed. Diana Fuss. New York: Routledge, 1991: 13–31.

Bynum, Caroline Walker. *Holy Feast and Holy Fast: The Religious Significance of Food to Medieval Women*. Berkeley: University of California Press, 1987.

Caramello, Charles. "Gertrude Stein as Exemplary Theorist." In *Gertrude Stein and the Making of Literature.* Ed. Shirley Neuman and Ira B. Nadel. Boston: Northeastern University Press, 1988: 1–7.

Case, Sue-Ellen. Introduction. *Performing Feminisms: Feminist Critical Theory and Theatre.* Ed. Case. Baltimore: Johns Hopkins University Press, 1990: 1–13.

——. "Toward a Butch-Femme Aesthetic." *Discourse* 11.1 (1988–89): 55–73.

Castillo, Ana. "Massacre of the Dreamers: Reflections on Mexican-Indian Women in the U.S. 500 Years after the Conquest." In *Critical Fictions: The Politics of Imaginative Writing.* Ed. Philomena Mariani. Seattle: Bay Press, 1991: 161–76.

——. *The Mixquiahuala Letters.* New York: Doubleday, 1992.

Chinosole. "Audre Lorde and the Matrilineal Diaspora." In *Wild Women in the Whirlwind: Afra-American Culture and the Contemporary Literary Renaissance.* Ed. Joanne M. Braxton and Andrée Nicola. New Brunswick, N.J.: Rutgers University Press, 1990: 379–94.

Cisneros, Sandra. *The House on Mango Street.* New York: Vintage, 1991. First published in a slightly different form by Arte Público Press 1984 and revised in 1989.

Cixous, Hélène. "The Laugh of the Medusa." Trans. Keith Cohen and Paula Cohen. *Signs* 1 (1976): 873–93.

Couser, Thomas. *Altered Egos: Authority in American Autobiography.* New York: Oxford University Press, 1989.

David-Ménard, Monique. *Hysteria from Freud to Lacan: Body and Language in Psychoanalysis.* Trans. Catherine Porter. Ithaca: Cornell University Press, 1989.

De Lauretis, Teresa. *Alice Doesn't: Feminism, Semiotics, and Cinema.* Bloomington: Indiana University Press, 1984.

——. "Sexual Indifference and Lesbian Representation." In *Performing Feminisms: Feminist Critical Theory and Theatre.* Ed. Sue-Ellen Case. Baltimore: Johns Hopkins University Press, 1990: 17–39.

——. *Technologies of Gender: Essays on Theory, Film, and Fiction.* Bloomington: Indiana University Press, 1987.

——, guest ed. "Queer Theory: Lesbian and Gay Sexualities." *differences* 3 (Summer 1991).

Deleuze, Gilles, and Félix Guattari. *A Thousand Plateaus: Capitalism and Schizophrenia.* Trans. Brian Massumi. Minneapolis: University of Minnesota Press, 1987.

De Man, Paul. "Autobiography as De-facement." *Modern Language Notes* 94 (1979): 919–30.

Derrida, Jacques. *The Ear of the Other: Otobiography, Transference, Translation.* Trans. Peggy Kamuf. New York: Schocken, 1985.

——. "The Law of Genre." Trans. Avital Ronell. *Glyph* 7 (Spring 1980). Rpt. *Critical Inquiry* 7 (Autumn 1980): 55–81.

Dolan, Jill. "'Lesbian' Subjectivity in Realism: Dragging at the Margins of Structure and Ideology." In *Performing Feminisms: Feminist Critical Theory and*

Theatre. Ed. Sue-Ellen Case. Baltimore: Johns Hopkins University Press, 1990: 40–53.

Dollimore, Jonathan. "The Cultural Politics of Perversion: Augustine, Shakespeare, Freud, Foucault." In *Sexual Sameness: Textual Differences in Lesbian and Gay Writing*. Ed. Joseph Bristow. New York: Routledge, 1992: 9–25.

DuPlessis, Rachel Blau. *The Pink Guitar: Writing as Feminist Strategy*. New York: Routledge, 1990.

Dydo, Ulla E. "*Stanzas in Meditation:* The Other Autobiography." *Chicago Review* 35.2 (1985): 4–20.

Eakin, Paul John. *Fictions in Autobiography: Studies in the Art of Self-Invention*. Princeton: Princeton University Press, 1985.

Felman, Shoshana. *Jacques Lacan and the Adventure of Insight: Psychoanalysis in Contemporary Culture*. Cambridge: Harvard University Press, 1987.

Felski, Rita. *Beyond Feminist Aesthetics: Feminist Literature and Social Change*. Cambridge: Harvard University Press, 1989.

Fifer, Elizabeth. "Is Flesh Advisable? The Interior Theater of Gertrude Stein." *Signs* 4 (1979): 472–83.

Foucault, Michel. *Discipline and Punish: The Birth of the Prison*. Trans. Alan Sheridan. New York: Random House, 1977.

——. *The History of Sexuality*. Vol. 1: *An Introduction*. Trans. Robert Hurley. New York: Random House, 1978.

——. "Nietzsche, Genealogy, History." Trans. Donald F. Bouchard and Sherry Simon. In *The Foucault Reader*. Ed. Paul Rabinow. New York: Pantheon, 1984: 76–100.

——. "Questions on Geography." In *Power/Knowledge*. Ed. Colin Gordon. Brighton: Harvester, 1980.

——. "What Is an Author?" Trans. Josué Harari. In *The Foucault Reader*. Ed. Paul Rabinow. New York: Pantheon, 1984: 101–20.

Freud, Sigmund. *Dora: An Analysis of a Case of Hysteria*. New York: Collier, 1963.

Fuss, Diana. *Essentially Speaking: Feminism, Nature, and Difference*. New York: Routledge, 1989.

——, ed. *Inside/Out: Lesbian Theories/Gay Theories*. New York: Routledge, 1991.

Gagnier, Regenia. *Subjectivities: A History of Self-Representation in Britain, 1832–1920*. Oxford: Oxford University Press, 1991.

Gallop, Jane. *Reading Lacan*. Ithaca: Cornell University Press, 1985.

——. *Thinking through the Body*. New York: Columbia University Press, 1988.

Gilbert, Sandra. "Purloined Letters: William Carlos Williams and 'Cress.'" *William Carlos Williams Review* 10.2 (Fall 1985): 5–15.

Gilbert , Sandra, and Susan Gubar. *No Man's Land*. Vol. 1: *The War of the Words*. New Haven: Yale University Press, 1988.

——. *No Man's Land*. Vol. 2: *Sexchanges*. New Haven: Yale University Press, 1989.

Gilmore, Leigh. "The Gaze of the Other Woman: Beholding and Begetting in Dickinson, Moore, and Rich." In *Engendering the Word*. Ed. Temma Berg et al. Urbana: University of Illinois Press, 1989: 81–102.

Gilmore, Leigh, and Marcia Aldrich. "Writing Home: 'Home' and Lesbian Representation in Minnie Bruce Pratt." *Genre* 25 (Spring 1992): 25–46.

Gubar, Susan. "'The Blank Page' and the Issues of Female Creativity." In *Writing and Sexual Difference*. Ed. Elizabeth Abel. Chicago: University of Chicago Press, 1982: 73–93.

Gusdorf, Georges. "Conditions and Limits of Autobiography." Trans. James Olney. In *Autobiography: Essays Theoretical and Critical*. Ed. Olney. Princeton: Princeton University Press, 1980: 28–49.

Haraway, Donna. "A Manifesto for Cyborgs: Science, Technology, and Socialist Feminism in the 1980s." *Socialist Review* 80 (April 1985): 65–107.

Heimmel, Jennifer P. *"God Is Our Mother": Julian of Norwich and the Medieval Image of Christian Feminine Divinity*. Salzburg, Austria: Salzburg Studies in English Literature, 1982.

Heinzelman, Susan Sage. "Women's Petty Treason: Feminism, Narrative, and the Law." *Journal of Narrative Technique*, 20 (Spring 1990): 89–106.

Hewitt, Leah. *Autobiographical Tightropes*. Lincoln: University of Nebraska Press, 1990.

hooks, bell. *Feminist Theory: From Margin to Center*. Boston: South End, 1984.

Hunter, Dianne, ed. *Seduction and Theory: Readings of Gender, Representation, and Rhetoric*. Urbana: University of Illinois Press, 1989.

Jacobus, Mary. *Romanticism, Writing, and Sexual Difference: Essays on "The Prelude."* Oxford: Clarendon Press, 1989.

Jaggar, Alison. *Feminist Politics and Human Nature*. Brighton: Harvester, 1983.

Jameson, Fredric. "Cognitive Mapping." In *Marxism and the Interpretation of Culture*. Ed. Cary Nelson and Lawrence Grossberg. Urbana: University of Illinois Press, 1988.

Jardine, Alice. *Gynesis*. Ithaca: Cornell University Press, 1985.

Jay, Paul. *Being in the Text: Self-Representation from Wordsworth to Roland Barthes*. Ithaca: Cornell University Press, 1984.

Jelinek, Estelle C., ed. *Women's Autobiography: Essays in Criticism*. Bloomington: Indiana University Press, 1980.

Johnson, Barbara. *The Critical Difference: Essays in the Contemporary Rhetoric of Reading*. Baltimore: Johns Hopkins University Press, 1981.

——. "My Monster/ My Self." In *A World of Difference*. Ed. Barbara Johnson. Baltimore: Johns Hopkins University Press, 1987: 144–54.

Johnson, Joyce. *Minor Characters*. New York: Pocket Books, Simon and Schuster, 1983.

Julian of Norwich. *Revelations of Divine Love*. Trans. and with an introduction by Clifton Wolters. London: Penguin, 1988.

Kahn, Victoria. "Rhetoric and the Law." *Diacritics* 19.2 (1989): 21–34.

Kairys, David, ed. *The Politics of Law: A Progressive Critique*. New York: Pantheon, 1982.

Kamuf, Peggy. "Replacing Feminist Criticism." *Diacritics* 12 (Summer 1982): 42–47.

Kincaid, Jamaica. *Annie John*. New York: Farrar, Straus and Giroux, 1985. First

Plume Printing, 1986. First published in slightly different form in the *New Yorker*, 1983.

——. *Lucy*. New York: Farrar, Straus and Giroux, 1990. First Plume Printing, 1991.

——. *A Small Place*. New York: Farrar, Straus and Giroux, 1988.

——. "Untitled Conference Presentation." In *Critical Fictions: The Politics of Imaginative Writing*. Ed. Philomena Mariani. Seattle: Bay Press, 1991: 223–29.

King, Katie. "The Situation of Lesbianism as Feminism's Magical Sign: Contests for Meaning and the U.S. Women's Movement, 1968–1972." *Communication* 9 (1986): 65–91.

Kingston, Maxine Hong. *The Woman Warrior*. New York: Pantheon, 1975.

Kofman, Sarah. *The Enigma of Woman: Woman in Freud's Writings*. Trans. Catherine Porter. Ithaca: Cornell University Press, 1985.

Knowles, David. *The English Mystical Tradition*. London: Burns, 1961.

Krupat, Arnold. *For Those Who Come After: A Study of Native American Autobiography*. Berkeley: University of California Press, 1985.

Lacan, Jacques. *Écrits: A Selection*. Trans. Alan Sheridan. New York: Norton, 1977.

——. *Seminaire XX*. Quoted in Stephen Heath, "Difference." *Screen* (1971): 51.

Lejeune, Philippe. *Le Pacte autobiographique*. Paris: Seuil, 1975.

Lerner, Gerda. *The Female Experience*. Indianapolis: Bobbs-Merrill, 1977.

Lévi-Strauss, Claude. *The Elementary Structure of Kinship*. Boston: Beacon, 1969.

Lionnet, Françoise. *Autobiographical Voices: Race, Gender, Self-Portraiture*. Ithaca: Cornell University Press, 1989.

Lispector, Clarice. *The Foreign Legion*. Trans. Giovanni Pontiero. 1964; New York: New Directions, 1992.

Lorde, Audre. *Zami: A New Spelling of My Name*. Trumansburg, N.Y.: Crossing, 1983.

McCarthy, Mary. *Memories of a Catholic Girlhood*. Berkeley Medallion Edition. New York: Harcourt, Brace, and World, 1966.

Martin, Biddy. "Lesbian Identity and Autobiographical Difference[s]." In *Life/Lines: Theorizing Women's Autobiography*. Ed. Bella Brodzki and Celeste Schenck. Ithaca: Cornell University Press, 1988: 77–103.

——. *Women and Modernity: The (Life)Styles of Lou Andreas-Salomé*. Ithaca: Cornell University Press, 1991.

Mason, Mary G. "The Other Voice: Autobiographies of Women Writers." In *Autobiography: Essays Theoretical and Critical*. Ed. James Olney. Princeton: Princeton University Press, 1980: 207–34.

Meese, Elizabeth. *Crossing the Double-Cross: The Practice of Feminist Criticism*. Chapel Hill: University of North Carolina Press, 1986.

——. *(Ex) Tensions: Re-Figuring Feminist Criticism*. Urbana: University of Illinois Press, 1990.

Meyjes, G. H. M. Posthumus. *Jean Gerson et l'assemblée de Vincennes (1329): ses conceptions de la juridiction temporelle de l'église*. Leiden: Brill, 1978.

Miller, D. A. *The Novel and the Police*. Berkeley: University of California Press, 1988.

Miller, Nancy K. *Getting Personal: Feminist Occasions and Other Autobiographical Acts*. New York: Routledge, 1991.

——. *Subject to Change: Reading Feminist Writing*. New York: Columbia University Press, 1988.

——. "The Text's Heroine: A Feminist Critic and Her Fictions." *Diacritics* 12 (Summer 1982): 48–53.

Mitchell, Juliet. *Psychoanalysis and Feminism*. New York: Pantheon, 1974.

Moraga, Cherríe. *Loving in the War Years: Lo que nunca pasó por sus labios*. Boston: South End, 1983.

Moraga, Cherríe, and Gloria Anzaldúa, eds. *This Bridge Called My Back: Writings by Radical Women of Color*. Watertown, Mass.: Persephone, 1981.

Nussbaum, Felicity. *The Autobiographical Subject: Gender and Ideology in Eighteenth-Century England*. Baltimore: Johns Hopkins University Press, 1989.

Olney, James, ed. *Autobiography: Essays Theoretical and Critical*. Princeton: Princeton University Press, 1980.

——. "Autobiography and the Cultural Moment." In *Autobiography: Essays Theoretical and Critical*. Ed. James Olney. Princeton: Princeton University Press, 1980: 3–27.

——. *Metaphors of Self: The Meaning of Autobiography*. Princeton: Princeton University Press, 1972.

Ostriker, Alicia. *Stealing the Language: The Emergence of Women's Poetry in America*. Boston: Beacon, 1986.

Pascal, Roy. *Design and Truth in Autobiography*. London: Routledge, 1960.

Paz, Octavio. *Labyrinth of Solitude: Life and Thought in Mexico*. New York: Grove, 1961.

Perry, Donna. "Interview with Jamaica Kincaid." In *Reading Black, Reading Feminist*. Ed. Henry Louis Gates. New York: Penguin, 1990: 492–510.

Pratt, Minnie Bruce. "Identity: Skin Blood Heart." In *Yours in Struggle*. Ed. Elly Bulkin, Pratt, and Barbara Smith. Ithaca: Firebrand, 1984.

Rabine, Leslie. "No Lost Paradise: Social Gender and Symbolic Gender in the Writings of Maxine Hong Kingston." *Signs* 12 (Spring 1987): 471–92.

Rich, Adrienne. *The Dream of a Common Language: Poems, 1974–1977*. New York: Norton, 1978.

——. "Notes toward a Politics of Location." In *Blood, Bread, and Poetry*. New York: Norton, 1986: 210–31.

Riley, Denise. *"Am I That Name?" Feminism and the Category of "Women" in History*. Minneapolis: University of Minnesota Press, 1988.

Rose, Jacqueline. *Sexuality in the Field of Vision*. London: Verso, 1986.

Rubin, Gayle. "The Traffic in Women: Notes on the 'Political Economy' of Sex." In *Toward an Anthropology of Women*. Ed. Rayna R. Reiter. New York: Monthly Review Press, 1975.

Ruddick, Lisa. *Reading Gertrude Stein: Body, Gnosis, Text*. Ithaca: Cornell University Press, 1990.

Ryan, Michael. *Politics and Culture: Working Hypotheses for a Post-Revolutionary Society*. Baltimore: Johns Hopkins University Press, 1989.

Sacks, Oliver. *The Man Who Mistook His Wife for a Hat*. New York: Summit, 1985.

Saldívar, Ramón. *Chicano Narratives: The Dialectics of Difference*. Madison: University of Wisconsin Press, 1990.

Scarry, Elaine. *The Body in Pain*. New York: Oxford University Press, 1985.

Schenck, Celeste. "All of a Piece: Women's Autobiography and Poetry." In *Life/Lines: Theorizing Women's Autobiography*. Ed. Bella Brodzki and Celeste Schenck. Ithaca: Cornell University Press, 1988: 281–305.

Schmitz, Neil. *Of Huck and Alice: Humorous Writing in American Literature*. Minneapolis: University of Minnesota Press, 1983.

Sedgwick, Eve Kosofsky. *Epistemology of the Closet*. Berkeley: University of California Press, 1990.

———. "Pedagogy in the Context of an Antihomophobic Project." *South Atlantic Quarterly* (Winter 1990): 138–56.

Segrest, Mab. *My Mama's Dead Squirrel: Lesbian Essays on Southern Culture*. Ithaca, N.Y.: Firebrand, 1985.

Smith, Sidonie. *A Poetics of Women's Autobiography: Marginality and the Fictions of Self-Representation*. Bloomington: Indiana University Press, 1987.

Smith, Valerie. *Self-Discovery and Authority in African-American Narratives*. Cambridge: Harvard University Press, 1987.

Sommer, Doris. "'Not Just a Personal Story': Women's *Testimonios* and the Plural Self." In *Life/Lines: Theorizing Women's Autobiography*. Ed. Bella Brodzki and Celeste Schenck. Ithaca: Cornell University Press, 1988: 107–30.

Spengemann, William. *The Forms of Autobiography: Episodes in the History of a Literary Genre*. New Haven: Yale University Press, 1980.

Spivak, Gayatri C. "Can the Subaltern Speak?" In *Marxism and the Interpretation of Culture*. Ed. Cary Nelson and Lawrence Grossberg. Urbana: University of Illinois Press, 1988: 271–313.

Stallybrass, Peter, and Allon White. *The Politics and Poetics of Transgression*. Ithaca: Cornell University Press, 1986.

Stanton, Domna, ed. *The Female Autograph*. 1984; Chicago: University of Chicago Press, 1987.

Steedman, Carolyn Kay. *Landscape for a Good Woman: A Story of Two Lives*. New Brunswick, N.J.: Rutgers University Press, 1987.

Stein, Gertrude. *The Autobiography of Alice B. Toklas*. 1933; New York: Vintage, 1961.

———. *Everybody's Autobiography*. 1937; New York: Cooper Square, 1970.

———. *Fernhurst, Q.E.D., and Other Early Writing*. New York: Liveright, 1971.

———. "Ada" in *Geography and Plays*. 1922; New York: Something Else Press, 1968.

———. *The Making of Americans: Being a History of a Family's Progress, 1906–1908*. 1925; New York: Something Else Press, 1966.

Steiner, Wendy. *Exact Resemblance to Exact Resemblance: The Literary Portraiture of Gertrude Stein*. New Haven: Yale University Press, 1978.

Steptoe, Robert. *From behind the Veil: A Study of African-American Narrative*. Urbana: University of Illinois Press, 1979.

Stimpson, Catharine. "Gertrice/Altrude: Stein, Toklas, and the Paradox of the Happy Marriage." In *Mothering the Mind*. Ed. Ruth Perry and Martine Watson Brownley. New York: Holmes and Meier, 1984: 122–39.

———. "The Mind, the Body, and Gertrude Stein." *Critical Inquiry* 3 (1977): 491–96.

———. "The Somagrams of Gertrude Stein." In *The Female Body in Western Culture: Contemporary Perspectives*. Ed. Susan R. Suleiman. Cambridge: Harvard University Press, 1986: 30–43.

Suleiman, Susan Rubin, ed. *The Female Body in Western Culture: Contemporary Perspectives*. Cambridge: Harvard University Press, 1986.

Tambling, Jeremy. *Confession: Sexuality, Sin, the Subject*. New York: St. Martin's, 1990.

Teresa of Avila. *The Life of Teresa of Jesus: The Autobiography of Teresa of Avila*. Trans. E. Allison Peers. Garden City, N.Y.: Doubleday, 1960.

Tillich, Hannah. *From Time to Time*. New York: Stein and Day, 1974.

———. Interview in *Contemporary Authors*. Vols. 73–76. Detroit: Gale Research, 1978.

Todorov, Tzvetan. *Genres in Discourse*. Trans. Catherine Porter. Cambridge: Cambridge University Press, 1990.

Weintraub, Karl. *The Value of the Individual: Self and Circumstance in Autobiography*. Chicago: University of Chicago Press, 1978.

Whitman, Walt. *An American Primer, with Facsimiles of the Original Manuscript*. Ed. Horace Traubel. Boston: Small, Maynard, 1904.

———. *Leaves of Grass*. Ed. David McKay. Philadelphia: Sherman & Co., 1900.

Williams, Patricia J. *The Alchemy of Race and Rights: Diary of a Law Professor*. Cambridge: Harvard University Press, 1991.

Williams, Raymond. *Marxism and Literature*. Oxford: Oxford University Press, 1977.

Williams, William Carlos. *Paterson*. New York: New Directions, 1963.

Winterson, Jeanette. *Oranges Are Not the Only Fruit*. New York: Atlantic Monthly Press, 1987. First published by Pandora, London, 1985.

———. *The Passion*. New York: Vintage, 1989. First published by Bloomsbury Press, London, 1987.

———. *Sexing the Cherry*. New York: Vintage, 1991. First published by Bloomsbury, London, 1989. First published in the U.S. by the Atlantic Monthly Press, New York, 1990.

Wittig, Monique. *Les Guérillères*. Trans. David Le Vay. Boston: Beacon, 1985.

———. *The Lesbian Body*. Trans. David Le Vay. Paris: Minuit, 1973. Boston: Beacon, 1986.

———. "The Mark of Gender." In *Poetics of Gender*. Ed. Nancy K. Miller. New York: Columbia University Press, 1986: 63–73.

——. "Point of View: Universal or Particular?" *Feminist Issues* 3.2 (1983): 63–69.

——. "The Straight Mind." *Feminist Issues* 1.1 (1980): 103–11.

——. *The Straight Mind and Other Essays.* Boston: Beacon, 1992.

Wong, Hertha Dawn. *Sending My Heart Back across the Years: Tradition and Innovation in Native American Autobiography.* New York: Oxford University Press, 1992.

Woolf, Virginia. *A Room of One's Own.* New York: Harcourt, Brace, 1929.

Zimmerman, Bonnie. "The Politics of Transliteration: Lesbian Personal Narratives." In *The Lesbian Issue: Essays from Signs.* Ed. Estelle B. Freedman et al. Chicago: University of Chicago Press, 1985: 251–70.

Index

Reading Women Writing

A SERIES EDITED BY

Shari Benstock and Celeste Schenck